Spiritual Awakenings

JOURNEYS OF THE SPIRIT
FROM THE PAGES OF AA GRAPEVINE

BOOKS PUBLISHED BY AA GRAPEVINE, INC.

The Language of the Heart (& eBook)
The Best of the Grapevine Volume I (& eBook)
The Best of Bill (& eBook)
Thank You for Sharing
Spiritual Awakenings (& eBook)
I Am Responsible: The Hand of AA
The Home Group: Heartbeat of AA (& eBook)
Emotional Sobriety — The Next Frontier (& eBook)
Spiritual Awakenings II (& eBook)
In Our Own Words: Stories of Young AAs in Recovery (& eBook)
Beginners' Book (& eBook)
Voices of Long-Term Sobriety (& eBook)
A Rabbit Walks Into A Bar
Step by Step — Real AAs, Real Recovery (& eBook)
Emotional Sobriety II — The Next Frontier (& eBook)
Young & Sober (& eBook)
Into Action (& eBook)
Happy, Joyous & Free (& eBook)
One on One (& eBook)
No Matter What (& eBook)
Grapevine Daily Quote Book (& eBook)
Sober & Out (& eBook)
Forming True Partnerships (& eBook)
Our Twelve Traditions (& eBook)
Making Amends (& eBook)

IN SPANISH

El lenguaje del corazón
Lo mejor de Bill (& eBook)
El grupo base: Corazón de AA
Lo mejor de La Viña
Felices, alegres y libres (& eBook)
Un día a la vez (& eBook)

IN FRENCH

Le langage du coeur
Les meilleurs articles de Bill
Le Groupe d'attache: Le battement du coeur des AA
En tête à tête (& eBook)
Heureux, joyeux et libres (& eBook)

Spiritual Awakenings

JOURNEYS OF THE SPIRIT

FROM THE PAGES OF AA GRAPEVINE

AAGRAPEVINE,Inc.
NEW YORK, NEW YORK
www.aagrapevine.org

*"The greatest gift that can come to anybody
is a spiritual awakening."*

— Bill W.
AA Grapevine, December 1957

AA Preamble

Alcoholics Anonymous
is a fellowship of men and women who share
their experience, strength and hope with each
other that they may solve their common problem and help others to recover from alcoholism.
The only requirement for membership is a
desire to stop drinking. There are no dues or
fees for AA membership; we are self-supporting
through our own contributions. AA is not allied
with any sect, denomination, politics, organization or institution; does not wish to engage in
any controversy, neither endorses nor opposes
any causes. Our primary purpose is to stay
sober and help other alcoholics to
achieve sobriety.

CONTENTS

CONTENTS *CONTINUED*

WELCOME

What a blessing, these stories from our companions in AA! For when we came to Alcoholics Anonymous, that is exactly what we heard—tales of the journeys those who were here before us had taken from the darkness of alcoholism into the fullness of new light.

Listening to such stories, freely given, how could anyone not be stirred? We wanted what we could see, however dimly, what these storytellers had. Some among us plunged right into a new life; others moved more slowly. But for all of us, the more we listened, really listened, the more a change came on.

We tried to live the Steps of Alcoholics Anonymous, and the change became more focused—a coming to life, an arousal, if you will, of some part of ourselves lying dormant all these years, perhaps an entire lifetime. So our search began.

For help we turned to our friends, to our sponsors, to readings inside and outside AA. And as we persisted, we began to find something, hard to pin down, at first—a sense that all our seeking now brought with it the dawning of arrival.

We found ourselves going about our many daily tasks with a different slant on things. Indeed, for some of us the world may have begun to seem entirely new. Oh, our old habits often banged into the new, but even so we found that life without alcohol, without some constantly beckoning spree, could be lived fully, joyfully, whatever came our way.

These, then, are our stories, our spiritual awakenings.

The Editors

Beginnings

❧

W e start with the voices of our cofounders, plus two early friends of AA. One friend, Dr. Harry Emerson Fosdick, one-time minister of the Riverside Church in New York City, talks about the "essential truths" of our Twelve Steps. "Just as around our bodies there is a physical universe from which replenishing power comes into us," he observes, "so around our souls there is a spiritual Presence in whose fellowship our lives can be sustained and our characters transformed."

A spiritual presence in which characters are transformed. According to psychiatrist Dr. Harry M. Tiebout, another early friend of AA, central to this transformation is our AA principle of anonymity. "The great religions are conscious of the need for nothingness if one is to attain grace," he writes, later adding, "the maintenance of a feeling of anonymity—of a feeling 'I am nothing special'—is a basic insurance of humility and so a basic safeguard against further trouble with alcohol."

Dr. Bob takes up the topic of humility when he speaks of the kitchen table, "that modest piece of furniture" around which so much of AA's early history was played out. "Experience has taught us," he says, "that simplicity is basic." Although, in Dr. Bob's words, "the ego of the alcoholic dies a hard death," in the transformation of sobriety we can find some measure of humility.

And finally, stirred by the simplicity of the gravesite where Dr. Bob and his wife, Anne, lie buried, Bill W. is led to comment that the real monument to his life is "one word only, which we AAs have written. That word is Sacrifice."

Spiritual presence, transformation, anonymity, humility, simplicity, sacrifice. What better foundation upon which to build new lives?

THOSE MARVELOUS TWELVE STEPS
June 1960

An interpretation of the Steps by an eminent scholar
who was not one of us—but was always one with us

It was no theologian, spinning theories about God, who wrote AA's Twelve Steps. They were hammered out of the hard rock of experience by men in desperate need. But, speaking as a clergyman who never was an alcoholic, I read those Twelve Steps with profound intellectual admiration. They state with amazing clarity and conciseness the essential truths, both psychological and theological, which underlie the possibility of transformed character.

It is not the alcoholic alone who comes to the place where he has to admit that he is powerless to manage his life. A nervous breakdown brought me there. Completely knocked out, in a sanitarium, my will power so far gone that the harder I tried the worse off I was, I had to admit that my life had become unmanageable. It was then, when I was powerless to save myself, that I desperately welcomed a Power from beyond myself. When I read Step Two—*Came to believe that a Power greater than ourselves could restore us to sanity*—that hit my target in dead center.

The Twelve Steps of AA are not true for alcoholics only; they are basic and universal truths. So it was when Robert Louis Stevenson was transformed from aimless, feckless, irresponsible living into a vigorous, purposeful life, and ascribed the change to "that unknown steersman whom we call God."

There are two techniques indispensable for a sane and healthy life. The first is will power—putting our backs into it and trying hard. The second is intake—hospitality to power from beyond ourselves, what Paul called being "strengthened with might through his Spirit in the inner man." The first is like a tree's fruit; the second is like a tree's roots. After many years of personal counseling, I am sure that, soon or late, every life runs into some experience where the first technique peters out and the second technique becomes critically necessary.

Here again, the Twelve Steps state a universal truth. Of course, we must try hard, but even physical output is not the whole story; intake—air, food, sunlight—is essential. My basic religious faith is that, just as around our bodies there is a physical universe from which replenishing power comes into us, so around our souls there is a spiritual Presence in whose fellowship our lives can be sustained and our characters transformed. So Step Eleven—*Sought through prayer and meditation to improve our conscious contact with God ...*—describes a universal need.

To be sure, one sometimes meets a self-confident, two-fisted man who thinks he needs no power but his own. He likes to quote Henley's "Invictus": "I am the master of my fate: I am the captain of my soul." That sounds splendid, but the story runs that Henley had a friend who knew him through and through, and who understood how weak as water he sometimes was when the temptations of the flesh assailed him. One day, this friend quoted that line to Henley, "I am the captain of my soul," and then added, "The hell you are!"

Many a man, proudly confident that he by himself alone is the master of his fate, needs to have it said to him: No! The Twelve Steps are right about that.

I can imagine a certain type of theological thinker who lifts his eyebrows at that italicized phrase twice used, *God as we understood Him.* I applaud it. It is more than an expression of tolerance which makes it possible for Roman Catholics, Protestants, and Jews to join in asserting the Twelve Steps. Once more, a universal and indispensable truth is involved.

God can be thought of as Absolute Being. He is that. But in a crisis, where a man grapples with an unmanageable habit or an abysmal grief, Absolute Being can be as distant, cold, and useless as the man in the moon. What we need in a crisis is the near end of God, God as we understand Him, God as an available resource close at hand, our unseen Friend, our invisible Companion. Granted that our diverse and partial ideas of God are inadequate! But anyone who, because of alcohol or for any other reason, has gone through the experience which the Twelve Steps describe, can understand at least a little what the psalmist meant when he said, "O God, Thou art my God."

Some time ago, I heard a man talk about God. He was not dogmatic. He was not a formal creedalist. But he was not indefinite, either. He had been in an immoral hole that seemed hopeless. All his friends thought it was hopeless. And in that hopeless situation, although he had always thought himself an agnostic, he threw himself back on any God that might be. And something happened to him, for which I know no better description than the phrase Virgil used when he led Dante up out of hell through purgatory and left him at the gate of paradise, saying, "Over thyself I crown and miter thee."

So this once-helpless man stood crowned and mitered. No theologian could have been more sure of God than he was. To him, God was not "a sort of something," or, as one college student described God, "an oblong blur." Rather, like the blind man whom Jesus healed, he had had an honest-to-goodness experience that no materialism could explain, that only a real God could account for, and that gave to his testimony certitude and definiteness: "One thing I know, that though I was blind, now I see."

It is this accent of realistic experience in the Twelve Steps that makes them so vital. Through them, one feels a gospel of hope: No man need stay the way he is. John Callender was a captain in George Washington's army, and at the battle of Bunker Hill, he was guilty of such rank cowardice that Washington publicly cashiered him, telling him that what he had done was infamous in a soldier, most injurious to an army, and the last to be forgiven.

So was that the end of John Callender? No! He reenlisted as a private, and at the battle of Long Island, displayed such conspicuous courage that Washington restored him to his captaincy. I will wager anything that, if John Callender could read the Twelve Steps, he would recognize the experience that he went through.

Especially impressive is the way the Twelve Steps avoid all self-pity with its inevitable accompaniment of blaming others for our failures. *Made a searching and fearless moral inventory of ourselves*—that is ethical realism and psychological common sense. And from there on, admitting *the exact nature of our wrongs*, being willing *to have God remove all these defects of character*, and the rest, the Twelve Steps trace a course of penitence, confession, and restitution which makes a personal counselor wish that a lot of other alcoholics would take the same indispensable path to moral transformation.

No words can adequately express the gratitude felt by many of us who have watched with admiration the amazing progress of Alcoholics Anonymous. Among the many factors which have contributed to this success, I am sure that one is central: The Twelve Steps represent the everlasting truth about all personal regeneration. Their basic principles are eternally so, not just for alcoholics, but for everyone.

Dr. Harry Emerson Fosdick

WHEN THE BIG "I" BECOMES NOBODY

September 1965

The AA program of help is touched with elements of true inspiration, and in no place is that inspiration more evident than in the selection of its name, Alcoholics Anonymous. Anonymity is, of course, of great protective value, especially to the newcomer; but my present target is to focus on the even greater value anonymity has in contributing to the state of humility necessary for the maintenance of sobriety in the recovered alcoholic.

My thesis is that anonymity, thoughtfully preserved, supplies two essential ingredients to that maintenance. The two ingredients, actually two sides of the same coin, are: first, the preservation of a reduced ego; second, the continued presence of humility or humbleness. As stated in the Twelfth Tradition of AA, "Anonymity is the spiritual foundation of all our traditions," reminding each member to place "principles before personalities."

Many of you will wonder what that word "ego" means. It has so many definitions that the first task is to clarify the nature of the ego needing reduction.

This ego is not an intellectual concept, but a state of feeling—a feeling of importance—of being "special." Few people can recognize this need to be special in themselves. Most of us, however, can recognize offshoots of this attitude and put the proper name to it. Let me illustrate. Early in the AA days, I was consulted about a serious problem plaguing the local group. The practice of celebrating a year's sobriety with a birthday cake had resulted in a certain number of the members getting drunk within a short period after the celebration. It seemed apparent that some could not stand prosperity. I was asked to settle between birthday cakes and no birthday cakes.

Characteristically, I begged off, not from shyness, but from ignorance. Some three or four years later, AA furnished me with the answer. The group no longer had such a problem, because, as one member said, "We celebrate still, but a year's sobriety is now a dime a dozen. No one gets much of a kick out of that anymore!"

A look at what happened shows us ego, as I see it, in action. Initially, the person who had been sober for a full year was a standout, someone to be looked up to. His ego naturally expanded; his pride flowered; any previous deflation vanished. With such a renewal of confidence, he took a drink. He had been made special and reacted accordingly. Later, the special element dropped out. No ego feeds off being in the dime-a-dozen category, and the problem of ego build-up vanished.

Today, AA in practice is well aware of the dangers of singling anyone out for honors and praise. The dangers of re-inflation are recognized. The phrase "trusted servant" is a conscious effort to keep that ego down, although admittedly some servants have a problem in that regard.

Now, let us take a closer look at this ego which causes trouble. The feelings associated with this state of mind are of basic importance in understanding the value of anonymity for the individual—the value of placing him in the rank and file of humanity.

Certain qualities typify this ego which views itself as special and therefore different. It is high on itself and prone to keep its goals and visions at the same high level. It disdains what it sees as grubs who plod along without the fire and inspiration of those sparked by ideals lifting people out of the commonplace and offering promise of better things to come.

Often, the same ego operates in reverse. It despairs of man, with his faults and his failings, and develops a cynicism which sours the spirit and makes of its possessor a cranky realist who finds nothing good in this vale of tears. Life never quite meets his demands upon it, and he lives an embittered existence, grabbing what he can out of the moment, but never really part of what goes on around him. He seeks love and understanding and prates endlessly about this sense of alienation from those around him. Basically, he is a disappointed idealist—forever aiming high and landing low. Both of these egos confuse humbleness with humiliation.

To develop further, the expression "You think you're something" nicely catches the sense of being above the crowd. Children readily spot young-sters who think they are something, and do their best to puncture that illu-sion. For instance, they play a game called tag. In it, the one who is tagged is called "it." You've heard them accuse each other saying, "You think you're it," thereby charging the other with acting as though he was better than his mates. In their own way, children make very good therapists or head-shrinkers. They are skillful puncturers of inflated egos, even though their purpose is not necessarily therapeutic.

AA had its start in just such a puncturing. Bill W. always refers to his experience at Towns Hospital as a "deflation in great depth" and on occa-sion has been heard to say that his ego took a "hell of a licking." AA stems from that deflation and that licking.

Clearly, the sense of being special, of being "something," has its dan-gers, its drawbacks for the alcoholic. Yet the opposite, namely, that one is to be a nothing, has little counter appeal. The individual seems faced with being a something and getting drunk, or being a nothing and getting drunk from boredom.

The apparent dilemma rests upon a false impression about the nature of nothingness as a state of mind. The ability to accept ourselves as noth-ing is not easily developed. It runs counter to all our desires for identity, for an apparently meaningful existence, one filled with hope and prom-ise. To be nothing seems a form of psychological suicide. We cling to our somethingness with all the strength at our command. The thought of be-ing a nothing is simply not acceptable. But the fact is that the person who does not learn to be as nothing cannot feel that he is but a plain, ordinary everyday kind of person, who merges with the human race—and as such is humble, lost in the crowd, and essentially anonymous. When that can happen, the person has a lot going for him.

People with "nothing" on their minds can relax and go about their busi-ness quietly and with a minimum of fuss and bother. They can even enjoy life as it comes along. In AA, this is called the 24-hour program, which re-ally signifies that the individual does not have tomorrow on his mind. He can live in the present and find his pleasure in the here and now. He is hus-tling nowhere. With nothing on his mind, the individual is receptive and open-minded.

The great religions are conscious of the need for nothingness if one is to attain grace. In the New Testament, Matthew, 18:3, quotes Christ with these words: "Truly I say to you, unless you turn and become like children, you will never enter the kingdom of heaven. Whoever humbles himself like this child, he is the greatest in the kingdom of heaven."

Zen teaches the release of nothingness. A famous series of pictures designed to show growth in man's nature ends with a circle enclosed in a square. The circle depicts man in a state of nothingness; the square represents the framework of limitations man must learn to live within. In this blank state, "Nothing is easy, nothing hard," and so Zen, too, has linked nothingness, humbleness, and grace.

Anonymity is a state of mind of great value to the individual in maintaining sobriety. While I recognize its protective function, I feel that any discussion of it would be one-sided if it failed to emphasize the fact that the maintenance of a feeling of anonymity—of a feeling "I am nothing special"—is a basic insurance of humility and so a basic safeguard against further trouble with alcohol. This kind of anonymity is truly a precious possession.

Harry M. Tiebout, MD

THE FUNDAMENTALS IN RETROSPECT

September 1948

It is gratifying to feel that one belongs to and has a definite personal part in the work of a growing and spiritually prospering organization for the release of the alcoholics of mankind from a deadly enslavement. For me, there is double gratification in the realization that, more than thirteen years ago, an all-wise Providence, whose ways must always be mysterious to our limited understandings, brought me to "see my duty clear," and to contribute in decent humility, as have so many others, my part in guiding the first trembling steps of the then infant organization, Alcoholics Anonymous.

It is fitting at this time to indulge in some retrospect regarding certain fundamentals. Much has been written, much has been said about the Twelve Steps of AA. The tenets of our faith and practice were not worked out overnight and then presented to our members as an opportunist creed. Born of our early trials and many tribulations, they were and are the result of humble and sincere desire, sought in personal prayer, for divine guidance.

As finally expressed and offered, they are simple in language, plain in meaning. They are also workable by any person having a sincere desire to obtain and keep sobriety. The results are the proof. Their simplicity and workability are such that no special interpretations, and certainly no reservations, have ever been necessary. And it has become increasingly clear that the degree of harmonious living which we achieve is in direct ratio to our earnest attempt to follow them literally under divine guidance to the best of our ability.

Yet there are no shibboleths in AA. We are not bound by theological doctrine. None of us may be excommunicated and cast into outer darkness. For we are many minds in our organization, and an AA Decalogue in the language of "Thou shalt not" would gall us indeed.

Look at our Twelve Traditions. No random expressions these, based on just casual observation. On the contrary, they represent the sum of our experiences as individuals, as groups within AA, and similarly with our fellows and other organizations in the great fellowship of humanity under God throughout the world. They are all suggestions, yet the spirit in which they have been conceived merits their serious, prayerful consideration as the guideposts of AA policy for the individual, the group, and our various committees, local and national.

We have found it wise policy, too, to hold to no glorification of the individual. Obviously, that is sound. Most of us will concede that when it came to the personal showdown of admitting our lives to Almighty God, as we understood Him, we still had some sneaking ideas of personal justification and excuse. We had to discard them, but the ego of the alcoholic dies a hard death. Many of us, because of activity, have received praise, not only from our fellow AAs, but from the world at large. We would be ungrateful indeed to be boorish when that happens; still, it is so easy for us to become, privately perhaps, just a little vain about it all. Yet fitting and wearing halos is not for us.

We've all seen the new member who stays sober for a time, largely through sponsorship. Then maybe the sponsor gets drunk, and you know what usually happens. Left without a human prop, the new member gets drunk, too. He has been glorifying an individual, instead of following the program.

Certainly, we need leaders, but we must regard them as the human agents of the Higher Power and not with undue adulation as individuals. The Fourth and Tenth Steps cannot be too strongly emphasized here, *Made a searching and fearless moral inventory of ourselves ... Continued to take personal inventory and when we were wrong promptly admitted it.* There is your perfect antidote for halo-poisoning. ...

So with the question of anonymity. If we have a banner, this word, speaking of the surrender of the individual—the ego—is emblazoned on it. Let us dwell thoughtfully on its full meaning and learn thereby to remain humble, modest, ever-conscious that we are eternally under divine direction.

Alcoholics Anonymous was nurtured in its early days around a kitchen table. Many of our pioneer groups and some of our most resultful meetings and best programs have had their origin around that modest piece of furniture, with the coffeepot handy on the stove.

True, we have progressed materially to better furniture and more comfortable surroundings. Yet the kitchen table must ever be appropriate for us. It is the perfect symbol of simplicity. In AA we have no VIPs, nor have we need of any. Our organization needs no title-holders nor grandiose buildings. That is by design. Experience has taught us that simplicity is basic in preservation of our personal sobriety and helping those in need.

Far better it is for us to fully understand the meaning and practice of "thou good and faithful servant," than to listen to "With 60,000 members, you should have sixty-stories-high administration headquarters in New York with an assortment of trained 'ists' to direct your affairs." We need nothing of the sort. God grant that AA may ever stay simple.

Over the years we have tested and developed suitable techniques for our purpose. They are entirely flexible. We have all known and seen miracles—the healing of broken individuals, the rebuilding of broken homes. And always it has been the constructive, personal Twelfth Step work based on an ever-upward-looking faith which has done the job.

In as large an organization as ours, we naturally have had our share of those who fail to measure up to certain obvious standards of conduct. They have included schemers for personal gain, petty swindlers and confidence men, crooks of various kinds, and other human fallibles. Relatively, their number has been small, much smaller than in many religious and social-uplift organizations. Yet they have been a problem and not an easy one. They have caused many an AA to stop thinking and working constructively for a time.

We cannot condone their actions, yet we must concede that when we have used normal caution and precaution in dealing with such cases, we may safely leave them to that Higher Power. Let me reiterate that we AAs are many men and women, that we are of many minds. It will be well for us to concentrate on the goal of personal sobriety and active work. We humans and alcoholics, on strict moral stock-taking, must confess to at least a slight degree of larcenous instinct. We can hardly arrogate the roles of judges and executioners.

Thirteen grand years! To have been a part of it all from the beginning has been reward indeed.

Dr. Bob

Anonymous to the End *January 1955*

Last summer I visited the Akron cemetery where Bob and Anne lie. Their simple stone says never a word about Alcoholics Anonymous. This made me so glad I cried. Did this wonderful couple carry personal anonymity too far when they so firmly refused to use the words "Alcoholics Anonymous," even on their own burial stone?

For one, I don't think so. I think that this great and final example of self-effacement will prove of more permanent worth to AA than could any spectacular public notoriety or fine mausoleum.

We don't have to go to Akron, Ohio, to see Dr. Bob's memorial. Dr. Bob's real monument is visible throughout the length and breadth of AA. Let us look again at its true inscription ... one word only, which we AAs have written. That word is Sacrifice.

Bill W.

PART ONE:

Seeking

⌘

A SEARCH FOR ENLIGHTENMENT

Here we encounter a remarkable group of AAs who are in the midst of what Carl Jung describes as "the spiritual thirst of our being for wholeness." The search may lead to a sudden, dramatic spiritual awakening—"an illumination of enormous impact and dimension," Bill W. writes—though for many the quest is long and the awakening gradual. One writer describes experiencing "a spiritual change without noticing it"; another a slow progression from self-loathing to "cleansing tears" of gratitude.

For some, the search begins with a simple *maybe*, a willingness to act *as if*, while for others it resides in AA meetings, in "the gift of the art of listening." Whether the Fellowship is seen as "the eye of the hurricane" or a new home where "shared darkness has become a shared light," here in AA we are able to accomplish together what we can't do on our own.

Along the way come the questions. What is a Higher Power? Where do I look for one? Who or what is God, if there is a God? As is the case with so much in AA, the answers vary with our experiences, and so concepts of a Higher Power range from "an infinity of kindness" to the Spirit of Love, from the "still, small voice" inside to a sensitivity for the Universal, from a Deeper Power to "God, the verb."

An awakening of the spirit defies definition and requires faith, says one writer, though sometimes the intense pursuit of it can of itself be the root of our troubles, says another. But probably all of us will agree with that one AA who observes that however we look at it, a spiritual awakening "flowers from the cultivating of all of AA's Twelve Steps."

THE BILL W. – CARL JUNG LETTERS
January 1963

Here is a vital chapter of AA's early history, first published in the Grapevine in January 1963. This extraordinary exchange of letters revealed for the first time not only the direct historical ancestry of AA, but the bizarre situation wherein Jung, deeply involved with scientists and with a scientific reputation at stake, felt he had to be cautious about revealing his profound and lasting belief that the ultimate sources of recovery are spiritual sources. Permission to publish Dr. Jung's letter was granted to the Grapevine by the Jung estate.

January 23, 1961

My dear Dr. Jung:

This letter of great appreciation has been very long overdue.

May I first introduce myself as Bill W., a co-founder of the Society of Alcoholics Anonymous. Though you have surely heard of us, I doubt if you are aware that a certain conversation you once had with one of your patients, a Mr. Rowland H., back in the early 1930s, did play a critical role in the founding of our Fellowship.

Though Rowland H. has long since passed away, the recollection of his remarkable experience while under treatment by you has definitely become part of AA history. Our remembrance of Rowland H.'s statement about his experience with you is as follows:

Having exhausted other means of recovery from his alcoholism, it was about 1931 that he became your patient. I believe he remained under your care for perhaps a year. His admiration for you was boundless, and he left you with a feeling of much confidence.

To his great consternation, he soon relapsed into intoxication. Certain that you were his "court of last resort," he again returned to your care. Then followed the conversation between you that was to become the first link in the chain of events that led to the founding of Alcoholics Anonymous.

My recollection of his account is this: First of all, you frankly told

him of his hopelessness, so far as any further medical or psychiatric treatment might be concerned. This candid and humble statement of yours was beyond doubt the first foundation stone upon which our society has since been built.

Coming from you, one he so trusted and admired, the impact upon him was immense.

When he then asked you if there was any other hope, you told him that there might be, provided he could become the subject of a spiritual or religious experience—in short, a genuine conversion. You pointed out how such an experience, if brought about, might remotivate him when nothing else could. But you did caution, though, that while such experiences had sometimes brought recovery to alcoholics, they were, nevertheless, comparatively rare. You recommended that he place himself in a religious atmosphere and hope for the best. This I believe was the substance of your advice.

Shortly thereafter, Mr. H. joined the Oxford Group, an evangelical movement then at the height of its success in Europe, and one with which you are doubtless familiar. You will remember their large emphasis upon the principles of self-survey, confession, restitution, and the giving of oneself in service to others. They strongly stressed meditation and prayer. In these surroundings, Rowland H. did find a conversion experience that released him for the time being from his compulsion to drink.

Returning to New York, he became very active with the "O.G." here, then led by an Episcopal clergyman, Dr. Samuel Shoemaker. Dr. Shoemaker had been one of the founders of that movement, and his was a powerful personality that carried immense sincerity and conviction.

At this time (1932-34), the Oxford Group had already sobered a number of alcoholics, and Rowland, feeling that he could especially identify with these sufferers, addressed himself to the help of still others. One of these chanced to be an old schoolmate of mine, Edwin T. (Ebby). He had been threatened with commitment to an institution, but Mr. H. and another ex-alcoholic "O.G." member procured his parole, and helped to bring about his sobriety.

Meanwhile, I had run the course of alcoholism and was threatened with commitment myself. Fortunately, I had fallen under the care of a physician—a Dr. William D. Silkworth—who was wonderfully capable of understanding alcoholics. But just as you had given up on Rowland, so had he given me up. It was his theory that alcoholism had two components—an obsession that compelled the sufferer to drink against his will and interest, and some sort of metabolism difficulty which he then called an allergy. The alcoholic's compulsion guaranteed that the alcoholic's drinking would go on, and the allergy made sure that the sufferer would finally deteriorate, go insane, or die. Though I had been one of the few he had thought it possible to help, he was finally obliged to tell me of my hopelessness; I, too, would have to be locked up. To me, this was a shattering blow. Just as Rowland had been made ready for his conversion experience by you, so had my wonderful friend Dr. Silkworth prepared me.

Hearing of my plight, my friend Edwin T. came to see me at my home, where I was drinking. By then, it was November 1934. I had long marked my friend Edwin for a hopeless case. Yet here he was in a very evident state of "release," which could by no means be accounted for by his mere association for a very short time with the Oxford Group. Yet this obvious state of release, as distinguished from the usual depression, was tremendously convincing. Because he was a kindred sufferer, he could unquestionably communicate with me at great depth. I knew at once I must find an experience like his, or die.

Again I returned to Dr. Silkworth's care, where I could be once more sobered and so gain a clearer view of my friend's experience of release, and of Rowland H.'s approach to him.

Clear once more of alcohol, I found myself terribly depressed. This seemed to be caused by my inability to gain the slightest faith. Edwin T. again visited me and repeated the simple Oxford Group formulas. Soon after he left me, I became even more depressed. In utter despair, I cried out, "If there be a God, will he show himself." There immediately came to me an illumination of enormous impact and dimension, something which I have since tried to describe in the book *Alcoholics Anonymous* and also in *AA Comes of Age*, basic texts which I am sending to you. My release from the alcohol obsession was immediate. At once, I knew I was a free man.

Shortly following my experience, my friend Edwin came to the hospital, bringing me a copy of William James's *Varieties of Religious Experience*. This book gave me the realization that most conversion experiences, whatever their variety, do have a common denominator of ego collapse at depth. The individual faces an impossible dilemma. In my case, the dilemma had been created by my compulsive drinking and the deep feeling of hopelessness had been vastly deepened still more by my alcoholic friend when he acquainted me with your verdict of hopelessness respecting Rowland H.

In the wake of my spiritual experience, there came a vision of a society of alcoholics, each identifying with and transmitting his experience to the next—chain-style. If each sufferer were to carry the news of the scientific hopelessness of alcoholism to each new prospect, he might be able to lay every newcomer wide open to a transforming spiritual experience. This concept proved to be the foundation of such success as Alcoholics Anonymous has since achieved. This has made a conversion experience—nearly every variety reported by James—available on an almost wholesale basis. Our sustained recoveries over the last quarter-century number about 30,000. In America and through the world, there are today 8,000 AA groups. (In 2003, worldwide membership is estimated to be over 2,000,000; number of groups, over 97,000.)

So to you, to Dr. Shoemaker of the Oxford Group, to William James, and to my own physician, Dr. Silkworth, we of AA owe this tremendous benefaction. As you will now clearly see, this astonishing chain of events actually started long ago in your consulting room, and it was directly founded upon your own humility and deep perception.

Very many thoughtful AAs are students of your writings. Because of your conviction that man is something more than intellect, emotion, and two dollars' worth of chemicals, you have especially endeared yourself to us.

How our society grew, developed its Traditions for unity, and structured its functioning, will be seen in the texts and pamphlet that

I am sending you.

You will also be interested to learn that, in addition to the "spiritual experience," many AAs report a great variety of psychic phenomena, the cumulative weight of which is very considerable. Other members have—following their recovery in AA—been much helped by your practitioners. A few have been intrigued by the *I Ching* and your remarkable introduction to that work.

Please be certain that your place in the affection, and in the history, of our Fellowship is like no other.

William G. W.

January 30, 1961

Dear Mr. W.

Your letter has been very welcome indeed.

I had no news from Rowland H. any more and often wondered what has been his fate. Our conversation which he has adequately reported to you had an aspect of which he did not know. The reason that I could not tell him everything was that those days I had to be exceedingly careful of what I said. I had found out that I was misunderstood in every possible way. Thus I was very careful when I talked to Rowland H. But what I really thought about was the result of many experiences with men of his kind.

His craving for alcohol was the equivalent, on a low level, of the spiritual thirst of our being for wholeness, expressed in medieval language: the union with God.

How could one formulate such an insight in a language that is not misunderstood in our days?

The only right and legitimate way to such an experience is that it happens to you in reality, and it can only happen to you when you walk on a path which leads you to higher understanding. You might be led to that goal by an act of grace or through a personal and honest contact with friends, or through a higher education of the mind beyond the confines of mere rationalism. I see from your letter that

Rowland H. has chosen the second way, which was, under the circumstances, obviously the best one.

I am strongly convinced that the evil principle prevailing in this world leads the unrecognized spiritual need into perdition if that is not counteracted either by real religious insight or by the protective wall of human community. An ordinary man, not protected by an action from above and isolated in society, cannot resist the power of evil, which is called very aptly the Devil. But the use of such words arouses so many mistakes that one can only keep aloof from them as much as possible.

These are the reasons why I could not give a full and sufficient explanation to Rowland H., but I am risking it with you because I conclude from your very decent and honest letter that you have acquired a point of view above the misleading platitudes one usually hears about alcoholism.

You see, alcohol in Latin is *spiritus*, and you use the same word for the highest religious experience as well as for the most depraving poison. The helpful formula therefore is: *spiritus contra spiritum*.

Thanking you again for your kind letter.

C. G. Jung

So <u>That's</u> a Spiritual Experience!

January 1977

I remember, early in my sobriety, feeling depressed because I had not had a spiritual experience. I was sure that I alone had not undergone a sudden change of heart.

This impression came from listening to some other members describe their spiritual awakenings. They described them simply and honestly. There had been, they said, no flashing lights, no burning bushes. But there had been a moment when they experienced total surrender, a sudden change of attitude. It was, they said, an experience that immediately changed their lives.

I assumed (erroneously, I later found) that all AA members had undergone a similar experience. I was sure that those who did not speak of their moment of truth were too modest to describe it. And I was also sure that I was the only one, even among the new members, who had not experienced an instantaneous change.

I believed that my entry into AA had been different. I had come in reluctantly, and had stayed reluctant for as long as possible. Only gradually, over a period of months, did I realize that I had no place else to go. There was never any sudden, joyful acceptance of recovery. There was, instead, a gradual, sad admission that I could choose AA or die. Not what I would have called a "spiritual" experience.

Fortunately, there was a small group of us who were all new to the program and very close. It was among them that I made a series of discoveries.

First, I discovered that I was not alone. All of us agreed that, whatever a spiritual experience might be, we certainly hadn't had one. We had all been waiting for it to happen, and by now, most of us were convinced that it probably never would. We were different. Unlike the older members, we had been too "sinful" in the past and were too secular in the present to be worthy of anything "spiritual."

Our second discovery was more exciting. We discovered that most of the other members had not undergone an instantaneous change, either. We learned, by listening at meetings and talking to our sponsors, that the majority of those we admired had undergone, like us, a gradual change. So we weren't inferior. We were with the majority.

The third discovery was a blockbuster. One of us read Bill W.'s discussion of the Twelfth Step in *Twelve Steps and Twelve Traditions*. There, he explains that there are many kinds of spiritual experience. Some are like the conversions of the great religious leaders of the past; others seem purely psychological. Some are sudden or instantaneous; others are a gradual learning experience. But all of them, whatever form they take, have one effect: They make a person capable of doing something he could not do before.

As Bill puts it, "When a man or a woman has a spiritual awakening, the most important meaning of it is that he has now become able to do, feel, and believe that which he could not do before on his unaided strength and resources alone."

For all of us, this was an important discovery. I was now capable of doing things that had been impossible for me before; I could not deny it. The obvious example was staying sober—by this time, I had been dry for several consecutive months. Before AA, several consecutive days had been impossible.

In other words, I had been undergoing a spiritual experience without knowing it. My confused questioning about a Higher Power, my changed mental attitude, and even my physical recovery had all been part of a spiritual awakening. Without knowing it, I had been in contact with the source of life, whatever or Whoever that might be.

Paradoxically, the realization that even I had experienced something spiritual was in itself a spiritual experience, and I am only slowly understanding its implications. What happened in the past, without my knowledge, is probably continuing now. And in the future, when tomorrow becomes today, it can go on and on. All that is required is a desire to stop drinking, and to stay stopped.

Ed O.
York, Pennsylvania

Learning To Listen   March 1979

I was alone, isolated in my misery and self-disgust, utterly without hope—helpless. From the depths of that despair, I uttered a groan rather than a prayer: "Please help me." It wasn't much, but it was probably the best, or the first, real prayer I had ever said. I had talked to God, not at Him. Despair had stripped away all pretense and, for a moment, even the veil of alcohol. For that moment, I was truly humble and empty. There was nothing left in me, and I knew it. And I knew only God could help me, and He did. I picked up the phone and called AA. From Him, I received enough honesty to admit my total helplessness and enough humility to ask for help. That was three years ago.

R.O.
Seattle, Washington

You're Welcome Here
April 1988

For my first two or three years in AA I found talking about the spiritual aspect of AA a real problem. I solved it in the only way I could at the time, by not mentioning the subject at all.

There were several reasons why I found it so hard to speak of God or spirituality. My personal relationship with my Higher Power was then, and still is, a very private thing to me, something I cannot talk about lightly. Also, my ideas of God were vague and unformulated. It wasn't that I didn't believe in God, only what, exactly, was I believing in? I didn't know, so I didn't talk about it.

Finally, I had heard older members caution against bearing down too hard on what they called "the God business" in working with newcomers. "You can scare them away if you sound as if you are trying to cram your religion down their throats. Soft pedal the spiritual a little until they've logged some sober time. Remember, spiritual progress isn't what gets us sober, it's what keeps us sober."

At no time did any of these long-sober and much respected members recommend what I was actually doing: avoiding the subject altogether.

I never doubted that spiritual progress was essential to my recovery, and to the recovery of the newer women I was trying to help. What worried me increasingly was whether they could be helped by someone unable to talk about the spirituality so basic to AA.

Presently I took my problem to an AA member with long experience, Timothy, sober for nearly thirty years. He did not seem at all disturbed by my confession that I had trouble talking to new people about my concept of God.

"Why should you tell them about your concept of God?" he asked. "Your idea of God isn't going to help them stay sober. Their own idea of God, or of a Higher Power, will. Our responsibility is not to offer our newcomers a ready-made God, but to encourage them to develop their own spiritual base.

"I think your problem lies in neglecting four very important words in our Steps. They are so important that they are the only ones carried in italics. You find them in Steps Three and Eleven, immediately following the word 'God.' They are: *as we understood Him.*

"Which means that the only idea of a Higher Power our new people need, or that will work for them, is their own. Not yours, not mine, not their parents', not that of the minister in the church down the street, but their own. In AA each individual has the absolute right to believe whatever he wants to believe, or can believe, and not one of us is entitled to tell him he's wrong, or try to force our beliefs on him."

Timothy sped me on my way with suggestions for some reading in two sections of the Big Book which he thought I might now read with greater understanding.

In chapter four, "We Agnostics," I found this statement: "We needed to ask ourselves but one short question. 'Do I now believe, or am I even willing to believe, that there is a power greater than myself?' As soon as a man can say that he does believe, or is willing to believe, we emphatically assure him that he is on his way. It has been repeatedly proven among us that upon this simple cornerstone a wonderfully effective spiritual structure can be built."

Timothy's other suggestion was the second section of the Appendices entitled "Spiritual Experience." In that section these words leaped out at me "... any alcoholic capable of honestly facing his problem in the light of our experience can recover, provided he does not close his mind to all spiritual concepts."

What wonderful freedom those passages give us. How widely they throw open the doors of AA to admit every sick, terrified, desperate alcoholic who wants to recover. For there is not one hint as to what we should believe, or what the nature of our Higher Power should be. That is entirely up to us. The alcoholic who is not prepared at this point to have faith in any kind of god and regards his AA group as his higher power, is welcomed into AA, gets sober, stays sober, grows along spiritual lines, and in general is a terrific success. He may, in time, develop a more conventional concept of God. We sometimes experience dramatic changes in ourselves as we live the AA program, year after year.

On the other hand, he may not. His spiritual growth may be in another direction, and he will remain agnostic all his long, sober life. We have the obligation to respect his right to hold his own beliefs, no matter how different they may be from our convictions.

A few days later I had the opportunity to thank Timothy for his guidance. "I feel a little better equipped to talk to new members now," I said. "If you have any other recommended reading I'd like to hear about it."

"I do, as it so happens—two of them," Timothy said slowly. "With these it isn't a matter of reading passages you hadn't noticed before. You know them well. Now you need to look at them in a new way, until you perceive their relationship to AA spirituality. One is the Third Tradition. The other is the first part of the Twelfth Step."

The Third Tradition. "The only requirement for AA membership is a desire to stop drinking." I had not thought of it in relation to spiritual growth before. I had long since observed that the Tradition says nothing about age, color, sex (or sexual preference), race, education or occupation. If you want to stop drinking AA doesn't care who you are or where you came from. Now, for the first time I noticed—really noticed—that the Third Tradition also says not one word about what your religion is, whether you believe in God, or who or what or where you think God is. If you want to stop drinking AA doesn't care whether you are a Christian, a Buddhist, a Jew, a Mohammedan, an atheist, an agnostic, or whatever. The door to AA is wide. Come right in. You're welcome here.

The first part of the Twelfth Step says: *Having had a spiritual awakening as the result of these steps* .... As *the result* of these Steps! I understood, at last, what the older members meant when they told me that spiritual progress isn't what gets us sober, it's what keeps us sober.

All this time I had thought that I, and the new women I tried to help, needed some kind of spiritual foundation for a proper start in AA. What I did not perceive, until Timothy guided my thinking, was that having a desire to stop drinking, that is, to make a drastic change in our lives, was itself a spiritual foundation—quite enough of one to get us started staying sober, one day at a time. Spiritual progress would come as we worked through the Steps. As a result of this action we would know a spiritual awakening into a satisfying life forever impossible to the drinking alcoholic.

Elizabeth E.
Tulsa, Oklahoma

A RUSH OF GRATITUDE
April 1983

How often I used to listen with envy to the words *Having had a spiritual awakening* ... as others told of their new spiritual lives! For me, there appeared no magical awakening, just a gradual lessening of anxiety and a little self-respect after several years in the program.

Don't get me wrong—those little changes were most welcome. They were a significant improvement over the self-loathing, nervous twit I was during my drinking years—but hardly something so grand as to warrant the label "spiritual awakening."

So I continued to attend my meetings and listened with awe and resignation as my sisters and brothers pronounced their Twelfth Step revelations. I hoped some of it might rub off, but no such luck. Oh, it wasn't a total loss. I was sober. My life continued to improve. I made some friends, solved some long-standing problems, and developed a positive credit rating for the first time in my adult life. But no thunderbolts or lightning, no Twelfth Step fireworks, no parting of the clouds, and no trumpeting heralds to signal a new spiritual awareness.

And so it went until one day when, as I completed a particularly difficult task, I felt tears fill my eyes and I heard myself muttering to no one in particular, "Thank you, thank you, thank you." The experience left me feeling cleansed and peaceful. As I reflected on it later, I wrote it off as bizarre—probably the reaction to some severe stress. But it happened again shortly after that: tears, mumbled thank-yous, and an exquisite feeling of peace and completeness. Thinking I might be cracking up, I called my sponsor. His response was laughter. "Cracking up?" he chuckled. "You've never been healthier, you meathead. You've finally experienced gratitude."

And so I did—for the first time in my life, I experienced gratitude. Never in my drinking years had I ever known this wonderful feeling. In those sick days, the most I could ever feel was relief if something bad didn't happen or I didn't get caught doing something destructive.

Now, I've got a brand-new feeling, gratitude—a feeling that has visited me more and more frequently—sometimes with the rush of cleansing tears—sometimes with just a serene flow of mental thank-yous for some small, God-given bonus in a routine day—sometimes with an overwhelming sense of thankfulness when one of my children does or says something touching or special—sometimes (often!) when I reflect on the beautiful new life and wonderful partner-spouse that AA has given me.

So for me, a "spiritual awakening" has become synonymous with the emergence of a brand-new feeling—gratitude.

M.B.
Minneapolis, Minnesota

THE HUMAN HANDS THAT HELP US
November 1997

Like many of us, I didn't believe in a power greater than myself. Not that I didn't want to. When, as a teenager, I began to have doubts, I went to my minister. He was supposed to provide me with certainty. Instead, he suggested that I read some books. But I'd heard him quote from those books in sermons that I didn't approve of, so I wasn't about to read them. Soon questions of faith and doubt were beside the point, for I went to college and discovered a new power and a new self through alcohol.

How I made it through college I don't know because I was nearly a daily drinker in those years. I graduated, married, worked, and went on for graduate degrees—all while drinking every day. In graduate school, my husband and I were known for giving great parties where I provided lots of food and the guests provided a bottle apiece. I still remember the night when one guest was crying because, having drunk one bottle of rum, he slipped and broke the second one as he was leaving. My only thought was, How could he be so careless?

Those should have been wonderful years. I was doing well in my studies. Everyone found my husband handsome and charming. And we continued to give those big warm parties where everyone got sloshed and sang and danced. Something was missing, however, and I thought I had found it when I met a theology professor who believed in God. He radiated a peace and joy that I'd never seen before in anyone. To the amusement of my husband, I started going to church. And I signed up for theology courses. I was going to learn how to get the faith that my professor had.

But all the theology I'd read made clear that faith was not a commodity I could purchase or a quality I could acquire. It was the gift of this God that I didn't believe in. I could not acquire it, the books agreed, I could only wait for it, using such means of grace as prayer and meditation and churchgoing. I was outraged. I was a busy person. I didn't have time to wait when the waiting itself was not even a guarantee that the faith would come. "I can't wait on this God," I said. "If he exists, then he can give me this faith when he wants to. Until then, I've got things to do."

With that I gave up all concern about God and went about my business. I finished graduate school, got a job, divorced my husband, and set about serious drinking. I was certain that I wasn't an alcoholic. No one with my professional status could be one. Besides, unlike my stodgy colleagues, I knew how to drink, how to relax and have fun. After a series of bizarre relationships, I met and married another alcoholic, who taught me to drink in the daytime and to appreciate the best vodka. Although that marriage also ended, I shall be forever grateful because it forced me to look at my life.

A drinking marriage is not fun. It is mornings of creeping around the house to see whether you have broken anything in a blackout. It is jealousy and fear and fights. After one fight that ended only when friends took me away to their home, my mother called to tell me that I had a problem. "I know I do," I answered. "Let me tell you what he's done now."

"No," she said, "you have a problem, a drinking problem." For the only time in my life, I hung up on my mother. I moved out of my house to sort things out with my husband and went to a motel. I called my mother. She told me she and my father loved me, but that no amount of money they might spend on me could cure me. "Go to AA," she said. "It is the only thing that has any success. Otherwise you will wind up in the gutter."

I set out to prove to myself and my mother that I could control my drinking. And I did it for one week. Then, to reward myself, I stopped at a friend's house for one vodka. I don't know how many we had, and neither does he, but we celebrated his first AA birthday last spring. What I do remember is coming to a stoplight in my little suburb of Atlanta to see a man and a woman stopped in a car beside mine. The man got out of his car and came over to my window. "Where do you live, lady? Do you know where you live?" And the next thing I knew I was at my house, and the man and the woman were driving off.

The next morning, my husband told me I'd cried that I had no friends. Driving back to the motel, I started to do what I had always done in the past, which was not to think about what had happened the night before but to tell myself that it didn't matter, today would be different. Only this time I stopped in the middle of telling myself that. For the first time in my life, I said to myself, "I must think about what has happened. I must try to remember."

There was precious little that I could remember. What stood out was the man at my car window. A man I did not know, whose face I could not recall, had interrupted his evening to make certain that I got home safely. He could as easily have mugged, raped, or murdered me. Instead, he helped me. As I drove down the road, shaking and with tears in my eyes, I—who did not believe in God and who had been too busy to await his grace—knew that grace had come to me. That free gift of guidance and protection from the stranger was grace. The moment when I knew that was an absolutely alien thought to me, not one I would have chosen to think. It just came to me that I was alive by the gracious act of a stranger and that this grace was from God.

And then I began to tremble because I knew my mother had spoken the truth. I was an alcoholic. I had been driving in a blackout. Not only could the man have done anything to me, but I could have done murder with my car and never have known it. Terrified of myself, I made it back to the motel, looked up and called the number for the central office. The line was busy. My eyes were so blurred by tears I could hardly read the page, but I called the next listing. It was an AA clubhouse near my motel. That morning I went in the clubhouse doors and my life began again. The AA members there welcomed me, they shared with me, they kept me with them while I dried out. Like the stranger, they offered me grace.

Since that morning on January 26, 1983, I've never doubted that there is a God. I don't mean to say I know anything about God. All I know is that I've experienced in my life a power greater than myself, and it has restored me to my sanity. For me, it is the power we refer to when we say,

"Keep coming back, it works." God for me is that "it." God is the "it" in "Get down on your knees and pray; it works." And "it" does—whatever we call it.

A man I know wouldn't pray to God, so his sponsor told him to pray to Stone Mountain or his cat or a lamp. It worked. Now he too calls "it" God because, as he says, he might as well use a term that's been convenient for so many people for so long. He knows and I know that we each mean something a bit different when we say "God," but then in AA we all know that "God" is a handy name for a powerful reality—the grace, the love, the power greater than ourselves, the it—that we first experience through the human hands that help us when we cannot help ourselves.

Sara S.
Decatur, Georgia

My Name is Gary and I'm a Human Being   February 2003

During my years growing up in an alcoholic home, as well as my years as a practicing alcoholic, I lost my sense of being a human.

The way I was treated and, subsequently, the way I treated others were inhuman. It wasn't until I entered the rooms of Alcoholics Anonymous that I was restored to sanity and welcomed back to the human race. The unconditional love and acceptance from fellow alcoholics reminded me at a deep level that I was human, that I had worth.

It was then that I could pursue an understanding of a power greater than myself. Until I understood and accepted my status as a human being, my effort toward seeking God was in vain.

Some of us take a long time to "come to" before we can "come to believe" that there is any hope for us.

Gary D.
Nanaimo, British Columbia

THE SENSE OF SOBRIETY

August 1959

> *Sense, v. The verb has been used for some three centuries in philosophic writing as a comprehensive form of see or/& hear or/& smell or/& taste or/& feel by touch, i.e., of "have sense perception of" ... also "become aware," perceive.*   — Fowler's Modern English Usage

In this unwieldy definition lies the total of what sobriety has come to mean to me. It embraces the life awareness that I knew only in fragments until I found sense in AA.

I searched for this simple and yet intangible truth in trying to explain to a newcomer why it was that our meetings are the very thing of life to us and why it was that for my first year I needed meetings every night, and still and always will require this refreshment periodically. Although this newcomer has admitted willingly that she is an alcoholic, and that having tried all the other ways she knew AA must hold her answer, she is still having trouble. She simply does not see why her knowledge of the program from an occasional meeting and full familiarity with all the books and literature cannot bring her a sustained sobriety. It is perhaps because she has not yet awakened to the *sense* of sobriety, and so cannot communicate with herself or with us.

To me this is such a tangible thing that I think I can actually feel it grow with each passing AA day. It is a special kind of communication without words and I *sense* it most acutely in AA meetings. I think it is what we mean when we say "and then I came to AA and it was like coming home"; "and then I joined AA and found there all I had ever looked for"; "I felt I belonged"; "these people had something I wanted."

How often we have heard these words, and what does it mean? I think it means that in this atmosphere we sense, if we are ready, this powerful communication—each with the other and the whole with our form of God. We sense that here is our place and these are our people because they are us—they speak our language. I don't think it is a verbal language we mean; I think it is a deep non-word communication based on all the dark experiences we have encountered in our lonely search for a home of the spirit. We sense that here in AA this shared darkness has become a shared light and we know that only the sharing of despair can bring us this illumination. Perhaps that is what we mean when we say "hitting bottom." Perhaps it means that our need to communicate has become so powerful that we are ready at last to begin to *sense*.

Perhaps, too, this readiness means that we are willing to accept the liabilities that go with total sensing. Perhaps it means we are now ready to pay the cost of surrender and to admit that we are no longer going to walk away from what full consciousness really implies. For it implies not only the willingness to receive the love and benefits AA has to offer, but also to surrender to the equally painful experience of exposure to ourselves, and others, of ourselves. I think that the amount of the desire and need to experience sensing is the measure of our sobriety. In it lies the challenge and the growth of our program. We have broken through at last into communication with our kind and we must either sustain these life lines and make them ever stronger or go back to the shadows of the non-sense world we inhabited before.

H.W.
Pleasantville, New York

WHERE THE WORDS COME FROM
May 1960

T he story in a recent issue (February 1960) of the Grapevine about AA life on an Indian reservation called to mind a true story that has almost become a legend out here in the Southwest. At a meeting in southern Arizona, three Papago Indians were in attendance one night. Two were very young, and one was very old. After the meeting, both of the younger men pumped the speaker's hand and thanked him very profusely. The old Indian also said something in his native tongue, and one of the younger men interpreted it to the speaker as follows: "He say he don't know what you say, but he like where the words come from."

We have learned the art of listening in this Fellowship, and how wonderful has been the result! It is one of the great dividends that many of us overlook. Have you ever sat in an easy, pleasant conversation with another of our Fellowship when things took a sudden turn? You each listened avidly to the other; then you found yourself saying things that astonished even you. Something seemed to emerge from it all, and there was a simple naturalness in the long pause that followed.

If this has happened to you, then you know that you come out of it with a feeling of rapture, a feeling that, for a minute, you have been very close to a higher power. Have you ever been writing a letter to an old friend in the Fellowship, when your thoughts and meditation about him came into focus and your writing took an exciting new turn? You have actually listened to memories; you have been listened to and heard; and your whole message is recast as a result.

Have you ever found yourself talking to an old-timer when the very quality of his listening seemed to change your whole course? Perhaps you were feeling awfully sorry for yourself and had intended to pour out all the agonies that had brought you to a current dry drunk. Perhaps you wanted a quart or two—of sympathy, at least. But then, with the understanding love of his complete attention, the true state of things gradually dawned on you. You no longer needed the sympathy.

Or, perhaps, you sought out this old-timer to confess something that you could no longer keep in your own heart. You were not at all sure of the courage to tell how low you had fallen, and you began in evasively safe regions, unsure of both yourself and your friend. But the complete and easy attentiveness of your friend lifted the latch on the gate; it opened quietly; and all that you were holding back tumbled out. Now it was out, now it was over, and you had died a little death, perhaps; but in the patient, kindly eyes of a great and understanding friend, into which you had hardly dared to lift your own in the beginning, you found that you were still loved and still living in a great sober life, which many never come to know.

Yes, one of the truly great gifts in this Fellowship of mutually concerned people is the gift of the art of listening. How many times have you heard people say that they have never seen an audience as intense and kindly as an AA group? And how true it is that almost everyone would rather listen than lead. But our need to listen goes beyond meetings and talks with friends. One of the ancients said, "No man can spend more in good works than he earns in meditation." We need Step Eleven and our greater conscious contact with the Divine Listener. Then will our serenity emerge; then will our help to others have quality.

K.C.

EYE OF THE HURRICANE

December 1992

My mother spoke spirituality. Her tribe did not believe that we owned anything; if she liked something she would give it away, as she would say that it was trying to "own" her. She encouraged me to watch and learn from the animals to see how they used different skills to solve problems and to study the ways of the universe and of the Great Spirit who would teach me if I would listen.

I was never accepted by the other children of the tribe as I was not a full-blood. I listened to the Germans, who worked in the oil fields with my father, when they came to sing the good German songs, drink the beer, and really have a good time. They were "my people." I did not want anything to do with the tribe. I refused to play cowboys and Indians if I had to be the Indian. Shame came early to my life.

World War II broke out and it was no longer popular to speak in German. The music was gone from my life and now I had more shame for my heritage. With the shortage of gas, food and legal booze, things got worse. The violence that came when my father's friends got together to drink became more unpredictable and more unpleasant. Fear became a companion to the shame. I still react to a slammed car door that was the sign for us children to scatter to the winds: My dad had got hold of some of that "fighting whiskey."

My mother's spiritual nature must have kept her isolated from the growing violence, the ugly incidents, the verbal and physical abuse. She always seemed to live in the eye of the hurricane, untouched by the madness around the house.

I found in my own drinking a release from the sense of shame and the fear. Booze was my solution, not my problem! Being activated for the

Korean War didn't make me an alcoholic but it allowed me to hone my drinking and surviving skills. It also allowed me to run away from any identification as an Indian and to escape the harshness of my father.

After coming home from that war, I made many attempts to stop drinking, which were never successful for long. The fears and shame demanded to be drowned in the next bottle, or the next. Images of childhood trauma came up—as I became worse than my father. But the fear in the eyes of those who loved me (and later left to escape a crazy man) became too much to drown in booze.

AA is spiritual, is the eye of the hurricane, is my refuge and my comfort. Today I can visit my mother, who talks to me in her native tongue and I do not understand, but she understands! I hear the voice of the Spirit in the winds, in the animals, and in AA meetings.

Today at an AA meeting I can be myself; I work on ways to touch those parts of me that were lost or thrown away. I can pray and meditate and hear the Great Father's moccasins as he walks through the halls of the AA meeting places. Thanks to AA for making a place for broken hearts and wounded souls.

Anonymous
Oklahoma City, Oklahoma

Between Two Cultures   *March 1984*

I was raised between the culture of the dominant society and of my own Indian heritage, one tyranny pulling me in one direction and the other in the opposite direction. I did not know my own identity nor where I was going.

One of the tyrannies was the Christian religion versus what I had learned from my elders about the Indian religion, which I believe to be true for me today. That is primarily why the AA program made sense to me: I could believe in anything I wanted to. I had known all along that the key to my recovery was spiritual or religious, and AA helped me differentiate between the two. Once the tyranny was lifted and I was free to believe the way I wanted, I was given the gift of sobriety.

C.H.
Santa Ana, California

THE SPIRITUAL KIND OF THIRST

August 1965

Alcoholics Anonymous suggested I choose my own concept of God. To choose a concept of God that made sense to me. I've since wondered why this hadn't occurred to me a long time ago. The idea made such sound, common sense. Then I realized that common sense is one of the most uncommon things there is. Like a miracle, the idea of a belief in God, as I understood Him, set my mind free. It was impossible to have any conflict of feelings or opinions if I accepted my own idea of God.

From this point on I was able to read books, to listen to sermons and accept those ideas which appealed to me and to reject those ideas which I could not agree with, without being angry or defiant. I was able to reject the ideas of others without feeling guilty or wrong. I was free to choose, and it's important I extend to everyone else the same privilege. In reality, AA opened a whole new wonderful world to me.

As I pursued the Eleventh Step, I came to realize that at some point in my life, years ago, long before I became alcoholic, long before I ever drank, perhaps somewhere in my mid-teens, I reached a stalemate where the meaning of life was no longer clear to me. I had become confused about the purpose of life. My whole being, consciously and unconsciously, sensed an inferiority, which I tried to overcome.

In my earlier years I had tried to find a comfortable solution to this sense of inferiority in churches and religions. And while at church, I indulged in the sentimental fallacy of shedding a tear and feeling compassion over abstract truth, justice, and beauty; I was never to know or recognize these qualities when I met them in the street because the circumstances made them vulgar. I was incapable of rationalizing the irrational concepts of organized symbolic religion and became more bewildered, confused, and hostile at every attempt to do so.

So, unable to find a satisfactory answer to my growing sense of inferiority in any formal religious affiliation, I tried to compensate for my uneasiness and confusion by studying science and engineering. I found a lot of satisfaction in the logic and reason of scientific principles and in the laws of science, but no gratifying or conclusive answer to the mystery of what life was all about. Knowing something of the wonders of the world around me left me feeling even more inferior. Then, over a period of years, I tried to calm and pacify this growing inferiority by trying to relate myself to the people around me first; then, by working hard for positions of prestige; then by becoming involved in the affairs of the community; and finally, by accumulating material things—by making money. All of this, over quite a long period of my life, repeatedly left me with only a growing uneasy emptiness. At times, the sense of inferiority was almost overwhelming, yet I secretly harbored feelings of superiority.

I was drawn irresistibly toward a personal goal of principle and perfection. I could not describe this goal in advance. I didn't know for sure what I was seeking. Repeated attempts to find the answer in different religions always left me feeling uncomfortable. I sought this uncertain principle in the works and books of philosophers and in psychology. I sought it in the euphoria of mild intoxication, and then, because I was or had become alcoholic, I sought this mystical goal in drunkenness—in the bottle. I don't believe I drank to get drunk, but always to seek in the next drink that peace for which a sick soul seems to thirst. As the search continued, I became more separated and overwhelmed with that awful sense of aloneness. I was led onward by a principle within myself that I could not see or understand.

The search ended for me in a rather sudden and climactic experience as I came to after my last drunk, which resulted in my asking Alcoholics Anonymous for help. Here, in AA, I'm certain I've found that which I had been seeking. Here I've found "The peace that passeth all understanding." I believe I've learned from Alcoholics Anonymous that all this time I had been seeking a concept of God that I could understand. A concept that made sense to me. A concept with which I could be comfortable. Through Alcoholics Anonymous I've found a way to discipline myself and to experience the wonders of sobriety and spiritual growth. I've found a deep spiritual sense of purpose and I know where I'm going. I find myself in comfortable harmony with God, as I understand Him.

I'm no longer puzzled or confused at the conflicting concepts of God as reflected by the different organized religions, because I find that among all the many temperaments and attitudes attributed to God by the multitude of sects and denominations, they all seem to agree that God is Spirit and that God is Love.

So, I've come to believe God is the Spirit of Love. I think of Spirit as being that calm feeling of buoyancy and exultation and elation and joy we often experience. It's what we see in others when we say, "He's high-spirited," or "He's full of life." It's what we feel within when we hum a happy tune or say, "My spirit sings within me." Love has come to mean anything but the popular Hollywood or sexy-magazine concept that fooled me for a long time.

Love, to me, is fourfold: it's caring, it's feeling respect for, it's feeling responsible for, and it's understanding. When we care what happens to ourselves and to other people; when we respect the rights and the feelings of ourselves and others, whether they're rich or poor, young or old, black or white, drunk or sober; when we feel and act responsibly for ourselves and others; when we understand ourselves and others—then we love ourselves and others. Without these feelings for ourselves there can be none for others. Love is doing and giving these things with no thought of reward or personal gain.

I suppose Love is recognized most easily by all of us in watching a mother's love for a child. To the degree that I get angry or feel resentments or fear or anxiety and frustration—to that degree I've separated myself from God. To the degree I feel the Spirit of Love within me, to that degree I've improved my conscious contact with God, as I understand Him.

In searching through all the AA books and literature, I've only found one place that indicates the kind of God we might expect to find in Alcoholics Anonymous. That's in our Second Tradition, wherein it states that our only authority is ... *a loving God as He may express Himself in our group conscience.*

So, while a total concept of God confined to being a Spirit of Love might seem too simple, and unacceptable to some people, I find that the essential ingredient of the Fellowship of Alcoholics Anonymous is a group of people who care, who respect, who are responsible and who understand. People who have a mature love for one another.

Don McF.
Los Angeles, California

WHEN OTHER PEOPLE CAME ALIVE

April 1974

Recently, during one of our AA meetings, I listened to a speaker describing his spiritual awakening, and my mind took me back to the desperate struggle for what I found to be my first spiritual awakening (in AA, that is).

After having used AA for almost three years as a vehicle upon which to ride away from family problems, job problems, and all the problems connected with my drinking, I consciously decided to go back to drinking. After all, my problems were well in hand now. I had no worries about my drinking; it was the problems that had made me drink too much, and they were behind me.

Needless to say, the next three years brought me back to the stark reality of the problems, tenfold. This time, I couldn't seem to find a way into AA, as I had the first time. I didn't realize that the so-called first time had been only a "half-measure." I had no past sobriety, only an empty water wagon which I had stayed on for three years.

My drinking became an uncontrollable obsession, and I lived with the terror of blackouts, sweats, and fear of not having a drink when I needed it—which was almost always. My job was disintegrating from day to day. Not only were my funds exhausted, but I had borrowed heavily to support my family. My resolve to quit drinking no longer kept me dry for a month, or two weeks, or a day. It was gone.

At this point in my life, I sat in the kitchen of one of the few friends I had left, looking at a half-empty bottle at three in the morning, without the will or the strength to pour myself a drink. "This is it!" I told myself. "This is the bottom, the point of no return." I didn't even have the strength to drive thirty miles to my home.

Some way, the Higher Power enabled me to get into my car after daybreak and drive to my hometown. I tried to find the courage to drive into a tree at high speed, so that my family could at least collect my life insurance. But I couldn't.

My first stop was at a recovery house to ask for help. The first person I met was Ray, whom I had met in AA what seemed to be a lifetime ago.

Ray said, "Hi, Willard. It's good to see you back." No admonitions, no look of shock at my appearance. Just "Hi, Willard. It's good to see you back."

The next year and a half was the longest period of my life. Many times each day, I decided I couldn't make it. I went to AA meetings daily—sometimes more often, but never less. I read the Big Book over and over, but couldn't seem to find the answer. My sponsor, Buck, kept after me almost daily. When I had to make a business trip to another town, I would call him as soon as I checked into my room, and he always made certain that I knew where the meetings were in that town. He often said, "You have to do your own roadwork, but if you stick around, you will find the answer you need—not necessarily the one you are looking for."

One night, I sensed something different in the meeting. I didn't know what it was; I just had an indefinable feeling that something was going to happen. There were forty-two (how well I remember) people in the room. It was a discussion meeting. It was almost my turn to comment, but instead of doing what was my custom—thinking about what I was going to say—I listened. I heard a new member of three or four months say, "You know, what I have found in AA is that other people care about me!" My skin tingled, and I felt a strange emotion.

The next speaker said, "Our Higher Power cares about all of us." My feeling became stronger. Finally, a newcomer, who had not too long ago been lying under a bridge with his muscatel, said, "What surprises me is that I care for *myself.*"

With that last utterance, my whole life seemed to come into focus. The people suddenly came alive before my eyes, where before they had all been lumps of clay. These same people with whom I had talked and gone to meetings were truly born before my eyes. I was, for the first time, seeing the miracle of birth. My emotion was so great that I ran out of the room, drove my car near the ocean, and listened to the whisper of the waves, as I sobbed and let all of my hatred and frustrations and lack of love for my fellowman and myself be swept out to sea.

After eighteen months of really trying, of taking the full measure of pain, of reality, something had happened—when I least expected it—to change my entire life. This was my first spiritual awakening! While it remains the most dramatic emotional upheaval of my life, it was not my last.

Now, after ten years of unbroken sobriety, I have the privilege of calling upon this spiritual awakening daily—especially at meetings where I see newcomers who, perhaps for the first time, come to realize that we care for them and that they care for themselves. As I sit in AA meetings, I never fail to marvel at this "miracle of birth," this constant spiritual awakening. In my estimation, it gives us living, ever-increasing awareness as long as we continue to be a part of the AA Fellowship. It is a promise of future spiritual growth.

W.B.
Monterey, California

Working Incognito
April 1994

When people learn that they are suffering from an incurable, progressive disease, they are said to follow a pattern of denial, anger, fear, and acceptance. I know that's what happened to me.

Following a court-ordered drug and alcohol evaluation, I was diagnosed as having severe alcoholism requiring in-patient treatment. I went through the evaluation report line by line, denying or explaining away everything that it said. I was able to get a recommendation for out-patient treatment and AA meetings.

Then I was shown the Twelve Steps and I said *that* I would not do. I didn't believe in God. Besides, only the First Step mentioned alcohol. I could choose my own Higher Power. "Like what?" I asked. "Anything. It could be AA, it could be a book, it could be an ashtray! Anything you want."

Somehow I avoided both treatment and AA for several years. Drinking continued to destroy my life. Every symptom was quickly rationalized. I had to buy another six-pack if last night's had only two left. When breaking yet another promise to drink only soda, my response was, "Someone offered to buy me a drink. What was I supposed to do? Say no?"

As my disease progressed, I became convinced that I had lost my mind. I could play a role in order to cope with work or family but I felt dead inside. Eventually, I concluded that I must have a multiple personality. My sober me could only remember what I did sober and my drunk me could only remember what I did drunk. That would explain those long blackouts.

Then I began a new job. I was fascinated by a coworker who was under house arrest. She wore an ankle-bracelet monitor. At lunchtime, I noticed that she always had two books with her. An avid reader myself, I thumbed through her meditation book occasionally.

I asked her where she got the book. "At an AA meeting," she told me. "You go to those?" I was astounded. "You probably have to go, right?"

"Actually, I like them. Would you like to go to one with me? Here, I'll give you a meeting list and I'll circle the meetings I like to go to. Maybe I'll see you there."

My first meeting was a large open speaker meeting. My friend wasn't there, but after walking through the coffee line, casually looking for her, I couldn't just put down the coffee and leave. I took a seat and listened to the lead tell her story. It felt like my story. The details were different but the symptoms were the same.

Came To Believe   *April 1968*

Way back in the beginning when I first came to meetings with a desire to stay sober, I listened little but I looked a lot. I didn't want to hear how the other man had got sober—I wanted to see that he was sober—and then I wanted to go back the next week to see if he was still sober!

If my fellow member had told me at this stage (and he probably did) that he had something good and I ought to get some of it for myself, I wouldn't have known what he was talking about. But I could see that this man had something which I wanted and the only way to get it was to keep coming back each week to see if I could find out, by just looking, what it was he had. As I looked and looked and looked—I listened once in a while.

And thus it was I came to believe ....

T.C.
England

I decided to research this program and the next day I went to the library. I typed "Alcoholics Anonymous" into the computer directory. It came up as a title. "Someone actually wrote a whole book about these people?" I thought. I went home and read the Big Book. There I learned that alcoholism is a disease of the mind, body, and spirit. "Maybe I should give this a try," I said to myself.

A couple of weeks later, at a beginner's meeting, I introduced myself. "I'm Sue. I'm an alcoholic." I had not only slipped out of denial, I had an identity. I began to enjoy meetings and the opportunity to explore this newfound sense of self.

Four months later found me back with the bottle. I had entered the anger phase. It wasn't fair. Why should I be an alcoholic? A lifetime without booze! Besides, I didn't get sober just to go to AA meetings. I was fortunate that I entered into fear rather quickly. I could drink but I couldn't get drunk. The old feeling returned that I was shattering inside into many people. I went back to meetings a much different person. I not only had a desire to stop drinking, I had a desire for that glimpse of a real self.

I began to listen carefully whenever I heard about relapses. I attended a lot of meetings and made a commitment to do so by accepting a service position.

One day our group was informed of the death of one of our members. His sponsor told us what had happened. He had gone out drinking one night and died the next morning.

He had literally drunk himself to death. Clearly, just going to meetings wasn't enough. I was told that the alcoholic will drink again if she does not change. I had to change. I became willing to go to any lengths.

I had accepted my disease on the physical and mental levels but not on the spiritual level. I understood the concept of a God but I wasn't close to a Higher Power as I understood him. My prayers began, "God, Higher Power, Great Spirit, or whatever the hell you want to be called ...." I was stuck on Steps Two and Three. I wanted to move forward but I couldn't define my Higher Power.

At a Step meeting one night, the discussion was on the Third Step. I'm sure a lot of wonderful things were said, but what I chose to hear was one man describing this Step as simply doing the next right thing as it came up. I knew I could do that.

By applying that principle as consistently as possible, I almost automatically decreased the amount of projecting into the future I had been doing. I was too concentrated on the present for that. I stopped philosophizing and complicating my Higher Power. My prayers became a simple formula. I began with the Serenity Prayer, threw in a "thy will not mine be done," and finished with a gratitude list.

I was amazed at the things I was grateful for: those painful situations that served to show me my character defects; the ability to accept and share my pain with others; the opportunities to do things I was afraid to do which gave me strength and confidence. Service made me feel useful. Twelfth Step work taught me to accept my past. This may be my greatest asset.

I realized that the many coincidences in my life seemed to be directed. I finally came to believe that a Power greater than myself could restore me to sanity. I had only to stop fighting and practice the rest of the AA program as enthusiastically as I could.

So how do I define my Higher Power now? I don't. My Higher Power works incognito, defying definition and requiring faith. Having faith has unlocked the barriers to the complete acceptance of my disease. Now I can dedicate myself to its treatment, the Twelve Steps of Alcoholics Anonymous.

Susan G.
State College, Pennsylvania

How an Atheist Works the Steps   March 2003

Atheism and AA's principles are not mutually exclusive, and if anyone tells you that you have to believe in God to stay sober or to remain in AA, he or she is dead wrong. I always tell nonbelievers who ask how they can do those God Steps to look for the goal of the Step and do whatever they can to meet its intent. And don't drink, no matter what happens. Nothing improves if you drink.

June L.
El Granada, California

A Crack in the Wall of Disbelief

April 1998

I sampled AA ten years ago but never really got past the First Step. Steps Two and Three smacked of religion and turned me off; after all, I was in charge of my life. I made some futile attempts at finding a power for living sober but never learned anything about spirituality or had much willingness to change my attitudes. About six years ago I hit another bottom and agreed to return to AA meetings because I refused to listen to the Employee Assistance Program Counselor when he suggested a treatment center he could get me into right away. I was afraid of that kind of commitment and thought that if AA didn't work again I always had treatment, like an ace in the hole. In fact, I didn't want to get sober for the rest of my life, only get some people off my back. Just because I couldn't get along with my bosses, coworkers, the union, or anybody else didn't mean I had a problem—I just needed some time to regroup.

First, I bought a Big Book and started to read it, and tried a Sunday Grapevine meeting and a Thursday Step meeting, where the topic was Step Two. An old drunk, a former schoolteacher named Howard, was leading the meeting, and I was trying to figure out how I was going to get past Step Two this time. He was talking about not having to believe but being willing to believe: don't say no, say maybe. He also talked about having one's own conception of God and then told a story about a nonbeliever who had a tall tree as his higher power. I laughed to myself and thought what a bunch of nonsense that was. That turned my mind off for the rest of the meeting. Later on at home I thought of how amusing the old guy had been—a tree for a higher power!—and wondered about the kind of bull that kept those people sober.

Suddenly I thought about a great place I'd discovered trying to trout fish where these huge rocks lay along a run above a nice pool, where everything was shaded and cool and peaceful in the summer. I realized that I already had my own tree. Only it was a bunch of big rocks and a stream that Mother Nature had put together. It made me feel good to be there, and that didn't happen often. Maybe I could believe in something—and this was a small crack in the wall of disbelief. A dash of willingness was all

I had, but it was enough to make a start. I had done as Howard suggested, changed to maybe, became willing to believe in something besides myself. I'm always grateful for the lesson I learned at that Step meeting, because it opened the door to learning more about myself and my alcoholism, and about AA. It helped me to grow in the program and in my spiritual awakening. Nothing has come fast and easy, but it has come and I'm grateful and sober today because of AA.

Anonymous
Mason City, Iowa

SMALL WONDERS

May 1987

They told me when I came to AA I had a threefold illness—physical, mental, and spiritual. As I went through withdrawal from alcohol, I quickly understood the physical aspect. It took longer to get used to the idea there was something wrong with me mentally. Eventually, though, I was able to see that the way I view the world is hardly "normal."

What I couldn't accept was that I was in trouble spiritually. How could I be, since, as far as I was concerned, God didn't exist; and if there was no God, then there was no spiritual side to human life? I had decided long before I came to AA that man was a physical entity who possessed an intellect, but there was no power he could depend on outside of his own ability to reason. I had stopped deluding myself about this mythical being called God. First I learned that Santa Claus wasn't real, soon after, the Easter Bunny went the way of Santa, and in time, I determined that believing in God was equally absurd. I had never seen, touched, or talked to Santa Claus, the Easter Bunny, or God; therefore, if I knew for sure that the first two were merely childhood fantasies, the other one must be, too.

The trouble was that while I didn't mind that Santa Claus and the Easter Bunny didn't exist, I deeply resented knowing there was no God. When I thought of all the hours I had wasted in Sunday school, catechism classes, and church services in pursuit of an illusion, I was furious. I was enraged at my parents who had forced me to attend church, at the ministers who had perpetuated the lie about God, at all the people who refused to admit that God was a fraud. My anger crystallized into one big resentment.

Nurturing this resentment, among many others, I came to AA. When I first arrived, I needed to find out how to stop getting drunk, but the people at the tables kept talking about God. It's true that they frequently used the words "higher power" or qualified God with "as you understand him," but I knew what they were saying: church, Christianity, religion. All my defenses leaped into action. If getting sober in AA meant believing in God, then I was either going to have to find another place to get sober or else stay drunk. Whenever someone at a meeting mentioned God, I stopped listening. Meetings on the Second, Third, Sixth, Seventh, and Eleventh Steps were occasions for me to daydream while others were speaking, and to pass when it was my turn to comment. I refused to repeat the Lord's Prayer at the close of each meeting.

Then a terrible thing happened. Someone suggested that if I didn't believe, I might try acting as if I did. In AA I had learned that you have to be honest, and now I was being advised to pretend to believe in something I positively did not believe in. How very dishonest, I thought, as I set out to prove that "fake it till you make it" wouldn't work. So I began trying to communicate with a higher power. I approached this power by saying: "If you're there, which I don't for a moment believe you are, could you help me, which I don't for a moment believe you can?" Just as I expected, there was no answer—no thunderclaps, no heavenly beings descending to me from clouds, no burning bushes. There was no higher power named God or anything else. I was on my own.

Then my life began to change. Problems started to resolve themselves. I was able to get up in the morning without fear of facing the day. I could go through a day without constant terror that catastrophe was imminent. Even though I didn't exactly love my job, I was able to handle it, and I even found that there were times when I could relax and enjoy myself. I could see the humor and the beauty of what was around me. I never had the leisure to do that before when the responsibility of running the universe was all mine.

So *that* was how the higher power worked. Because I was watching for miracles on an epic scale, I didn't recognize the small wonders that were occurring every day. This was a higher power I liked—gentle, quiet, steady.

This was my kind of God, one I could understand, one in whose hands I was willing to place my life, because I knew he wasn't going to turn on me if I made a mistake. This was a God who was going to accept all of me, not the God I had heard about before, who would be angry with me if I ever showed any doubt or weakness. This was a God I wanted to live with.

I have come to believe in a power greater than myself, which I choose to call my Higher Power. I can't refer to this power as God. To me God still suggests church, Christianity religion; and my Higher Power isn't connected with those things. Maybe I'm only playing with words; after all, does it matter what you call it as long as you have faith in it? Maybe the rebel that still lives inside me warns me that calling my Higher Power God would mean giving in to all those church people whose teachings I vigorously resisted. All I know is that today, one day at a time, I can depend on my Higher Power, whoever or whatever it may be. By letting go, by allowing my Higher Power to manage my life, I have more control over myself than I've ever had before.

K.B.
Palos Hills, Illinois

It Starts with the People   *July 1987*

I thought the "God" that I learned about through my Catholic upbringing hated me for all the terrible things I had done while I was drinking. Today I know better. God loves me unconditionally, just as the people at my first meeting did. They asked no questions. They just welcomed me and allowed me to take or leave the suggestions they made. They believed, and I came to believe.

So today when a newcomer says to me, "I don't believe in this God stuff," I usually say, "That's okay. Don't drink, go to meetings and just try to look around the meeting rooms at the faces of the people who are trying to stay sober one day at a time. Believe that they believe in a Power greater than themselves and give yourself time!"

L.M.
Springfield, Massachusetts

A Candle of Hope

April 1991

Healing comes in many forms. This is written as a part of my healing, in the hope that it may help someone else.

My search (in drinking and sobriety) has been for a belief in something beyond the tangible—a spirit of oneness with others—a Higher Power, I suppose. This search has taken many diverse routes—college, seminary, graduate school, Christianity, existentialism, atheism, agnosticism, and finally alcoholism. I came to AA about eight-and-a-half years ago, a scared, bitter, angry, hurt woman, carrying the scars of alcoholism. I could not talk, so I listened. I felt pretty hopeless. Thoughts of suicide had often been my companions during the drinking days, and just not drinking did not change that very much. But I came to meetings, I sat, and I listened. I heard of a God in which I did not believe. I heard from some that I needed their God or I would get drunk. I did not get drunk and I did not believe in their God. I still knew the sense of despair of an alcoholic hitting bottom but I still did not believe.

My lack of belief had been sealed the night I heard a fine lady say that my grandfather's years of suffering were caused by God. My grandfather had been my childhood idol and I certainly wanted no part of such a God. Years later, I still had no intention of turning my will and my life over to the care of such a being. I might be an alcoholic, but I wasn't stupid!

I read AA literature, talked with my sponsor, and found that my interpretation of a Higher Power was all that was needed.

About a year after I came to AA I went to a treatment center and was helped to continue on the road to spiritual and emotional recovery. This road too has taken diverse routes—lots of meetings, readings, talks with AA members, discussion groups, psychotherapy, and the beginning of sharing. The keys seemed to be listening and sharing—the spirit at work. I also went through the Statue-of-Liberty stage of recovery—"Bring me your tired and your lonely and I'll make them sober—whether or not they want to be." As a result, I began to accept my own limitations and the free will choices of others. I also went through the "boredom" stage of recovery and learned to reach out anew, to have more patience, and to put value on old friends.

There came a time when I began to wish I believed as most of my AA friends did. I was so much a people-pleaser I rarely shared how I felt about the Higher Power issue. I was still fearful of rejection. Then I heard a woman who shared thoughts similar to mine and we became AA friends. I talked with a man who had relapsed after twelve years' sobriety who felt his relapse was partly related to pretending to believe in the Higher Power of other AAs. This time he vowed to be honest and make his own search. We have had many marvelous talks. I began to believe in a Higher Power who is the spirit of the universe—a tremendous and dependable source of strength. This spirit does not cause tragedy or find me parking places. This spirit is always with me unless, as the Big Book suggests, I allow resentment to separate me from the sunlight of the spirit. My Higher Power has been born for me through sharing and hope. Every day, hopeless, helpless alcoholics walk into AA meetings, grab onto hope, and begin a renewal of their spirit.

I needed to write this tonight. It is Christmas Eve—the season of hope and sharing in the Christian tradition and my ninth season of hope after many years of often feeling little hope. Last December my sister-in-law, with whom I was very close, committed suicide. Three months later my brother, her husband, followed suit. They lost hope, even the possibility of hope. They could no longer share, and they felt no love. They once again felt the despair that we alcoholics know so well. Apparently, they needed this program more than they wanted it. I loved them, I shared with them, I tried to be helpful. I learned about my limitations and the limited free will of others.

I am glad I struggled to begin a concept of Higher Power that works for me. I am grateful for a program of recovery that is large enough to include all alcoholics with all sorts of beliefs or lack of belief. I am grateful for those who shared with me and believed when I could not—because I have had a Higher Power through all this. I have also experienced sharing and hope. Tears did not come during my brother's funeral but they came when I walked into an AA meeting the night I got home. I was free to share at that meeting.

I have learned a lot. I have learned that accusing myself of having a "pity party" is no excuse for not sharing the many intense feelings that accompany personal tragedies. I have learned to be more "a part of" than "apart from." I am infinitely more grateful for the gifts of sharing and hope.

Tonight I went to an AA meeting. Someone told me the name of an AA who was going through an experience similar to mine. I got this person's number because I've been there. Perhaps I can share my experience, strength, and hope. Perhaps I can help light another candle of hope in someone else. After all, that is what Alcoholics Anonymous is all about, isn't it?

Anonymous
Cleveland, Ohio

OKAY, GOD ...

October 1985

When I first came to AA, all I wanted was to quit drinking. I knew that my drinking was killing me and that AA could tell me how to quit. One day at a time, I learned how to not drink, but my problems seemed to be getting worse instead of better. That is, I got sober enough to want to live again, but I couldn't seem to remember how to live. Soon, I was healthier than ever before; my finances improved with the money not spent ruining myself at happy hour; my home life improved; but I just wasn't comfortable.

"AA is a way of life," my sponsor explained, with that confident good humor everyone in AA seemed to have—everyone but me. "Try thinking about God instead of not drinking."

Well, everything became perfectly clear to me then—I was convinced my sponsor had gone bananas. God was something that got people together every Sunday morning, and certainly God didn't really care whether I drank or not, right?

"Wrong," my sponsor said. "Who do you think got you to AA in the first place? You only need to have a willingness to meet God, and you'll be more comfortable."

After a few more days of misery, I decided maybe I shouldn't give up until I'd tried this God thing, and I was very close to giving up the sobriety routine. I got out my AA books and read over what I called the God Steps. How was I going to meet God? I tried praying, but there were no thunderbolts. I tried meditating, and there was no blinding light from heaven. Apparently, I decided, God just didn't realize the seriousness of my situation.

"Okay, God," I explained, "this is important to me—you and I are going to have to get together right now if I'm going to stay sober." God didn't make one single response—not even one good gust of wind or ray of sunshine. I decided to give God a formal introduction. After all, maybe I wasn't handling this divinity properly; maybe I needed a different approach. So I politely invited God to spend the day with me (like a visiting relative or friend), and instantly began a mental dialogue with God.

As we stood together in the freezing cold waiting for the crosstown bus, I looked around the city with God and silently explained why I was riding the bus. We discussed the weather and decided it really wasn't all that cold after all. We sat together on the bus (of course, I didn't save God a seat except in my mind), and as we looked at all the people, I realized I really enjoyed riding the bus in the morning.

At work, I introduced God to everyone I knew. In explaining exactly what I liked and didn't like about my co-workers, I found myself saying some pretty silly things to God—things I'd be embarrassed to tell a person—but I quickly realized these were things I had been telling myself for weeks. By lunchtime, God and I were getting along pretty well, and I seemed to be getting along much better with several people I'd had resentments against. By the end of the day, I found myself wondering if having God along had anything to do with why I hadn't been bored, angry, or upset all day.

That evening, after a heavy discussion about traffic and car repairs, God and I pulled into an AA meeting. For a moment, I thought I saw God smiling, and I realized that in the process of introducing myself to God, I was getting a good look at who I really was.

I saw my sponsor at the meeting and explained that I had taken God to work with me. With a wide smile, she asked, "And when was the last time you thought about not drinking?"

This time, I smiled. I hadn't thought about a drink all day. My mind was too full of God thoughts. It was a first for me. God had changed my life. Or maybe my life was still the same, but I had changed. Either way, another day had passed, and I was now both sober and comfortable. Miracles really do come in many guises—just as God does.

K. S.
Houston, Texas

Journey of the Spirit
April 1994

Fortunately for me, I met a sober member of Alcoholics Anonymous just before my entire life fell apart due to my drinking. This AA told me about the program Alcoholics Anonymous. He said that if I ever felt my drinking was a problem and I wanted to stop, I should call the local central office. In July 1984, when I was emotionally, physically, mentally, and spiritually spent, I did just that and asked where the next closest meeting was being held. That night, I walked through the door of the meeting hall and into a new life.

Once the fog of drinking cleared, I noticed the Steps on the wall. Most of them seemed okay to me with the exception of the third one: *Made a decision to turn our will and our lives over to the care of God* as we understood Him. I knew this would be some trouble for me. I had been raised with religion but had long since lost my faith in God.

During my early sobriety I listened intently whenever someone shared about Step Three. It seemed that everyone subscribed to the same concept: 1) The Steps needed to be taken in order. 2) Step Three was essential. 3) If you failed to take all the Steps you would drink again. So I knew that I had to come to believe in the God that everyone spoke about. I knew that for me to drink was to die. I didn't want to do either.

My sponsor directed me to get down on my knees and pray. She said that I didn't need to believe, just do the action and the feelings/belief would come later. I continued to follow her direction for years and prayed on my knees every morning and every night. After a few years of sobriety, I began to share about Step Three as best I could. But looking back, I realize that I was mainly restating what I had heard.

The people who befriended me were sober alcoholics and most were Christians or believed in the Judeo-Christian God. I was invited to church, and eventually I joined. My life was full of activity. I went to work, AA meetings, and church events. I had little time for anything else. This went on for more than three years. I convinced myself that I believed. I got married. I had a good job. Things were good. I attributed it to the God to which I prayed every morning and evening. I lost my job. My marriage failed. Nearly everything that I had acquired in my four-and-a-half years of sobriety was gone. I realized that my belief in God was gone too. I never really believed. But I was still sober.

The next year was a lonely year. All my sober/Christian friends wanted nothing to do with me, because I was talking about my true feelings. I told them that I didn't believe in their God. Occasionally, someone would call to see if I was still sober, always adding that if I didn't return to belief in God I would surely drink. I decided to do the things that made me happiest.

Since I was no longer spending all my time running from one event to another, I had time to spend with myself and to go out away from the city. I took long walks. I traveled to many beautiful places. I got in touch with myself and with nature. I found that I loved to be with plants and animals. I found a peacefulness in nature that wasn't in the city. I found a feeling I hadn't had since I was a small child. I learned about flowers and trees. I reconciled myself to being alone in the meetings and in my life because I thought no one would understand. At the very least I was finally honest with myself and with everyone else, and I was sober too. I began to experience moments of great calm deep within me.

My life began to change and to get really good. I found my soulmate and we have two children together. We moved to a rural area. We have three dogs and some land. We planted some flowers and vegetables. Things are better now than I could have ever imagined. I spend my time with my mate, kids, animals, and plants. At nine years of sobriety, life is better than ever, even though I still don't believe in "God."

I am grateful that the people in AA showed me how to live sober. However, I have learned many things from other sources. I learned about quiet from the breeze floating through the grass on a warm summer day. I have learned unconditional love from my animals. I have learned how to have wonder of the world from my children. I have learned that all things have tremendous power. My teachers have taught me to have respect for all living things, rather than a reverence for a concept within church walls.

I write this to anyone who may feel similarly. You are not alone in your feelings. The Judeo-Christian God is not what will keep you sober. There is a power greater. Believe in yourself. There are many wonders that await you on the journey. God speed to you.

Kathleen O'M.
Albuquerque, New Mexico

No Secondhand Gods

February 1996

I came to Alcoholics Anonymous beaten down by gin and depression, barely clinging to a thin and unhappy belief in God and trying desperately to talk myself back into my childhood faith. It wasn't working.

I was an ex-nun whose faith had fallen apart in the convent—partly because the order's strict policy on alcohol had prevented me, for the first sustained period in my adult life, from drinking away troublesome doubts and questions.

The first thing AA people told me about spirituality stopped me cold: they told me if I wanted to live, I needed an honest relationship with an honestly envisioned Higher Power. Ill-fitting secondhand Gods need not apply. I found this both liberating and terrifying. Terrifying because I'd been taught to hang onto my religion like grim death whether I felt honest doing it or not; liberating once I discovered I was genuinely more afraid of drinking again than of going to hell for unbelief.

The ensuing few years were an incredible revelation. My sponsor has an interest in comparative religion, and some of her books introduced me to a marvelous new faith, one that made me exclaim, "So *that's* what I've been all my life!" I became a practitioner and eventually a clergywoman of this faith, and it has given me the sort of relationship with my Deeper (for me, a better term than Higher) Power I could only have dreamed of.

Nevertheless, I have a solid granite derriere on the subject of keeping religion per se out of Alcoholics Anonymous. So I've never gone to meetings and tried to preach my religion to anyone. I've seen the damage that can do to groups and the confusion and pain it can cause newcomers.

But I do try to be honest about my Deeper Power; and it isn't easy. You see, I envision that Power as female, and I call her Goddess, not God. And in some AA meetings, you'd think I'd thrown a stinkbomb into the circle every time I refer to my Deeper Power in this way.

I was careful where I began saying it. For the most part, my home group didn't mind the new phrasing, so I tried it out at another meeting where I'd heard various people's Powers referred to as God, Allah, the Tao,

Religion Is Personal   *May 1982*

I feel we are getting away from AA's "Higher Power," "God as we understood Him" concept. Recently, I have heard opening-meeting prayers in Jesus Christ's name, and the Bible referred to as not being a religion but bringing the same message as the one in our Big Book.

Not that I see anything wrong with anyone else's belief. But to me, it is personal. Anything other than the "Higher Power" stressed within our Fellowship tends to limit us and to keep away some of those who may want to seek us out for help.

My understanding is that when the manuscript of the Big Book was written, it was decided that "Higher Power" and "God as we understood Him" be adopted. Belief in some power greater than ourselves was seen to be vital, but only as it came to each of us individually.

The newcomer is the important one in AA, and I recently learned from a newcomer that some of these religious references were disturbing to him. I guess all I am really trying to say is: Let's keep it simple; it works so well.

J.R.
Chatham, Ontario

the Great Maybe, and Eddie. All had gotten reasonable respect, even Eddie, so I was totally unprepared for the roar of derisive laughter that greeted me when I spoke one evening of "the Goddess as I understand Her."

I was thunderstruck, and tears came to my eyes. "I nearly died trying to find a Power I could believe in," I told them. "I would never laugh at yours; please don't laugh at mine."

I tried it again at other meetings. At about a third of the meetings, I got either ridicule or after-meeting conversation pitches. I wondered if it was just my area that was unusually closed to the idea, until I began hearing stories from other women of my faith on the Internet. All confirmed my impression that female deity-language is the one kind that elicits laughter or hostility ("You'll go to hell for that New Age stuff, you know!") at AA meetings.

For a while, I tried dancing around the issue with terms like "the Creator" and "the Divine." I didn't wear my religion's symbol around my neck at meetings, even though some Christians and Jews often wore theirs. Eventually, I stopped dancing; that's one tango not required of the more "mainstream" believers in our ranks, and I truly don't understand why it should be required of anyone.

I've watched for years now as this problem has driven desperately ill newcomers away from the program. They have had to fight the prevailing society so hard for a faith that fits, and it is so hard for them to face being laughed at or scorned for it in what is supposed to be a place of safety when they're barely out of detox.

Please, next time you're tempted to have a contemptuous (and audible) reaction to somebody else's deity, think: if it's what's keeping her alive, do you really want to knock it down?

Anonymous
Kentucky

Is There Room Enough in AA?

October 1987

Recently my twenty-eight-year-old son began to recognize his growing problem with alcohol (an episode with the law helped get his attention) and went to his first AA meeting on his own behalf. As a child he had been to meetings with me, now sixteen years sober in AA. Over the years he has watched the improvements in my life and I am sure he knows of AA's high success rate for alcoholism recovery. When he was about eighteen and I spoke to him about alcoholism and the strong potential for him to become an alcoholic he said, "Don't worry. If I find out I've got it I'll just go to AA."

This time has come for him, but his initial visit to AA for himself was a disaster. He says the only member there who approached him was a woman, well-meaning no doubt, who began telling him the first thing he has to do was find a belief in God. This woman's suggestion that God would bring about his recovery from alcoholism is about as absurd to him as a suggestion to use bloodletting or a few voodoo treatments would be to most of us in the modern Western world. You see, my son, like me, is an atheist.

When my son told me of his encounter, I tried to point out to him that I and an agnostic woman he knows have had success with AA's program. But his comment was: "Maybe you can handle that stuff but I don't want to waste my time with it. I'll just have to find some reasonable way to work this out." Like many alcoholics he may still be somewhat uncertain about whether he wants to make a commitment to sobriety. The heavy-handed religiosity he found provided exactly the excuse he needed to bolt and run. Unfortunately his assessment of AA as a group of religious fanatics was supported by two of his friends who had also sought help from AA and had rejected it for the same reasons after similar experiences.

The experience of my son and his friends led me to consider why and how I was able to find compatibility between AA's teachings and my own atheistic philosophies. My background prepared me better, I think. I had been raised in a religion—one that I rejected, but also one that I understand and do not feel any particular animosity toward. I simply do not regard belief in God as supportable by evidence, rational, nor necessary for happy living. That was true for me when I got to AA and continues into my long sobriety. I suspect that my earlier contact with religious people whom I loved and trusted made me more tolerant or at least less suspicious of their ideas. Also the man who urged me to call AA was an atheist in AA and had forewarned me of the strong God-orientation of many people. This AA member had suggested I reveal my ideas at once and ask that I be referred to someone with similar ideas.

Furthermore, I think my first call to AA was crucially different than my son's. I told the woman who came to take me to a meeting of my atheism and my concern that AA might not work for me. She respected my attitude and pointed out to me how AA, regardless of God or higher power, had a great deal to offer that was very practical. AA would (and did) provide friendly counseling from people who had followed the same path as I. In the nurture of the Fellowship I could develop living skills that I had neglected for so many years. The Fellowship would be an immediate source of social contact with those who also did not drink. AA could teach me to be a social being without having to use the drugs I was accustomed to. She told me the Twelve Steps could be liberally translated to be an excellent guideline for reasonable and harmonious living with others and with myself. Not that first night, nor in the years of our friendship since, did she tell me that I must find God in order to stay sober.

Over the years I have been reticent about my atheism at AA meetings because I know it goes against the grain of most members and is contrary to AA literature. The chapter to the agnostic is quite clear in its message—that somehow all of us will eventually find God—that such belief is fundamental to humans. I do not agree, but when God or higher power is discussed at meetings I tend to pass, except at the small close-knit home group I attend. Otherwise, my contributions are mostly limited to topics which address practical sobriety. I have refused requests to speak at meetings for several years because I didn't think I should speak openly of how AA works in my life.

Perhaps that was wise of me when I was still quite mad and when the benefits of AA were not so obvious in my life. It seemed unacceptable to state that sobriety is possible without believing in God when my sobriety was so short-term and my mental and emotional equilibrium was so tenuous. But years have passed and all the promises of AA have come to me. My life is richer than I could have ever imagined and I owe it entirely to the AA program. You see, AA's Twelve Steps and the exchange of ideas with other recovering alcoholics are so effective in combating this disease that, for some of us, these tools alone are enough to gain a rewarding sobriety. It concerns me that many do not realize this fact.

Rarely do I hear anyone else admit to nonbelief in God, and I have held the impression that very few atheists remain in AA. The man who sent me to AA subsequently abandoned the Fellowship. Often I have wondered whether the atheists commonly go away or if they finally conform out of greater willingness or more determination to believe than I have. Recently I have come to suspect that neither is the case. I hear so little from atheists in AA because those of us who do not believe in God keep quiet about it. I have done so partly out of timidity and partly to avoid the comment that the admission of atheism frequently brings: that I will someday believe or I will get drunk.

We all need to be able to explain to newcomers how AA works in terms that particular alcoholic can understand. Never would I seek to explain AA in my own atheistic interpretation to an alcoholic who believes in God and suggest that he would do well to modify his perception in order to get and stay sober. Instead I can speak to the person about God from the many references and explanations which abound in AA literature. Yet it is probably more difficult the other way around. A God-oriented AA member doesn't have a large supply of ideas from atheists available to share with the newcomer atheist. Too few of us state our positions in meetings; too little is written in AA's literature.

J.L.
Oakland, California

HONEST DISBELIEVERS

May 1983

Frequently at meetings, the discussions that develop around the topics of prayer and spirituality can leave sincerely atheist members feeling that they are second-class members of our Fellowship. I know that I need to remember—and I often forget—where I came from. A great number of us were atheists or nonbelievers of one kind or another. Even if we have now come to believe in God, it seems that God in His wisdom wants AA to work for the few still unable to believe—provided that they are honest or true to themselves. Remembering my own journey helps in encouraging the newcomer who also has problems with faith.

In my drinking years, I took an atheistic stand toward life. I claimed that I did not believe in God. It was only in desperation that I followed the AA suggestion to make an experiment with the existence of God. My scientific training found an experiment along the lines of disbelief vs. belief to be acceptable, especially as I was making no progress at the time. To me, God was merely an "it," initially. I could concede that something out there was bigger and more ordered than I was, and that I needed help.

I was impressed at the difference that the concession made in my life. Without any formal prayer, with merely the yielding to some form of higher power, it became possible for me to be freed from my obsession. Suddenly, I was able to do something I had been unable to do before: to abstain from alcohol.

All the things that have happened to me since then are explainable through a naturalist rationale. After all, I have never talked directly on a hot line with God. Neither have I received any supernatural sign from him. He does not seem to operate outside natural phenomena. I have, of course, been astounded by the import of many, many signs in my life that things were not as they were before. I do personally prefer to see and to believe that these signs are the manifestation of God's love for me—but I insist that this part of my life is private. There is no need to discuss the form or lack of form that my conception of God takes—at least, not at an AA meeting.

What does unite all members in the program is a common sincerity.

We are all seeking the truth; we are trying for honesty. In practice, any useful conception of God must relate to this idea of truth. Some people would say that God is truth—no more and no less.

Those members of AA who sincerely cannot subscribe to the language used by the more God-conscious still have this common denominator: the language of honesty which we all identify with. They can apply this program to their lives so long as they are true to themselves.

So far, I have been talking about reasoning, the use of language. There is also the realm of feelings. I do experience feelings of gratitude sustained by the continuing blessings in my life. I can feel the harmony that was not there before. I am in rhythm with universal truths, in sync with the order that surrounds me. Most atheists in our program can identify with such a description of what is happening in our lives.

When I see and identify with other peoples' emergence from the painful morass of our illness, I am sometimes overwhelmed with feelings of joy at their recovery. Those feelings can be called the love of God overwhelming me—an affinity for goodness. My sense of identification with atheists and other honest disbelievers is no less warm and overwhelmingly pleasant, for they are in truth first-class AA members.

S.M.
Santa Monica, California

IT'S ALWAYS DARK AT THE BEGINNING
August 1998

We had a meeting on the topic of Higher Powers, and I didn't speak, but I kept thinking about it. I was frustrated that I hadn't been able to come up with anything at all to say about the most essential part of the AA program. And I wanted to tell newcomers who were skeptical of religion that this was something totally different, something they would come to rely on. I wanted to explain how it differs from the God-concept of the religion in which I was raised, and why it is so reassuring to me. But I couldn't figure it out myself.

I remembered what one man, Bob, who has since died, used to say about his Higher Power: "If it were small enough for me to understand, it wouldn't be big enough to do me any good." I guess his words explain my problem in articulating anything about who or what my Higher Power is, and how it works in my life. But I still want to explore my own beliefs and try to clarify my thoughts.

When I came into AA, and for a long time afterward, I reacted to the word God in much the same way that I react to the taste of a slice of lemon—with a wince and a shiver. That had been true for many years, ever since college, when I stopped going to church and decided that religion was simply irrelevant.

I didn't believe in God anymore. I didn't see any reason to. For one thing, he had never responded to my pleas about my parents' drinking. He was all-powerful and completely loving, but he chose not to do anything at all to change that situation. I couldn't understand that. So instead of continuing to accept the mysterious way of God's love, I decided to give up on it, and to focus instead on doing what gave me pleasure.

The only problem was, I did too much of it, and I did it for years and years, long after it had stopped being fun and after it had caused me and other people a good deal of pain.

I was increasingly dependent on alcohol and really lost in the big adult world. Unable to cope with the problems of daily life and suffering periods of severe depression, I grasped at spirituality from time to time. Eastern religions appealed to me. I took some yoga classes and was intrigued by this physical, mental, emotional, and spiritual discipline.

But I continued to drink and was unable to sustain any of the practices as a way of life. I could do it for a while but then I'd get drunk.

After coming to AA, I was still wary of the word "God" for a long time. But I could accept the group as a power greater than myself; I could feel the strength there. Again, Bob had an explanation. He used the word "synergy." It explains a process in biology by which two or more organisms together are able to achieve an effect that neither can achieve individually. That made sense to me. I saw it happen, week after week, as we went around the table and created a spirit that couldn't be found anywhere else.

I was told that I could use whatever Higher Power worked for me, and I did. I liked the Native American Great Spirit that showed itself in nature. From early sobriety I found nature to be a wonderful place to find serenity.

I've heard people say that a higher power can even be a doorknob. Personally, I don't understand how a doorknob can be a source of serenity but I do understand that a higher power can be anything that keeps you sober, anything in your world that gives you hope and strength, that has meaning for you.

One time I adopted a character from a children's movie my daughter was watching, "The Never-Ending Story." In it, a beautiful little princess, who must have been eleven years old, calmed some nervous adventurers by saying, in her lovely soft voice: "It is always dark at the beginning." I adopted her right then as a Higher Power. Her words and her gentleness have come back to me again and again at times when I needed them. We all have our own personal inspirations.

After I did my Fourth Step, I began to listen to the "still, small voice" inside me that gave me guidance according to how honest I was with myself. I had denied myself access to that truth when I was drinking. It hurt too much. Now, when I was sober, those difficult feelings were the key to my spirituality and my serenity, the material from which to make my new life. Somehow that truth inside me, I knew, was the voice of my Higher Power.

When I had been coming to AA meetings for several months, I had an insight that made me feel much better than I had in a long time. Surprising myself, I said at a meeting, "God loves me." I was embarrassed after I said it. I figured everyone around the table was wincing and grabbing onto their doorknobs. At the same time, that announcement was a beginning for me. I knew that I had a Higher Power who loved me no matter what—whether I was a failure or a success, whether things were going well or badly. That was more than I could say for myself. I was a fairweather friend even to myself.

Before I came into AA I was able to stay sober on my own. But then things would go badly, and I'd drink again. "Why should I keep up this self-denial for nothing? Am I crazy? I'll never get my life together. I might as well drink." Or things would go well. "Look at me! I'm doing great! Why am I sitting home alone?" And I would drink. I can't stay sober just depending on myself, because I change too much. The same with other people. I cannot let my sobriety depend on them, because they change too. I sabotage myself if I attach my sobriety to people, places, or things. I can't, for example, pay too much attention to any material gains or successes I may have as a result of sobriety. What if I lose them? I might think I have a reason to drink.

And yet I seem to need something to hang on to. That's where my Higher Power comes in. Even though I still don't know exactly who he/she/it is, I know that it doesn't change with the weather or the circumstances of my life or the phases of the moon. I also know that my Higher Power loves me just as I am and has a plan for me. Maybe that plan included being hurt enough by my parents' drinking as a child to recognize the same patterns in myself, seek help in AA, and share my experience, strength, and hope with others who want to get sober.

I know it doesn't sound logical. But it works. It's just too big for me to really define. And I thank God for that.

Lynne D.
Carbondale, Illinois

God, the Verb

April 2002

To get to Step Two, you have to get past Step One. That was what I was told when I first came into the Fellowship of Alcoholics Anonymous. It made sense to me. The Steps are in order; they build upon one another. It was logical. My drinking, my attempts to control it, and all of the damage done in the process made it clear enough to me that I had more than a little drinking problem. So taking Step One was easy.

But taking Step Two was a much different story. You see, I came to AA as a proud agnostic. In retrospect, taking pride in doubt was pretty boorish. But that's how I arrived, and how I was when I started the transition from Step One to Step Two. Being an agnostic wasn't enough. I had my ego wrapped around it! I was proud that I was willing to ask the tough questions about God's existence. I had long before decided that if I was going to believe in a god, that belief would have to be well-grounded in logic.

For me, that meant to take Step Two, really take it, I would need a bit of time. Would you believe nine years! For nine long years, I clung to the phrases, "Fake it until you make it" and "Act as if you believe," just to stay sober and to work the other Steps.

Over the span of those nine years of living one day at a time, I used AA as my Higher Power, and it worked. I stayed sober. While AA worked as a power greater than myself that could restore me to sanity, it did not fill the bill of being the God I wanted so much to understand. You might say I had only enough to take Step Two, but not quite enough to honestly take Step Three.

On many occasions I talked about it with my sponsor, Jack, only to receive the same knowing smile and admonition: "Douglas, as smart as I am, and as smart as you are, together we don't have a brain big enough to get a hold of that one. Don't worry about what God is, just do the next right thing. It'll come to you. And, if you don't know what to believe, just believe that I believe. Know that it has worked for me and it is working for you. It's all the proof you really need."

For nine years, I heard him sing the same tune. To his credit, as many times as I brought it up to him, he never got irritated with me, or judged me, or preached his or any other gospel to me. He always listened and continued to encourage me to behave as the God I dearly wanted to have might have me behave. That was an interesting twist on the AA ideas "Act as if you believe" and "Fake it until you make it."

As it happened, I started sponsoring a man who made my agnosticism seem like it was in the peewee leagues. He was truly a major league agnostic, and even more disconcerting to me was the fact that he wasn't even proud of it! His agnosticism was just sort of "out there" for him.

If you have ever heard of the expression "still waters run deep," you could see living proof of it in this guy. John was one of the most intelligent people I have ever met. He was a very quiet, shy college professor, internationally published, and highly regarded for his teaching ability. John's capacity to reason and comprehend vastly exceeded my own and that of most people. He told me he thought about "the God thing" from time to time but never dwelt on it. Nevertheless, he was able to take Steps Two and Three and has now put together seven years of continuous sobriety. Ironically, through AA, he has come to believe in miracles, because, as he says, "I am one."

It hasn't been what John thought or believed (or didn't believe) that helped me through my agnosticism. John's behavior is what turned out to be the key that opened the door to Step Two for me.

John's life has never been easy. He has experienced the death of his twenty-three-year-old daughter, confronted the pain of caring for a wife dying from Alzheimer's disease, and experienced emotional abandonment from others who were dear to him. Yet through all of this, John has never been bitter toward the driver who killed his child; was faithful in providing the best care possible for his wife (now dead), and sought to understand, without malice, the side of those who had abandoned him. In other words, he behaved in a manner much like the God I would like to have might have me behave.

Something in the Wind   *April 1987*

An old school friend visited me and left two books by Dr. Harry Emerson Fosdick. Too ill to read them, I left them on the bedside table. However, at home, I opened one. It told the story of a boy on the coast of Maine in the United States who asked an old sailor: "What is the wind?" The old man scratched his head. "I don't know," he said, "I can't tell you. But I know how to hoist a sail."

Although the old sailor didn't know what the wind was, he had learned how to harness some of its great power.

Wasn't this what many in the Fellowship of Alcoholics Anonymous had done? Metaphorically speaking, they had hoisted a sail and caught hold of something, and that "something" was doing for them what they previously couldn't do for themselves.

Many called it God—some their Higher Power, while still others saw it as the strength of the Fellowship. As one man said, "I would be a fool not to want what those people had."

W.R.
Sydney, Australia

Recently, while in a deep meditation on a personal retreat, I was able to couple together John's behavior with Jack's admonition to behave as God would have me. When I say deep meditation, I'm not talking about the usual intellectual debate that goes on in my head. I'm talking about a meditation that reached into the deepest levels of my being to search for answers to such questions as, "Why am I alive? Is my life worth anything to anybody else but me? And if so, why?"

That was when I finally took Step Two—I mean really took it. I suddenly realized, at a level never before known to me, that working the Steps (that is, taking actions) was what had been leading me to sanity for the last nine years.

My vision of a Higher Power suddenly took on a very clear image of God being love, the verb. Until then, I had focused on God the noun. I became aware that my real purpose in life was not just to be a person capable of loving, but to be a loving person. My purpose is not to be centered around a concept of love, but instead around the action of love.

Another product of the meditation was the awareness that I focused on the wrong word in the familiar phrase, "act as if." Until I experienced the epiphany on the retreat, I had focused on the word "if." This is consistent with my agnosticism. But when I put the emphasis on the word "act," I came to discover that it was how I behaved that showed people I loved them. Jack, for all those years had been saying, "*act* as if," and I had been hearing, "act as *if.*"

Once I realized this, I could look back over the previous years to comprehend what John really meant when he told me he believed in miracles. By his actions, he had taken the leap of faith called for in the Second Step.

To me, the trapeze artist serves as the best metaphor for taking such a leap. It isn't a leap of faith when you know the trapeze bar is behind you, waiting for you—it is a leap of faith when you let go of the one you are now holding to reach for the one you do not yet see. It is when you act on faith that you actually have it.

It is now clear to me that the miracles John believes in—his, mine, and countless others'—have come from something we cannot see, but nonetheless exists. Those miracles have come from something deep within us that is much larger than any one of us.

The miracle of my sobriety is real. It did not come from my will; I had exerted all the will I had before I got to AA. It did not come from hearing or reading the Twelve Steps; I had done that before I got to AA. My miracle occurred when I became willing to go to any lengths to take action. Like the trapeze artist, it wasn't the knowledge of it being there—it was the action of letting go.

Doug B.
Lexington, Kentucky

The Lonely Emergencies
July 1958

Reason has moons, but moons not hers/ Lie mirrored on her sea,/ Confounding her astronomers, But O! delighting me. —Ralph Hodgson

"It is only in the lonely emergencies of life that our creed is tested," wrote William James. "Then routine maxims fail, and we fall back on our gods." The words say truly and beautifully what people often suppose they mean by that—to me—hateful banality: "There are no atheists in foxholes."

The atheists have been as brave in the foxholes as the conventionally devout, for atheism is itself a creed, or has the force of one in high-mindedness and virtue, and anyone but a bigot will acknowledge that many an atheist in history was nobler than many a professed man of God.

My dislike of the atheists-in-foxholes bit, apart from the polemical unction it usually goes with, is that it involves fear as the ultimate—indeed the only—religious motive. I have had enough to spare of a religion of fear, and it took the lonely emergency of touching bottom after twenty-five years as a drunkard to bring me by mystic chance into AA and free me from, among other fears, the fear of the religious big stick waved over my head by the well-intentioned teachers of my youth. I grew up in one of the authoritarian creeds, whose name doesn't matter, since other people may well believe that their childhood religion was the most severe.

But the bitterness is gone now—most of it. A silt remains, I suppose, as the residue of many another drunken unhappiness rises up in my heart sometimes and washes an uneasiness over my serenity. Then I go to an AA meeting, or find an AA friend; or if neither is possible at the time, I make a meeting for myself with memories of meetings, with the Serenity Prayer and the Twelve Steps.

Touching bottom was for me what, for all I know, it is for everybody: the collapse of pride under the accumulated horrors of the drinking years—the one delirium tremens too many, the convulsions, the shakes that seemed bigger than they had ever been before, the hotter and smellier sweat, the leg cramps no longer bearable; worse than all, the sense of inward disgrace, of humanity ruined past mending.

But here is the mystery: it only seemed the worst, for actually I had lived on that bottom for years and never made a move to lift myself from it by death (for which I had always more than a half-wish) or by seeking out AA.

I knew sobriety was possible in AA; I even knew it was possible for me only in AA—and this in spite of the fact that my only acquaintance in the fellowship was a zealous member of the church I had rejected, who proselytized for my return to the church and joining AA as though they were one and the same thing.

The little I knew about AA, in short, was all wrong. I thought of it as something that worked for "religious" people, which left me out; yet still I knew sobriety for alcoholics like me (I knew I was one) existed nowhere but in AA. In a way it seemed hard lines that "superstitious" people could sober up, and "enlightened" people like me were trapped in drunkenness.

It was not reason or will that brought me to AA, then; it was, in the phrase already used and now diffidently repeated, "mystic chance." The physical and mental torment were what they had long been, but I saw that I was on a bottom and could not live there. I knew I would be better dead than dead drunk. I was willing to die, without anger, even without sorrow, when a virtual stranger took me to the AA ward in Knickerbocker Hospital.

No act of intellect kept me sober day by day after I left the hospital; no act of will, in any usual sense. I knew no more than I had ever known; and sobriety had not come with some sudden welling from secret reserves of virtue. The reserves, if they existed at all, had long since been used up.

I had no virtue. I had nothing.

But I was sober day after day, within the day, and happy to let it go as mystic chance, without nagging for explanations. I never knew why I had to drink, and I didn't need to know why I was staying sober. If for "mystic chance" you want to read "dumb luck" that's all right with me. Better people than I am, including a greatly loved friend, had died of their alcoholism; better people than I am are still hooked.

But I never felt my sobriety challenged, except fleetingly and mostly in dreams. Within the day, whatever the day was like otherwise, I knew I would be sober, and I had a deep sense that something was working itself out, that another mystic chance was in the making; for by now, in spite of the surface illogic of the term, I took it for granted that logic of a kind beyond my understanding was involved in my sobriety, in the experience of Bill W., and in the whole history of AA.

Another lonely emergency: serious illness sent me to the hospital from which this is written. AA became richer for me through considerable suffering. I had tried not to bargain, to haggle, to chaffer with life and its creator, or to demand rewards beyond sobriety itself. The appeal of AA, right from the start, had been its very modesty, with no one, at least no one with any sense, promising me anything, even sobriety except upon imponderable conditions.

My heart grew lighter in the hospital as the days showed me how nothing had changed in the mystic chance that made me sober. I was still living a day at a time, and if a day came when I would no longer be living, what of that? Acceptance of life is also acceptance of death, since life as we know it must always end. The First, Second and Third of the Twelve Steps repeated themselves over and over in my mind through the worst of the illness—in that order—after I had said the Serenity Prayer; later the Eleventh Step joined the procession.

My creed was tested, and the wonder was that I had a creed to test. It was there all right, and there was nothing of fear in it. I was not a terror-stricken convert in a foxhole but a soul willing to go on to whatever might happen next. I don't know that I was any closer to death than I ever am, but death's possibility is more dramatic during an operation: it is perhaps the loneliest emergency of all, this side of eternity.

As to the creed: it is a little, maybe a skimpy creed, but it stood up, and skimpy or not, I mean to keep it if I can. It is a belief in a benevolence behind or within creation, an infinity of kindness that encompasses me as its creature. This I believe against every doubt of my skeptical mind (and it is skeptical by habit), against every difficulty the evil in the world can hurl against it.

I am content to bide my time, or my eternity, for the explanation of this as of other mysteries. Reality meanwhile seems to me to be better than it is bad, and goodness must be served in the face of every demon of distraction. My small creed has no dogma and no canon, but only an intuition of God, shyly held. I can use that contentious word with a full heart, so it be clear it is God *as I understand him*, with the italics respected.

Joe C.
New York, New York

AA's Steps Lead to — *Spiritual Awakening*
May 1967

I think I have heard and been a party to more disagreements, puzzlements, and confusion about the term "spiritual awakening" than any other in the program—including "God." And most of my difficulty was unnecessary. It could have been avoided just by paying more attention to what the Twelfth Step itself says and less attention to my "old ideas" about spiritual awakening.

First, a small point that made a big difference in my understanding. The Step does not say, *Having had a spiritual awakening as* a *result of these Steps;* it says, *having had a spiritual awakening as* the *result of these Steps.* So a spiritual awakening is not just one of several results of working the Steps. It is the totality of what the Steps are all about, what they are aiming at. Therefore, to define spiritual awakening for myself in Alcoholics Anonymous, all I have to do is describe the results of my work on the first eleven Steps. The work has involved: letting in the truth about my situation as an alcoholic and a loser in life; becoming willing to accept help, not on my terms, but on the terms offered; facing and accepting responsibility for my shortcomings and misbehavior rather than blaming Mums, Dads, my First Sergeant, the boss, the Twentieth Century, or fate. The results of this work have been sobriety, stability, and responsibility which have, in turn, produced a degree of meaning, satisfaction, and joy in my life which were never there before.

I have not yet mentioned God or Higher Power in connection with waking up spiritually. This is not because I want to apologize for or leave out God. The reality of God permeates and is the essence of spiritual awakening, but in order to begin to have experience of the reality, it is *not* first necessary to come to terms with the word *God* or even the words *Higher Power*. As long as one remains open-minded and willing about the words, experience of the reality does not have to and indeed ought not to be postponed.

One of the early fathers of the Christian church said, "Do you wish to know God? Learn first to know yourself." This is the key which opens up the opportunity for recovery in AA to so many of us. Spiritual awakening can begin in the absence of much knowledge or understanding, but it begins with knowledge and acceptance of the truth about ourselves.

A Slob's Guide to Spiritual Growth   *April 1982*

What right do I have to expect perfection and efficiency in my spiritual growth when the rest of my life is so full of ups and downs, ins and outs, and backs and forths? Throughout this whole adventure, the only consistency I have maintained is an absolute and total faith in AA, come what may.

Happiness happens when results exceed expectations. Maybe this is working after all. Deep down, there is also a warm, small ball of faith, always there, never dimmed, unexplainable, asking nothing, but giving much. To define it or try to bounce it would distort or destroy it. It just is, that's all.

As St. Augustine said, "God is closer to me than I am to Him." I don't know exactly what that means, but it sure is true.

C.H.
Fairfield, Connecticut

So I am learning, when looking for signs of spiritual awakening in myself, to look, not for bright lights or emotional upheavals (although I'm sure there is a place for these too), but for sobriety, stability, responsibility, meaning, satisfaction, joy. These are the marks of the beginning of spiritual awakening, and they come as *the* result of work with the Steps. If they fail to come or, after a time, begin to disappear, the answer is no mystery; it is more work with the Steps.

The first 100 members of this Fellowship, who hammered out the Twelve Steps, knew what they were doing. They could have made it two steps or ten steps or twenty-five steps, but they didn't. I don't think they put anything in they didn't think they needed. They were working the whole program, not because they were saints, but because they were drunks who wanted to get well. I have no reason to suppose I'm any less sick than they were; I have no reason to suppose I need any less of the program than they did.

I think I want to "keep it simple" as much as the next guy, but I also think my sobriety, my sanity, and my very life depend on keeping all of it.

T.P., Jr.
Hankins, New York

What a Spiritual Awakening Means to Me

April 1956

Recently I have heard more and more speakers remark, "It is easier to get sober than to stay sober." In my opinion this need not be so. For more than seven years I have worked with a number of fellow alcoholics who had trouble with the program. Almost invariably they had forgotten, or never actually grasped, the principles in our program that aid spiritual growth and promote a happy sobriety.

Ralph Waldo Emerson wrote, "Every man is an open door through which the Infinite passes into the finite; through which the Universal becomes individual." Certainly, to realize any measure of this heritage, I must have some degree of spiritual consciousness.

Years of progressive alcoholism laid me on the doorstep of AA, a physical and spiritual wreck. Like all alcoholics in my condition, I needed some kind of spiritual awakening to absorb the program.

What then is a spiritual awakening? There are many versions, perhaps because a spiritual awakening is a profoundly individual experience. Some report it as an illuminating flash. Others associate it with some deeply significant happening in their lives. Many experience it hardly aware of any immediate change. An ancient Stoic philosopher once said, "Great things are not created suddenly; let there be time. First, let it blossom, then bear fruit, then ripen." My own spiritual awakening developed concurrently with a gradual change in character, after I began to work the AA program.

Psychologically speaking, we are defined, in technical terms, as reacting mechanisms. Theoretically, we are supposed to respond to environmental influences according to a progressive formula: stimulation-integration-reaction. The pattern of my spiritual awakening closely followed this formula: AA fellowship and faithful striving with all the Steps became the stimulus for my spiritual development. Trying my best to exercise the first three Steps stimulated humility, hope, and faith. The Fourth, Fifth, and Tenth Steps laid down a pattern of growth for honesty with myself. Working the Sixth and Seventh Steps awakened remnants of moral courage and reestablished sincerity in relating myself to a Higher Power.

Following through with the Eighth and Ninth Steps validated my sincerity with those whom I had harmed, and paved the way for me to forgive myself.

A little reflection will show that a sincere attempt to exercise these first ten Steps brings into play some of the finest virtues in the human character: humility, hope, faith, honesty, courage, and sincerity. There is an old saying in AA: "If you don't get AA, keep coming and AA will get you."

In other words, some of these good character traits are bound to rub off. Whatever did rub off, integrated with a changing personality. I now felt eligible to try for higher spiritual rewards abiding in the Eleventh Step: *Sought through prayer and meditation to improve our conscious contact with God* as we understood Him, *praying only for knowledge of His will for us and the power to carry that out.*

Where could this profound exercise lead me? To the ideal expressed by

Emerson? If this sublime experience is indeed our heritage, what finer preparation could I make for it than by prayer and meditation to improve my conscious contact with God as I understood him?

How do I begin? It is written somewhere in the Talmud that "a man comes into the world with his fists closed, wanting everything." In the Eleventh Step we approach God with open hands, wanting nothing but the knowledge of his will and the power to carry that out.

Consistent striving with the Eleventh Step has sharpened my awareness and my appreciation of all creation and its glorious presentation, as the manifestation of supreme genius. "Behold I have placed before you an open door and no man can close it." I revere the soft glow of twilight and the gleam of countless worlds hovering remote in the heavens, as the splendorous source of spiritual stimulation, the bloom of infinite power. When the new day kindles in the silky tinted sky, I am conscious of its supreme endowments, significant to my growing spirit.

What then is my spiritual awakening?

It is a growing sensitivity of my spirit to the infinite and the universal, nurtured by illuminating glimpses of spiritual beauty. It flowers from the cultivation of all of AA's Twelve Steps.

Ever fresh in my heart is a song of thanksgiving for my expanding sobriety, as the opening door to timeless truth.

J.A.L.
Jackson Heights, New York

MESMERIZED BY SANITY

February 1997

When I first became a member of AA, all I did was stop drinking. This was a long time ago, and it was what the Fellowship around me advocated: you stayed away from the first drink a day at a time, shared at meetings, and this state of sobriety would enable you to solve all of your life's problems. My friends in AA, having been sober for some time, had something I wanted so I did what they did.

It worked fine, for a while. Then it stopped working. I became more and more discontented but denied it. After all, I was sober, wasn't I?

Too much of a coward, I didn't drink again but developed a second compulsion that brought me to my knees. This compulsion was only a symptom of my huge emotional problems: I was angry, fearful, totally self-absorbed, manipulative and dishonest in my relationships, I loathed myself and the world, and most of all, I was deeply unhappy. I had created a normal life, living like my peers did, achieving in my profession, and dying inside.

At this point I moved abroad, and it was in the first AA meeting there that I had what I can only describe as a spiritual experience. I guess I was terrified of the new situation, alone in an unfamiliar environment, and that made me open-minded. I listened to a speaker sharing about her relationship with God (they spoke a lot about God at that meeting), and she had such clear, fearless eyes, she radiated such happiness and contentment, that I was mesmerized. Suddenly I understood what had happened to me: the reasons for my drinking not having been treated, my alcoholism had come back with a different symptom. I felt an incredible joy and relief, and a wave of self-love and acceptance. I could see now I was presented with the very tools that would help me overcome my alcoholism. I now think that my "relapse" was quite a healthy reaction. If I look at human beings as systems, mine had had to cease functioning. I'd so mistreated myself by imposing standards of perfection, thus making self-acceptance impossible, and I'd denied all spiritual and emotional needs, that the system had to signal—with my new compulsion—that all was not well. I was forced to take notice and act. I could regret the wasted years, or I could get on with life and get well.

My real recovery started that very moment. I started AA all over again, got a sponsor, and worked the Steps in the order given.

The program promised me sanity, and it became something very desirable. I saw sanity in people I actively sought out in the meetings. It meant peace of mind, contentment, and self-acceptance. No more fighting the world and being eaten up by the rage, no more having to be Ms. Perfect who had all the answers. Looking back, I had no doubts that I could not do it by myself. I recognized that help had to come from a power greater than myself. Or, as I once heard at a meeting, "The mind can't cure the mind."

So I thought about the power greater than myself that I wanted to trust and whose care I could turn my life and my will over to. Again, I was helped greatly by those who were there before me. The well people all had a very personal relationship with God, and clear ideas about what their God was like. I listened, tried, erred, and changed my ideas when necessary. For some time now, my ideas about my Higher Power haven't changed but my understanding has deepened.

Has it all been plain sailing then? Of course not. Over the years, much has happened, and I'm getting older. I find one pattern coming up again and again. When all is well, I get complacent. Prayer stops being a priority, I do my Tenth Step less thoroughly, and going to a meeting becomes a burden. Fortunately, my threshold for self-inflicted pain is low these days, and I return to God as the source of sanity sooner rather than later. I've had some spectacular experiences of instant relief when asking God to take away obsessions. On the other hand, I've also experienced times when I had to ask again and again for the willingness to apply self-discipline to let go of self-destructive thoughts and actions.

These days I find that nothing is as precious as my sanity. I used to be addicted to drama and could only function on excitement and high levels of adrenaline. It's very different today. I really appreciate the quality of my life. I go through life at an even pace and enjoy being just one of the human race. I strive to serve in my work, to be a good friend and a responsible citizen. It's all very ordinary and average and sane, and I wouldn't trade it for anything.

E.M.
London, England

THE LORD OF SONG
April 2002

When I had been in AA only a few weeks, I dared talk with an old-timer about that amazing concept of a power greater than myself. "Please, tell me," I asked, "am I completely free to choose? You see, I need this program even if it requires a kind of conversion or something. Please, tell me the truth, because I'm ready to do anything!"

He smiled. Then he spoke compassionately: "You maybe think we are evangelists?"

"I'm not really sure."

He was still smiling. Then he put on his glasses and handed me his Big Book. "Bill's Story, page 12," he said. "Read aloud the words in italics."

I did. He repeated after me: "Your own conception of God ... Only a matter of being willing to believe in a Power greater than myself." "My own conception of God is silly," I almost screamed.

"But it's yours," he said. "And in this program, we're not supposed to believe as others do; we're simply encouraged to believe as we do ourselves."

At last, I was convinced. And I began working the program with my own conception of God. I was happy because now I was released.

In those days, the only God I was able to believe in was a God of songs. Perhaps this was a naive idea from my early childhood, but this was the only God I could love and believe in with all my heart.

AA was very open-minded on this subject: "A power greater than myself," said the Step. Just this. The Fellowship didn't care how I defined it.

Thereafter, I've never been judgmental about my own conception of God and worked the program as effectively as the members who belong to a particular religious body, I suppose. And with time, my conception of Higher Power developed and took more mature forms with every book I read on the subject.

Much later in my sobriety, thanks to a visitor, I came to know that there is a holy book called *Bhagavad Gita* (Holy Song, or Lord's Song). This visitor was an old-timer and like Dr. Earle, the author of "Physician, Heal Thyself" in the Big Book, he had been to India. After the meeting, I invited him to dinner, and we talked at length about the spiritual side of the program. He was a yogi and had been sober for more than ten years.

David (not his real name) told me that he understood the meaning of the first chapter of the *Bhagavad Gita*, which is called the Despondency of Arjuna, to be the conviction of hopelessness. Arjuna was the name of the hero and a whole chapter, the very first chapter, was dedicated to describing in detail the hopelessness of a hero in the middle of a battlefield that symbolizes life itself.

"I'm not a scholar," he said. "I'm just a recovering alcoholic. But I've met scholars who cannot understand the teaching of this sacred book simply because they are not familiar with something like the First Step of our AA program. I've also met people who think the AA program is purely Christian, simply because this is the only religion they are familiar with. My philosophy has concepts such as reincarnation, karma or dharma, which may seem hard to accept for many Americans. But you know alcoholism is no respecter of nation or religion. In America or Europe, we may be mostly Christian. But in other parts of the world, billions of people believe and think differently. To them, religion, holiness, and the sacred mean different things.

"I think that our program is universal. It is universal because, besides Hindus, Buddhists, and Christians, we also include agnostics and atheists and we mean it. And I'm very grateful for this open-mindedness."

I am very grateful to David. He helped me see that my own conception of God in my early sobriety wasn't unique, and something much more important: the program gave me full freedom on this matter.

In AA, I've met people who believe in a goddess or in extra-terrestrials as well as people who believe their Higher Power is a state of awareness or consciousness. I've even met a Freemason who understands the program as an extraordinary tool for building what he calls "the temple in man" out of the wreckage of the past.

To me, these were simply other alcoholics. Personally, I don't like labels. "Alcoholic" is the only label I can accept easily in an AA meeting. Every religion or belief system has its own language, terms, and definitions. I don't have to think about such things when working the program. In AA, I've found a freedom I'd been longing for since my childhood.

The program, I think, requires a little more than how we think or believe. We're not dealing with religion, but with spirituality. As said in the Big Book, "The spiritual life is not a theory. We have to live it." And as Bill W. put it in the June 1961 Grapevine: "We cannot grow very much unless we constantly try to envision what the eternal spiritual values are."

Ercan A.
Istanbul, Turkey

SEARCH FOR CLOUD NINE

April 1977

Remember the instant it dawned on you that you were a drunk? Remember how clear you were about it, the relief you felt, the freedom you experienced? You were no longer fighting. Booze had crushed you to the bottom. There was nowhere to go, nothing to do but experience the relief of the truth: "I'm a drunk, not a social drinker!"

How long you had resisted that truth! And as you lay there, the truth became clearer: You had been fooling yourself. Now you knew it. Every cell in your body ached and hurt, but at last every part of you knew you were a drunk. Through and through. Your search had ended. At the bottom, everything was clear. The truth had brought serenity and peace. It felt good. You had never felt so beautiful before.

Remember how you as an entity faded? What remained was an individual who knew surrender: the peace of stopping the driving, burning search. You seemed to float in a sea of bliss, connected to everything else in a boundless universe. For the first time, you felt in love with life.

You could barely wait until you got to an AA meeting to tell others what had happened. Remember how excited you were?

Eagerly, you awaited recognition by the chairman. Gleefully, you related your experience at the bottom, and faces lighted up in recognition. How good it was to be a part of the AA program. Here, people understood.

Remember how, sometime later, a guy (or was it a gal?) approached you and warned you that you were on Cloud Nine and would soon return to reality? This excitement was natural, happened to everybody, you were told, but soon reality would emerge. Staying sober might then become difficult for a while, but it would be worth it. Then your friend patted you gently, smiled, and walked away. You wanted to say something, but the words turned to ashes in your mouth.

Remember slowly trudging home that night? You felt let down, lonely, confused. Some of your old aches and pains returned.

"But," you reasoned, "he must know! He's been sober longer than I have." Deep down, though, you felt frightened. Somehow, there should be a way to keep the peace you had felt at the bottom. "It shouldn't fade like this," you murmured. You began to feel distant from some of your fellow AA members. They'd nod at you as though to say, "He's up on a cloud now. Let's be available when he crashes."

Remember how you became a little guarded, because you wanted to be a good AA member? The only way, you reasoned, was to be careful of what you said at meetings, so you would be well liked.

Your length of sobriety increased in weeks, then months, then years. You felt good about that, even though some of the old tensions had returned. Everyone liked you very much. "These AA members are great people," you said to yourself. "They understand."

Still, you yearned for the bliss and serenity you had felt at the bottom, at the point of surrender, when you first knew clearly that you were a drunk. But most of the peace had gone. You were alive, sober, but uncomfortable.

"I guess I've come down from Cloud Nine," you thought. "I suppose they were right. I'm down. Sober, but down!"

At that point, you made a secret decision. You decided to start a search for the old blissful feeling. You had to have it! Sobriety was wonderful, but you needed serenity too.

For weeks, months, perhaps years, your search took you to many places, meetings, authorities, and books, along many promising paths. Although you didn't know it then, the search itself was the root of your trouble! But that is getting ahead of the story.

Remember how you got hold of new books that offered answers? You devoured every word, hoping to recapture the lost peace. You assumed new roles, hoping to learn new ways that would bring peace. Sometimes you acted the clown, sometimes the wise man, sometimes the aggressor, sometimes the shy violet who sat in the back row at a meeting.

Remember how you prayed more (or prayed less), or went to more AA meetings (or fewer), or went to church (or stopped going to church)? A thousand things you did trying to recapture Cloud Nine and the sense of peace that had once filled you.

In spite of your hidden misery, you felt grateful to be sober (a long time by now), but the frantic search for serenity kept driving you. Each and every thing you found and tried did help for a while, but only for a while.

You just couldn't hold on to the good feelings for long; they were elusive; they slipped easily through your fingers, and sooner or later the misery returned!

So you picked up the pace. You found and read more new books, tried on more new ideas, searched harder, became more determined to recapture bliss. (Or did you call it happiness, or serenity, or peace, or God, or truth, or beauty, or a Higher Power? It really doesn't matter.)

The harder you searched for serenity, the worse you felt. Sober, yes. But inwardly at war. And somehow you seemed to know that this new obsession was splitting you apart.

One day, you found yourself alone, maybe in your room, maybe walking down the street, in a restaurant, at a meeting—it doesn't really matter. You were crying and couldn't keep back the tears. You were ashamed, but you felt depressed, in shreds, blown totally apart. Never had you felt so bad. You hated everything, sometimes even AA members!

You prayed that you would die—now. Life simply wasn't worth it! In spite of sobriety, you knew that you just couldn't keep going. Your search for peace had taken you everywhere, but you hadn't found it. Peace, maybe, wasn't to be yours, and that made life worthless, useless. Your crying broke into sobs.

Remember how you slumped into a chair, or fell onto your bed exhausted, sick to death of everything, deeply despising your life? How you hated it!

You relaxed a little and just lay there beaten, wanting to die.

And then a strange thing happened. The obsession seemed to fade away. The urge to desperately try subsided. The deep need to find answers dropped away. Only stillness remained.

As you lay there, inwardly quiet but emotionally beaten by your own hand, having stopped searching for anything or trying anything, a deep sense of peace filled you. Serenity and bliss returned. How this had happened, you didn't know.

But the reason didn't really matter. You didn't have to know the why of everything. Feeling serene was no longer a goal. Looking for peace was over. Somehow, you had given up. And you felt peaceful!

A light began to dawn, and you said to yourself, "This is another bottom, just like the one I felt years ago when I knew I was a drunk." And this thought came to you over and over again. It penetrated deep into your heart and soul. Remember, as you lay there, another light dawned, and a question slowly took form in your mind:

"Is my real home here at the bottom? Are the bottom, peace, serenity, Cloud Nine, and the top all the same thing?" Strange new idea.

But somehow you didn't really care whether that question was answered or not. Looking, searching, and waiting had ended.

Remember how a wonderful drowsiness came over you as you left all those questions to be answered by someone else? If they ever could be answered. It no longer mattered to you.

Finally, your body relaxed and you fell deeply asleep. Your first sleep in a long, long time. And you didn't know it, but you had fallen asleep with a great big grin on your face.

E.M.
Hazard, Kentucky

Spiritual Good Manners   *April 1959*

For me there was no easy or sudden help. Weighed down by the rejected symbols of my past, ridden by guilt for churchly dogmas left behind and scattered, I was without a home. Months passed and it was a Jewish friend leading a closed meeting one night who broke the spell. I saw what AA said so clearly. It was God as each of us understood Him. My intolerance, a sort of spiritual myopia, was a crippling thing. I, too, was freed to choose, to find my way. Listen, I thought, to those who talk of the Old Law, the prophets; to those who share with me the wisdom of Buddha the Enlightened One—they too move in the clear light along with those who see the Man of Nazareth enshrined. Listen to him who also appears in unbelief for he, too, brings gifts I cannot see.

Now I am a part of this Fellowship. Now I must take these gifts of understanding and return my own.

Mary B.
Chappaqua, New York

PART TWO

Finding

Encounters with a Higher Power

"God was about to introduce himself," one AA writes, in this case through a "dirty, panhandling wino." But as these stories attest, similar encounters have come about in so many equally unexpected ways—in a grandmother's love and concern, in a rose bush that keeps flowering through every drunk and hangover, in a big old refrigerator in a state hospital in Minnesota, in the brilliant round orange sitting on a dreary breakfast tray, and in "the resonating voices of countless men and women in AA."

As Bill W. writes, "Sooner or later, every AA comes to depend upon a Power greater than himself." One writer describes the process as "an awakening of my human spirit," what another depicts as "the gradual realization of who I was, where I should be headed." Doing the Steps, accepting the misfortunes that come into our lives, making difficult amends, getting involved in AA service—these are some of the routes that can lead us to a Higher Power of our understanding, whatever name we may choose to use.

As we understood Him—what an incredible variety of human experience that accommodates! "AA as a whole is my Higher Power," one writer declares; another observes that her Higher Power is more powerful than "any mere human or collection of humans, even AA as a whole; that's what makes it higher." Some find an Immanence, others a "little flicker of light," still others the good that is in all of us. And of course there's always love, lots of love. Perhaps, whatever else we discover, it's that love that helps us find our way, for as one writer puts it, here in AA, "love is our glue."

BILL W. ON THE SECOND TRADITION
January 1948

> *For our group purpose there is but one ultimate authority—a loving God as He may express Himself in our group conscience. Our leaders are but trusted servants; they do not govern.*

Sooner or later, every AA comes to depend upon a Power greater than himself. He finds that the God of his understanding is not only a source of strength, but also a source of *positive direction*. Realizing that some fraction of that infinite resource is now available, his life takes on an entirely different complexion. He experiences a new inner security together with such a sense of destiny and purpose as he has never known before. As each day passes, our AA reviews his mistakes and vicissitudes. He learns from daily experience what his remaining character defects are and becomes ever more willing that they be removed. In this fashion he improves his conscious contact with God.

Every AA group follows this same cycle of development. We are coming to realize that each group, as well as each individual, is a special entity, not quite like any other. Though AA groups are basically the same, each group does have its own special atmosphere, its own peculiar state of development. We believe that every AA group has a conscience. It is the collective conscience of its own membership. Daily experience informs and instructs this conscience. The group begins to recognize its own defects of character and, one by one, these are removed or lessened. As this process continues, the group becomes better able to receive right direction for its own affairs. Trial and error produces group experience, and out of corrected experience comes custom. When a customary way of doing things is definitely proved to be best, then that custom forms into AA Tradition. The Greater Power is then working through a clear group conscience.

We humbly hope and believe that our growing AA Tradition will prove to be the will of God for us.

Many people are coming to think that Alcoholics Anonymous is, to some extent, a new form of human society. In our discussion of the First Tradition, it was emphasized that we have, in AA, no coercive human authority. Because each AA, of necessity, has a sensitive and responsive conscience, and because alcohol will discipline him severely if he backslides, we are finding we have little need for manmade rules or regulations. Despite the fact that we do veer off at times on tangents, we are becoming more able to depend absolutely on the long-term stability of the AA group itself. With respect to its own affairs, the collective conscience of the group will, given time, almost surely demonstrate its perfect dependability. The group conscience will, in the end, prove a far more infallible guide for group affairs than the decision of any individual member, however good or wise he may be. This is a striking and almost unbelievable fact about Alcoholics Anonymous. Hence we can safely dispense with those exhortations and punishments seemingly so necessary to other societies. And we need not depend overmuch on inspired leaders. Because our active leadership of service can be truly rotating, we enjoy a kind of democracy rarely possible elsewhere. In this respect we may be, to a large degree, unique.

Therefore we of Alcoholics Anonymous are certain that there is but one ultimate authority; "a loving God as he may express himself in our group conscience."

Bill W.

Waking Up Sober   *July 1990*

The "spiritual awakening" of the Twelfth Step is for me an ongoing process. It grows and flourishes and becomes richer and deeper as I struggle my way through life one day at a time. I'm still a slow learner, and I certainly am not yet fully awake spiritually. The Higher Power gradually reveals himself through the working of our group, as we are told in the Second Tradition. And it is by my contact with the group, and through prayer and meditation, that I become ever more aware of his action in me and in my group. That, for me, is part of the "spiritual awakening."

Dan J.
Cochabamba, Bolivia

Two Messengers

February 1978

I felt trapped in my hotel room, imprisoned by my own anxiety and inde-cision. The events of the previous night had severely jolted the already shaky spiritual foundation of my AA program. For nearly four years, I had stayed sober despite the qualifications I attached to acceptance of a power greater than myself. Now, I was filled with the fear of abandonment by a God whom I had never really believed in.

The room emphasized my despair. It was a hideout. I was hiding from my boss, whose challenge to my faith had left me feeling helpless and alone. And I was hiding from everything outside those walls, because my insecurity made everything and everyone a threat. It was like some of the old days, when the best I could manage was to take my bottle to a secret place and shut out the world.

But the knowledge that I was hiding only increased my torment. Where else could I go? Where could I find escape from my doubts about all the beliefs I had previously been afraid to question? At an AA meeting, my sober experience told me. I found the number in the Chicago telephone directory. But I didn't call, and I knew I was withdrawing from the very Fellowship that had saved my life.

My mind drifted back to the night before. The sermon had begun at dinner and continued late into the night. My boss had enthusiastically ex-pounded on his fundamental Christian beliefs. The strength of his convic-tions and his exhortations that I should embrace his faith only served to expose my avoidance of surrender to anything except AA as a source of help for alcoholics.

Reacting in self-defense, I had countered his arguments with the phrases I had learned: ... *God as we understood Him ... Came to believe that a Power greater than ourselves ... His will for us ....* But they were words spoken from the head, not the heart. They were released as a smoke screen to hide my inner doubts. As we talked, the power of the distress sig-nals increased. My days of paying lip service to Steps Two and Three were coming to a close, and I could feel the encroaching vacancy in my soul.

"How," I asked myself, "do you begin believing in something that you have professed to believe in all along?"

I thought again of going to a meeting. But I was afraid, frightened by my own hypocrisy, fearful of its exposure. Even if I could find comfort there, surrounded by the only power I had been willing to accept, I was unwilling to experience the empty loneliness that would come after leaving God, as I understood him, behind at the meeting.

The need to get out of my room became more urgent. But where would I go? To the restaurant in the hotel? Perhaps even to the bar for a soft drink, just to feel a part of something? Neither was acceptable. Finally, I decided to leave the hotel to find a sandwich shop somewhere. The decision didn't make any sense, and I knew it. A blizzard raged outside. Chicago was an unfamiliar city. I wasn't even hungry. Still, I dressed—suit, tie, and topcoat—and plunged into the snowy night. I had no idea where I was going. But Someone did.

God was about to introduce himself.

I crossed Michigan Avenue and had walked just a few feet beyond the curb when a man emerged from a shadowy doorway. He was unshaven and wore dirty, long-unchanged clothes. There were holes in the grimy stocking cap pulled down tightly around his ears to ward off the freezing cold. His hands were thrust deeply into the pockets of his faded, grimy, Army fatigue jacket.

"Hey, mister, can you help me out?"

My initial reaction was to ignore him. But on an impulse, I stopped. He was much younger than he appeared at first glance, perhaps in his late twenties.

"Can you loan me fifty cents for a hamburger, sir? I haven't eaten since yesterday."

As he spoke, the old, familiar smell of stale wine flooded over me, overpowering the freshness of falling snow. Part of me wanted to refuse him. I knew the money would not be spent for a hamburger. But I remembered how it was, how the need for a drink could churn your guts and make your skin ache all over. I remembered how the first long pull could quiet the demons, if only for a little while.

I pulled out a dollar and shoved it into his shaking hand. I wanted to say something more, something about having a choice. But I couldn't.

"Thanks, mister."

I mumbled that it was okay, and started to turn away.

"Hey, mister, do you know where I can find an AA meeting around here?"

The words struck me with a thunderous force. A throbbing numbness passed through my body. I distrusted my ears. "What?" I asked incredulously.

"An AA meeting. I ... I can't stop drinking."

The incongruity of the situation was overwhelming. Why would a dirty, panhandling wino ask a respectable-looking businessman about an AA meeting? How could he think that I would know?

Yet, as I looked at him in stunned silence and saw the desperation that had been mine for so many years, I knew the answer. Who better?

"I don't know," I managed to say. I felt suddenly buoyant. "But we'll find one together. I'm an alcoholic, too."

We found a pay phone nearby. I called the intergroup office for the location of the nearest meeting. My wino friend had to tell me where we were.

"The Mustard Seed Group," said the friendly female voice. "You're only a block from there."

Another shock. While looking up AA's phone number in my room, I had noticed a separate listing for the Mustard Seed Group. It struck me as an interesting name, and I had wondered about it. But with my ignorance of Chicago geography, it could have been ten miles from my hotel. It wasn't. It was less than two blocks away.

A discussion meeting was in progress as we entered the room. We were directed to two chairs on the outer edge of the semicircle of participants. A hand microphone was being passed around as each person shared. My mind was reeling. It was some time before I became aware of the subject under discussion.

It was Step Three.

I felt as though I was living a fantasy, caught up somehow in a conspiracy of coincidences beyond my understanding. I flashed back to my first days in AA, when I was told to pray, whether I believed in it or not. I had been an atheistic daily drunk, unable to stay dry more than a few days at a time on my own will-power. With sobriety at stake, I had been willing to try. For the past four years, I had prayed because I was afraid to do otherwise. But I still didn't believe in it.

Now, trying to comprehend the events that had led me to this meeting, this particular meeting, I wondered. Could it be possible?

The microphone was suddenly in my hand. Before I spoke, I thought about the words of the Third Step: *Made a decision to turn our will and our lives over to the care of God as we understood Him.*

I knew then. This wasn't a fantasy. There had been no coincidences, no accidents of fate. In my anguish, God had sent me two messengers: one to show me that I was lost, the other to show me the way.

I shared. I talked about my earlier torment, about my feelings of withdrawing into myself, about my fears. I told them about discovering the name of this group, without knowing the meaning of that discovery. I told them how I had met my new friend, who was now beside me. And about how God, as I was beginning to understand him, had brought us here to this meeting.

R.H.
Culver City, California

Rambling Rose

December 2001

I have recently been thinking of how, in my drinking years, I tried various types of meditation and how I would practice one method and then get up, go into the kitchen, and reach for the bottle. I didn't know alcoholism was a disease—I only knew that as I tried so desperately to talk and listen to the God I had grown up with, the further I would sink into the loneliness and despair that only a soul like mine knew—or so I thought.

Then, through the grace of a God I had tried to touch for so long, I was carried quite literally into the rooms of Alcoholics Anonymous. I went to my first meeting drunk and a man and a woman propelled me through the doors to a new way of living.

Only when I had worked the Steps that first special time did I begin to find a Higher Power that would fill my soul with love, hope, and a design and purpose for living free of alcohol.

Today my Higher Power has led me to a new way to meditate. Outside my bedroom window is a rambling rose bush. When this room was added to the house, a rose garden had to be cemented over, but somehow one climbing rose bush grew out from under the concrete. Every spring during my drinking years, that bush would grow and the birds would sit in its branches; in my alcoholism, hating the sounds of the birds singing so early on those mornings when I came to, I went out and kept chopping down that bush. Yet the bush always grew back stronger and more beautiful than ever.

Now I treasure that rose bush that shelters birds and chipmunks and provides sweet flowers where the bees come to feast. There are even hummingbirds in some years since I've hung feeders in and near the bush.

When I awaken these days, before I even get up, I can turn my head to see all the wonders that my Higher Power has provided and the tremendous persistence that was there through all those years—drawing me ever nearer to those quiet, still moments that I know are for connecting to the God of my understanding.

No longer do I "come to" but rather wake up, and can truly feel from my soul, "Good morning, God" and not "Good God, morning."

This afternoon after a day out there trying to practice these principles in all my affairs, I was able to stretch out on my bed and look out the window and renew my spirit and conscious contact with a spirit that not only made me and loved me, but still loves me—loves me, birds, flowers, bees, and even that rose bush.

K.G.
Salem, Virginia

Power of Prayer   May 1968

The most wonderful thing I have discovered is that prayer works as truly and surely as I live and breathe! I am beginning to think of Allah as a most loving Creator who is specially interested in me—otherwise he would not have led me to AA or given me so many chances to come out of slips. He keeps on throwing the ball at our feet—so that we may play ball with him.

F.H.
Karachi, Pakistan

SPIRITUAL SPECTRUM
April 1980

Spirituality is a changing word for me. When I was first introduced to it, nobody told me about it. They simply let me feel it. They surrounded me with it, and I felt the first comfort I had felt in my life. After fourteen years of religious schools, I was finally introduced to God at my first meeting of Alcoholics Anonymous. We've been friends ever since.

If I were to pick a color for the changing nature of the spirituality that has grown around and in me, the color would not be the same for different periods of my life. Prior to AA, there was no color. I was plagued with self-doubt disguised as sensitivity and intellect. I knew how the mad people in hospitals felt and understood why some cultures think that dementia is a sign of being touched by God. The only difference was, I felt we were all touched by his archenemy, the Devil. The only thing to do was have another drink and ponder bleakly about it.

Then came my personal crash. When one wakes up in a state psycho ward tied down, one becomes willing to consider alternatives to one's previous life pattern. They fed me a mushy breakfast. Everything in that ward was dull brown or beige, but smack in the middle of the breakfast tray was a big, bright orange. I couldn't take my eyes from that orange. It looked so startling and healthy. I put it in my pocket and submitted meekly when the guard suggested I go to an AA meeting.

It was all so strange. What I experienced for the very first time in that room was harmony. I was pleasantly puzzled by the invisible link of happiness that seemed to connect the AA people there. I was caught up by it, and although I recall little of what was said at that meeting fifteen years ago, I still feel that moment of truth and the peace they gave me. It happened instantly. It caught my attention the way that orange had.

My first sponsors instructed me lovingly on how to maintain that spiritual experience. They told me again and again that faith without works tends to wither and die. They said that I must become active to keep my spirituality as green as grass. They told me to read the Big Book of Alcoholics Anonymous. The first time I read it, I had to move slowly. I couldn't retain more than a few paragraphs at a time. I have read it once a year since then, to stay green.

My first spiritual sponsor said that he could never accept God until he decided what God looked like. He had to know what he was praying at. He finally agreed with the thought that man was made in the image and likeness of God and commenced praying to a God who resembled himself. Our phrase *as we understood Him* allows for this and many other ideas. There are days when I feel that this is too narrow for me and that the primary divine source of spirituality is more like the wide blue sky about me.

I tend to get too busy. The problem is that when I tire, I lose sight of the gentle advice to practice these principles in all my affairs. I must remember that this includes business affairs. I can't meditate and read the Big Book and then go to work and cheat or assassinate the character of an opponent. This is a big red warning light that I am flirting with danger. I am not capable of negating the spirituality of another person and staying cozy myself. What I do to the next soul, I do to myself, and as day follows night, I suffer spiritual or emotional hangovers. When that red light flashes perilously, I check my tongue and shut up and listen for answers. They always come. I always experience calm when I listen.

I can always still the chaos by concentrating on God's unfolding enough time for me to do everything I am meant to accomplish. No more and no less. God's will unfolds smoothly; somehow, my schedule allows for all those things I must do. At my busiest, I can usually find time, for instance, to sit still and read the Big Book. It's easy, really—just turn off the red light, sit down, open the book, and read.

This does not mean that I hypnotize myself into laziness and doing nothing. For me, work is definitely a form of prayer. One friend of mine recently said that his wife called service work in AA a fine example of love and gratitude made visible. He said that he advises people to love God and then do as they please. If I am filled with love and gratitude and do as I please, I know I will do a good job for everyone, including myself.

Bill writes in the Big Book about the spirituality that is essential to recovery from the insane obsession with alcohol. He tells us repeatedly in these pages that we must find God in order to stop drinking and to grow as human beings with a spiritual nature. I was the recipient of this spiritual Fellowship's gifts, even when I did not acknowledge why. Eventually, I had to realize what was keeping me sober. Sooner or later, I had to discover that AA was not just group therapy. All the trick sayings and clever sponsors in the world would not help if I did not recognize the spiritual core of everything. Perhaps it was nice to hear at meetings that I could pray to radiators and bedposts; but to grow in life, I had to give God back his job. He does it better than anyone I know, including me.

This wonderful spiritual path began for me with an orange, and from the hilltop I stand on now in Alcoholics Anonymous, it is possible for me to keep my eyes on all the colors of the rainbow or focus on them one at a time. I am free to decide. I can't think of a color for freedom, but I know what it feels like, and it's glorious. Freedom for me began with that orange and with spirituality.

E.S.
New York, New York

Turning On the Power *August 1977*

God is truth. I can find Him only through honesty, and the honesty must begin with where I am as a human being. Sometimes, it has meant starting with honesty about my dishonesty. With painful slowness, I've come to understand that the Steps will speak to my condition wherever I am in sobriety. Fresh work with all of them created fresh experience. The demands of the program are specific and the rewards equally precise. Do the work, and collect the benefits.

The Big Book charts a vivid, vigorous course for personal change and growth. It's simple, direct, and precise. The program's transforming power is linked with its simplicity. AA's message promises healing and wholeness for any alcoholic who will pay the price. The price is simply to accept the help that will save our lives. In the process, AA gives us everything we really want but could never find anywhere else.

P.M.
Riverside, Illinois

A Gift That Surpasses Understanding

April 1970

When I first came into AA, the good people in the program told me that, if I was alcoholic, I had a very real sickness, that I was sick physically, mentally, and spiritually. I do not remember anyone ever telling me that I was sick religiously or that, because I was a priest, I could not be sick spiritually. And how right they were in refraining from saying that I was sick religiously! In my descent down the skids of booze and pills, I never had any serious difficulty with my religion or my priesthood. It is true that I was less than vigorous in the practice of both, but I sensed that my sickness was on a level much more basic than these.

And yet it was by no means clear to me what it meant for me to be spiritually sick and at the same time not to be religiously sick. Like many others in AA, I was uneasy with the word "spiritual" as it is used in the program. But when it dawned on me that the term "spiritual" is derived from the word "spirit," things started to clear up. I was comfortable with the word "spirit," because I had lived with it all my life. This spirit, this soul, this principle of life, call it what you will, was given to me long before I had any knowledge or practice of a formal religion, long before I had the slightest idea what profession or vocation I might want to pursue.

This is the spirit that was infused into me at the moment of my conception, the thing that would automatically give me membership in the human race. This spirit is the rational part of me that endowed me with dignity, nobility and a separate identity. My spirit or soul gave me the power to think, to make judgments, to wish, to will, to love, to reach out for the infinite. This spirit of mine gave me all these wonderful powers and something more—it gave me my total personality, which in the years to come would be molded and shaped, for better or worse, by environment, education, and circumstances.

The environment, education, and circumstances of the intervening years can be briefly telescoped. I had all the advantages of a good home, a better-than-ordinary education, a life with pleasant surroundings. My priesthood, which I loved (and still love dearly!), should have enhanced all these advantages. But life does not always work according to a definite blueprint.

Somewhere along the line, fears, self-doubt, and a sense of inadequacy began to manifest themselves. Then I discovered those two "friends," alcohol and tranquilizers, which seemed to quiet the fears and self-doubt and restore the sense of adequacy. The classical, insidious pattern started to form and continued growing over a long period: more and deeper fears, loss of interest in work and in life, gradual withdrawal from people and activities, deep-seated loneliness, panic, near despair. In this process of slow death, there was no one to whom I could turn except my two "friends."

The climax was occasioned by an enforced withdrawal from both the alcohol and the pills during hospitalization for major surgery. I went into DTs for a period of eleven days. After emerging from this pleasant interlude, I was immediately shipped to a "special-type" hospital (nut factory). About six weeks after being released from this institution, I went in and out of hallucinations, a delayed withdrawal symptom, and I soon found myself in the alcoholic ward of a state mental hospital. It was here that AA came to me.

Life had taken a tremendous toll on my spirit, my soul. I came into AA broken in spirit, soul-sick. If the ray of hope that I heard had worked for so many thousands in AA was to warm up my heart and light up my life, it would have to penetrate, not into the areas of my religion and my priesthood, but into the much deeper, more basic area where I was really sick—into my human spirit. Had there been in the AA program any suggestion of theology, formal or otherwise, I would have picked up my weak carcass and broken spirit and headed back to the desert outside. Having formally studied theology for four years under good professors, I was, according to ordinary standards, something of a professional theologian. At that time, I needed more theology about as much as I needed a third thumb.

What I did need and need desperately was, not more knowledge about God, but, with God's help, a deep, penetrating knowledge about myself. How could I learn to live, not ecstatically nor even euphorically, but with at least a modicum of peace? How could this spirit of mine find some kind of interest, enthusiasm, self-fulfillment? I was to discover that AA had the answer for this plain, ordinary, human craving of my heart.

I followed the suggestions of the AA people in the hope that I might emerge from the jungle, as they had, and enjoy a kind of resurrection. I went and still go to many meetings; I talked with many people, a newly discovered pleasure; I read a great deal of the available AA literature. These were immensely helpful and will always be necessary for me, to a certain extent. But if these techniques are to have any real meaning, body, and flavor for me, they must rest on something as substantial, vigorous, and life-giving as the Twelve Steps.

When I studied and started to live these Steps, it became clear that, at least for me, the "spiritual awakening" mentioned in the Twelfth Step had to mean "an awakening of the spirit"—i.e., no matter how swift or prolonged the process might be, I had to come awake, alive in my spirit as a human being. From that time on, I have had very few, if any, hang-ups with the word "spiritual" as used in the AA program.

I was greatly impressed with the order, the logic, and the thoroughness of the Steps. They seemed to be an all-or-nothing deal. If I had taken the First Step and settled for that, I would have been guilty of the "selective surrender" spoken of by that pioneer friend of AA, Dr. Harry M. Tiebout. In his wonderfully perceptive brochure "The Act of Surrender in the Therapeutic Process," he makes this comment about one of his patients: "His surrender is not to life as a person, but to alcohol as an alcoholic."

Had I merely surrendered to alcohol as an alcoholic, this would have been good, but not nearly good enough. True, it would have meant that alcohol and pills, two deadly substances for me, would have gone out of my life—no small blessing! But the trouble with me was that everything was going out of my life—friends, activities, my sense of values, the meaning of life, love, laughter, and beauty. My human spirit was indeed desert-dry, and now, with booze and pills gone, it would seem a more arid, barren wasteland. If I was to recover the wholeness, the oneness of my personality, if I truly wanted a rebirth of my human spirit, a taste of the joy of living, then, in accordance with Dr. Tiebout's formula, I had to surrender, not only to alcohol as an alcoholic, but to life as a person.

But Chapter V of the Big Book, "How It Works," assured me that this awakening of the spirit was the natural, orderly result of studying and living the Twelve Steps. "Rarely have we seen a person fail who has thoroughly followed our path," it says. Here was a safe, secure, comfortable framework within which I could move forward gradually and gracefully toward a new way of life, toward something of the peace and serenity that I saw in other AA people. Here was a mode of living fashioned, not from pure theory nor in the halls of academe, but from the rough, tough, raw experience in life of the first hundred members of AA, who had desperately wanted the same kind of awakening of the spirit that I was searching for.

This awakening of the spirit is set down so naturally and confidently in the Twelfth Step that it seems to carry this implicit warning: "If you are not having at least the beginnings of a spiritual awakening, it would be well to look back over the Steps and find out where you are failing." And there

---

What Does Surrender Mean? *April 1963*

Surrender is a disciplinary experience.... In recent articles, I have shown that the ego basically must be continuously forging ahead and that it operates on the unconscious assumption that it, the ego, should not be stopped. It takes for granted its right to go ahead and in this respect has no expectation of being stopped and no capacity to adjust to that eventuality. Stopping says in effect, "No, you can't continue," which is the essence of disciplinary control. The individual who cannot take a stopping is fundamentally an undisciplined person.

The function of surrender in AA is now clear. It produces that stopping by causing the individual to say, "I quit. I give up my headstrong ways. I've learned my lesson." Very often for the first time in that individual's adult career, he has encountered the necessary discipline that halts him in his headlong pace.

Actually, he is lucky to have within him the capacity to surrender. It is that which differentiates him from the wild animals. They may be cowed but are never really tamed. They never develop the love for the power of their master that we humans can for the Master who rules us all. And this happens because we can surrender and truly feel, "Thy will, not mine, be done." When that is true, we have become in fact "obedient servants of God." The spiritual life at that point is a reality. We have become members of the human race.

Harry M. Tiebout, M.D.

are no qualifying words, such as "maybe," "perhaps," or "perchance." On the other hand, there is a kind of built-in guarantee that, if you are living the Steps to the best of your ability, no matter how difficult it may be at times, you will eventually have this awakening of the spirit. What a tremendous source of encouragement!

I feel that anyone who comes into AA wants to "get better," whatever this term may specifically mean to him. It may mean getting out of trouble, placating the family or others, retaining his sanity, etc. The reason for a person's coming into AA is not important; any reason or even excuse will suffice. But it strikes me that the reason for his or her staying in AA is immensely important. Getting out of trouble, placating the family or the superior, etc.—all of these may be good for the time being. But for the sustained, lifetime work of handling this deadly, progressive disease of alcoholism, experience has shown that such motives are inadequate, short-lived, or too fragile; they do not meet the problem head-on, and under pressure they will snap or wither. The family, the boss, the probation officer, collectively or singly, are not the problem.

The problem is me (ungrammatical and humiliating as this may be). I am truly grateful that there was a fellowship, a group of warm, understanding people, to whom I could bring this "problem of me." Nobody lectured me; nobody gave me the moral wheeze; nor, on the other hand, did anybody stand in awe of me. The black suit and the Roman collar were merely the accidental and, therefore, unimportant attire of a sick human being. The important concern of the AAs was to reassure me that they knew what and how I was suffering and that I would "get better," as they had.

I somehow sensed immediately that the God of my understanding was present in AA by a special presence, a presence by which I could ask for and receive graces to handle my alcoholic problem, a presence that gave me these graces with and through AA people. I am grateful that within this apparently formless AA Fellowship, where only "suggestions" are made (famous last words!), there was a structured program of recovery where I would not be on my own. The Twelve Steps were there to guide me. And just over the horizon in the Twelfth Step was the promise, almost the guarantee, of something for which I had been searching over the years—a spiritual awakening!

Whatever this spiritual awakening may mean to anyone else in AA, to me it means that the God of my understanding has given me, by His special presence in AA and through AA people and the Twelve Steps, a gift that surpasses understanding—an awakening of my human spirit!

A Priest

GRANDMA'S TWELFTH STEP WORK
August 1999

In 1985 I was introduced into the AA Fellowship. I don't remember much about that first meeting but I knew that I belonged—I just wasn't ready yet. During the next ten years, I relapsed many times and was in and out of AA.

During that time, the "yets" came true. I lost a loving wife of sixteen years, a good job, and my home, and I faced a lengthy prison sentence. Worst of all, my grandma, whom l loved with all my heart, was in the hospital, expected to die.

In mid-August 1995, I was staying at the hospital at night with my grandma (my brother stayed with her during the day—we didn't want her to be alone). One night at about 2:00 A.M., my grandma woke up and said to me, "Son, there's something I want you to do for yourself. You have been very unhappy for a long time. Your drinking is killing you. Only you can stop. You need to get your life straightened out. Get married again and enjoy your life." She told me that whether she was here or in heaven, she'd be watching to see if I was okay. After that she went back to sleep. It was the hardest thing in my life to hear how I was hurting her. I felt like someone just reached into my chest and pulled my heart out. Here she was on her death bed, worrying about me.

I went outside to cry. There wasn't anyone around. I sat down at a table and put my head down and cried like a baby. For the first time in my life I saw myself for what I really was. It wasn't a pretty picture.

Then I felt a hand on my shoulder. I looked up to see a man standing there. He asked me if I was okay. I said, "I just have a lot of problems and my grandma is very sick." This guy then said the Serenity Prayer. I said, "How did you know I'm an alcoholic?" He said, "I didn't know. I just asked God what to say and he told me." I found out later he was in AA.

The next day I shared what had happened with my sponsor. He said that I'd had a "spiritual experience." I knew that he was right because things felt different. I knew everything would work out. By the end of August I knew I had truly surrendered. I was tired of hurting.

About a week later my grandma, still very sick, came home. On September 12, 1995, I was sentenced to five years and two months in prison. I went straight to treatment and started working a program of recovery from behind the walls. I wrote my grandma every week. I told her that I was doing very well. My mother came to see me and told me my grandma was doing well. She was back to normal and she wasn't going anywhere until she knew that I was okay.

I was allowed two phone calls a month. At first I didn't talk to Grandma because I was afraid she'd get too upset. After six months, I called home and Grandma answered the phone. We talked and laughed

Filet of Soul   *August 1987*

I finally decided my soul was where that empty space was deep within me, that hollow spot that was always craving something to fill it. But nothing could satisfy it. It was a lingering hunger, but for what I never knew. So I decided that if I did indeed have a soul it had a huge hole in it. A hole as big as a hula hoop, I decided. More hole than soul. It was a wounded soul aching to be healed.

Love is what the soul thrives on and I began to find it in Alcoholics Anonymous. I'm still finding more and more of it and I try to put it to work in my everyday life. And the more of it I use, the more of it there is.

I don't expect the hole in my soul to ever be filled completely and permanently, because I can't achieve that kind of perfection. But love as I am learning it and witnessing it in Alcoholics Anonymous seems to be the only thing that is coming close to making my soul whole.

E.K.
La Canada, California

like old times. I made sure she knew I was okay. At the end of my ten minute call, I told her I loved her and not to worry, that I was doing very well. Three days later she passed away.

I'm so grateful that I was able to put her mind at ease. She knew I was okay and I know she is watching over me. I thank God for his hand in this and a special thanks to Grandma. I have been sober for forty months now and will be going home soon.

Billy Ray M.
Hope Mills, North Carolina

What We Cannot Do for Ourselves

August 1999

Gratitude is one of the first gifts I received from Alcoholics Anonymous, since just the simple act of not putting alcohol in my system gave me almost immediate results. When I was a month sober, I looked in the mirror and didn't recognize the reflection: I had a sparkle in my eye that had never been there before. I was also able to pay a few more bills because all my money wasn't going into the bottle.

As time passed my gratitude list grew. At six months I noticed I had lost thirty pounds. At about a year my shaking began to subside. Within a couple of years I began to experience a relationship between myself and a Higher Power of my understanding.

I'd been sober a little over nine years when my sister called to tell me that my seventeen-year-old nephew, Matthew, who had muscular dystrophy, was not expected to live much longer. She told me he had questions about God. She said he was afraid because he hadn't gone to church much in his short life and wondered what would happen to him when he died. She was having a lot of trouble answering him because she had a lot of anger toward God for taking her child. She asked me to write to him and share my thoughts and beliefs about God.

Even though I felt inadequate, I told her I would write him. When I was hanging up, I thought, "Are you crazy? You're a drunk. You spent your whole life thinking only about yourself and you don't even go to church.

What can you say to help this boy?" I called my sponsor, I went to a lot of meetings, I read my Big Book, and I prayed almost constantly for a couple of weeks—then I wrote to Matthew.

I told him about my problems with God and how I had come to realize that God had been with me through all those years of drinking and hurting people. I told him that God had loved me and brought me to AA, despite the fact that I'd done nothing to deserve it. I don't remember everything I wrote that day, but Matthew got the letter a couple of days before he died and my sister said it helped him. I had almost been too late. If I'd waited any longer, he would have died with those questions still in his heart.

The gratitude from that is still with me today. I am grateful that I was able to make amends to my sister for not being there for her all those years. I am especially grateful that AA members shared their experience, strength, and hope with me so I could learn to share it with someone else.

I spent years running away from the topic of God. When I saw the word *God* in the Twelve Steps on the wall of my first meeting, I almost turned around and walked out the door. It was only because of God's grace that I didn't. I am grateful that my desperation made me willing enough to stick around long enough to see that God will always do for us what we cannot do for ourselves.

Lisa B.
Central City, Arkansas

The Result Was Nil

February 1998

The Big Book spells out the terms for a successful day-by-day recovery from the disease of alcoholism. But I believed I was unique. When I found AA, I bounced between the Fellowship and the bars for the first six months. I read the Big Book through the haze of alcohol. I attended meetings drunk, or would go to a meeting sober and then drive straight to a bar when the meeting was over.

As a last resort I went into a treatment center. There, I acquired a sponsor and a counselor. I attended five to seven meetings a week and saw my counselor twice a week, compliments of the court system (I'd gotten a DWI). I called my sponsor every day. I worked the Steps. I wrote in my journal every night. I read the Big Book. I got into service with hospitals and institutions. I desperately wanted to work the AA program perfectly. I finally stayed sober long enough to put together eighteen months of continuous sobriety.

I sort of left out the "Higher Power" part of the program because I grew up fearing a punishing, vengeful God. I was trying to stay sober by my own strength, without God's help. But my program stagnated. I could not grow. My problems didn't go away; in fact, some of them got worse.

So I threw myself a pity party and went out and got drunk. The worst part was that I gave up eighteen months of sobriety and I didn't even enjoy myself. While I was desperately trying to party, phrases from AA kept running through my head, which made me very aware that I'd messed up the best thing I'd ever done for myself. I tucked my tail between my legs and went crawling back to AA, where I fessed up and started over.

I'm celebrating my fifth AA birthday this week. I went to my women's meeting tonight and ended up reading a portion of Chapter Five, "How It Works," during the opening format. All of a sudden a phrase leapt right out of those familiar words and danced before my eyes. I realized that my whole attitude about working this wonderful program had changed. The phrase was: "Some of us have tried to hold onto our old ideas and the result was nil until we let go absolutely." My relapse came about because I was holding onto my old ideas about God and refusing to let go absolutely.

A few days after my relapse I was feeling soul-sick and willing (finally) to go to any length to stay sober. A friend suggested that I begin creating a new concept of a Higher Power by looking at the beautiful things of nature. I went outside and sat looking at the stars. I was heartsick and miserable and angry with myself and God. As the pain welled up in my heart, I shouted out at God, "Okay, I surrender!"

Oh, what peace settled over me. I felt like a ton of weight had been taken off my shoulders. At that point I began a relationship with my Higher Power whom I choose to call God.

Over the last five years I've still had problems, including sickness, surgery, and watching two close friends die. I'm not rich and famous, and I doubt I'll ever be able to work a "perfect" program. But I've enjoyed many days of serenity, even in the face of crisis, because I'm now able to turn things over to a loving, wonderful God. He takes good care of me. He loves me and has my best interest at heart. He has given me some incredible learning experiences through my times of pain or of just being down.

I love this program. It has given a better me in exchange for the old drunk me. I have friends whom I care deeply about, including a loving supportive women's group. I actually have feelings and I'm able to identify them and allow myself to feel them. With God's help I no longer stuff those feelings down where they would keep me very sick.

I'm happy and content a good part of the time. I owe my life to AA, God, and the people of AA. I wish you all a long and joyous recovery.

Cynthia Y.
Nampa, Idaho

That God Could and Would ...
April 1973

At my AA meeting, I have been waiting for you. You see, I am an alcoholic. By the grace of God, one day I sought help. Of course, I didn't really want to stop drinking, for alcohol was not my problem. You were part of my problem. You created pressures that caused me to drink too much; my family caused pressures; my profession, my childhood, my parents, and life in general caused pressures. I needed a way to reduce these pressures. But my efforts to flee these pressures eventually sent me to AA. You and everybody else seemed to think that alcohol was my problem. If I made a move that appeared to answer you, perhaps you and the others would get off my back.

A strange development took place after I had listened to the gentle souls around the tables: I became aware that I was an alcoholic and, indeed, that alcohol was compounding the unmanageability of my life, actually causing the worst of pressures.

As time progressed, all sorts of wonders came about, not the least of which was my enjoyment of being dry. Then I began to live as I had never imagined possible. My dryness became soberness and finally sobriety. As the multitude of benefits piled one on another, I increased the vigor of my pursuit of the AA program, and things got even better.

The weeks passed into measurable years. Awareness of the depth of AA became greater. With this discovery my life became a daily proof of one of the tenets of the AA program: "that God could and would if He were sought." In my earlier AA days, I had tried to convince you that you, too, needed AA.

Now I stopped badgering you. I shifted my emphasis (though imperfectly) from you and your alcoholic problems to me and my defects. You didn't understand the change. Often, you will recall, you thought I didn't give a damn, because I did nothing to prevent you from going on a bender. Nor did I reprove you or chastise you or scold you. How could you know that the change was really a part of my growth, that I had not lost interest in you and your problems? I hardly knew what the hell was going on myself.

As time passed, I learned that prayers—others' and my own—were working on me and bringing about growth. So I increased my prayer life. Suddenly, I was going to more and more AA meetings, making coffee, picking up ashtrays, welcoming people, giving talks. In essence, I began to live AA.

How often you remarked, "I don't understand the change in you." How often I wished I could spare you the misery and horror of those final years. But I prayed, and in meditation I realized I couldn't spare you anything. Only God could. For the desire had to be within you. Being human, I could not change conditions, except within myself. In trying to spare you, I was hanging on to "old ideas." As the Fifth Chapter of the Big Book says, "the result was nil." I was wrong in my approach. I was going to do something about your alcoholism. That was alcoholic thinking, and obviously the result had to be nil. So I released you to God, and that was good for you and for me.

Now here you are. It wasn't I who helped you. It was God. Rather, you have helped me to grow. Now you want what we have. As long as you have the desire, you know that AA will work, for here I am, and here are the hundreds of thousands who were just as hopeless as I was, and look at what we have achieved.

So tonight I welcome you. Before long, you'll find yourself wondering what you can do to spare someone else the horrors of the final years. The simple answer is: Just stick around, and your light will eventually shine into the dark corners of some alcoholic's mind, and he or she will be spared exactly the proper amount of the final years—according to God's will. Stick around and find out about the dark corners of your mind, and you'll understand how much you really have been spared, just as I have.

D.W.R.
Michigan

AA AND THE RELIGION TURNOFF

September 1977

A friend of mine, a fellow alcoholic, died last month. He needn't have. He could have joined AA. The reason he didn't is the reason I nearly didn't, many years ago, and his death recalls the feeling I had then toward the program.

My friend, Tom, and I worked for the same newspaper. In our youth, we contributed heavily to the fortune of a greasy tavern owner in an alley behind the pressroom. Tom and I were lean and cocky in those years. The thought of a drinking problem for either of us would have been ridiculous. Tom went on to become a well-known correspondent and editor. After we left the paper, we kept in touch, and whenever our paths crossed, the encounter would occasion a glorious and usually prolonged drunk.

Eventually, though, we knew we had a problem. Not knowing how to "frame" it, see it in its true perspective, we called it booze, and let it go at that. We thought it went with the territory. Tom had remarried several times, his wives leaving him because of his drinking. I'd been in and out of several hospitals. Tom and I would lament the passing of the good old days and mark our observance by getting drunk.

Once, over a couple of prairie oysters to aid us through a horrendous hangover, I remember suggesting, half seriously, that we try AA.

"Not those Holy Rollers," he replied.

Several of our acquaintances had joined the program by then, but we saw little of them. On getting sober, they had a habit of avoiding the watering holes they'd helped make famous. Tom would bomb in from some far-flung war and call my place, and we'd hold a wake for those poor lost souls.

"Whatever happened to Ted?"

"Ah, the silly man got religion and joined AA."

"Is that a fact? The saints preserve us. Timothy, give us two more of the same. Drink up, me boyo. Our work's cut out for us."

As I recall, drinking was becoming work. An uphill fight all the way. All at once, it seemed, we had grown too old for chasing down Third Avenue in pursuit of rheumatic ghosts and the faltering legends of youth. Marathon drinking, to catch the blood-red sun over the East River, was no longer the lyrical experience it had been. Nor even running plays with a professional quarterback, or composing dirty limericks with a famous poet among the pillars of the El, some silver dawn.

But Tom and I had a grudging—perhaps the word is sneaking—respect for AA. Ironically, it was through Tom that I'd first become aware of the Fellowship. He'd written an article on alcoholism, mentioning the successful "cure" found by so many in AA.

Tom's and my attitude at that point could be summed up by saying we thought the program was okay for the people in it, but for ourselves we couldn't buy the God bit. The program, in our view, smacked of Christian fundamentalism, even evangelism. Then, too, while we were admitted drunks—defiantly so—we didn't admit to having the problem of definitive "alcoholics," as AA members labeled themselves.

For my last birthday, my wife gave me the latest—the fourth—edition of the Columbia Encyclopedia, hailed as the best one-volume encyclopedia in the language. I looked up AA, and there it was—Tom's mistake, repeated for the nth time. The program was described as a means for "curing" alcoholism. My old copy, the second edition, doesn't even have an entry for AA, and I'm not sure which is worse—misinformation or no information.

It seems to me that we editorial types share with other professionals what is so frequently a fatal misconception about the program. A misconception going beyond the careless reporting and editing that allow "cure" instead of "recovery." It goes to the heart of the matter, explaining why so many of us, like my late friend Tom, fail to make it into AA.

Our liverish, bloated egos feel insulted by what we don't even intellectually understand. We think the program is reserved for the poor, the ignorant, the uninformed. (G.K. Chesterton was fond of saying that intellectuals were seldom intelligent.) We think—even by the time we're driven to the desperate realization that something is the matter, something is killing us—that AA may be okay for the next guy, but we're too sophisticated for anything like that to work for us. We need something more complicated, more subtle, more suited to our peculiar genius, the exquisite refinements

A Gift of Prayer *November 1967*

I have come to know and to cherish many of the ways of my ancestors. They, too, lived without "firewater." They, also, guided by their "Great Spirit of the universe," lived by a set of principles similar to our Twelve Steps.

One of the prayers of a great chief of my people has been handed down through generations. It has been a source of guidance and inspiration to me and I would like to share it with my AA brothers and sisters:

O! Great Spirit! Whose voice I hear in the winds, and whose breath gives life to all the world, hear me! I come before you, one of your many children. I am small and weak; I need your strength and wisdom!

Let me walk in beauty and make my eyes ever behold the red and purple sunset. Make my hands respect the things you have made; my ears sharp to hear your voice. Make me wise so that I may know the things you have taught my people—the lesson you have hidden in leaf and rock.

I seek strength not to be superior to my brothers, but to be able to fight my greatest enemy—myself. Make me ever ready to come to you with clean hands and straight eyes, so that when my life fades, as a fading sunset, my Spirit may come to you without shame.

From an AA of North American Indian heritage

of our pain. Something, let us say, that sounds more medically or scientifically impressive.

And so, like Tom, we elect to die.

My recovery began with a fantastic awakening. I realized that it is possible to believe in a Higher Power, in the efficacy of prayer and meditation, in making a conscious contact with a Higher Power as those concepts, privately understood—or not understood—are suggested in AA, without the loss of one iota of my precious identity.

Instead of loss, the dread void of what to do in place of drinking, there is gain. A spiritual redeepening of the self, through the affirmation of AA principles that stem, not merely from Christianity, but from all the great faiths and philosophies. A sense of humility, the reapportioning of what is really important for the remainder of my life. Best of all, a new understanding of simplicity, of keeping things simple, of knowing truth, the truth that works for me. It could never have been found through the complicated search that always ended in despair when I drank.

I'd been looking for a reality that doesn't exist outside today!

Tom never knew this. He never really knew what time it was. Never, that is, knew that the time is always forever Now.

I attended his funeral and looked on the stranger in the casket. Yet not entirely a stranger. Assuredly, it was not the Tom of old, with whom I'd run and drunk and sung. It could have been, incredibly, myself lying there, except for a grace and power beyond my telling here. He died for both of us (and all those that read this now).

As I left the funeral home on Madison Avenue, I was joined by another battered survivor, whom I hadn't seen in years. There was little left to see. He looked almost as bad as the one we'd come to mourn. We chatted on the corner. His watery eyes searched out a bar half a block up.

"C'mon, let's hoist a few."

I hesitated, not because I was tempted but because, after all this time in the program, that's still my reaction to friends and acquaintances who might also have a problem—and don't know how I've solved mine. One day at a time.

"I don't drink any more, Charlie. I'm in AA."

I saw the familiar start, the gleam of fright that crossed his face. We talked for a minute or two longer, then said goodbye. Charlie wanted to be rid of me, and how could I blame him, knowing so well what he was feeling? He didn't look back. Braving crowds and traffic with unswerving accuracy (he could have been crossing a minefield and it wouldn't have mattered), he disappeared under the neon sign of El Dorado, dreams, music, and that old black magic called oblivion. He left his life waiting in the street outside, like a dog tied to a lamppost.

I said a prayer for Charlie—for all of us, for Tom lately departed, for the living trapped in their denial and loneliness, in their embittered, cynical selves. I prayed that Charlie might get it. And suddenly the city blazed with a great beauty that throbbed and thrilled through me—that thing, that high I'd sought and never found in the bottom of a bottle. I felt the fierce, sweet joy of gratitude, standing there in the sunlit afternoon.

Maybe, I thought, maybe he'll come out before it's too late. God's will, chance, and change bear wondrous fruit. Just maybe what I said to him, the seed, will take hold and sprout. I recalled Tom's old tale of a miracle "cure" for what had ailed us both.

Now he was free of it. And dead.

I still had it, but was alive and well.

You never know.

J.W.
New York, New York

Conscious Contact *April 1990*

The God I know today is not an eminence ... not an Everest I must scale, but an Immanence, as close as the next breath or heartbeat. It is a presence in which I find myself, just as I am.

Jim N.
West Springfield, Massachusetts

Cold Sober

February 1991

For fifteen years, almost every time I work or think about our Second Step, considering the Power greater than ourselves, I am reminded of a large refrigerator in a ward at a Minnesota state hospital. It's not really idol worship, but it is a way for me to gratefully recall who I am and how amazing it is that I'm sober today by the grace of God. The Second Step is for me the Step of expecting good things and expecting them not from me but from a Power greater than myself.

I was sober just a couple of weeks in a sanitarium for alcoholic priests. After fighting tooth and nail against going into treatment, my head began to clear and I started to listen. The proposed stay in the sanitarium was three months, and like everything else in life, I thought I could speed things up if I went to as many meetings as they would allow. I signed up to be taken out to a meeting at the nearby state hospital. I was picked up by a man whom I've never seen before or since, but he reminded me of the traveling salesman in "The Music Man" or maybe a character out of *Main Street* by Sinclair Lewis.

He was giving the talk at the hospital meeting and was telling everyone about the Power greater than ourselves. He told everyone that the Power could be anything, even this refrigerator he was standing next to. And then he said: "Isn't that right, Father?"

It was many years ago, but I can still feel the anger rip through my insides. Here I was sitting quietly; nobody knew I was a priest. Here comes this traveling salesman pointing me out, me with my advanced theological degrees, asking me to say that a refrigerator could be used as a Power greater than myself to restore me to sanity. Oh, how mad I was as I gamely smiled at this man I now considered a complete idiot. But something all of a sudden hit me.

I looked at this smiling speaker. He had the keys to his own car. He wasn't three hundred miles from where he lived. No one had to sign him out of an institution to travel a few miles to another institution. I'd better listen, something inside me said. All my great knowledge about God, my retreats, years of prayer, my consultations with psychiatric experts and wonderful spiritual directors—none of it had gotten me sober and kept me sober. I better listen to this guy and to these other people.

And so I try to, one day at a time. I know now that once I accepted that First Step, there was hope in the Second Step. And the Power was not me nor mine.

I have confidence now that it is the God who loves me and all of us.

But every once in a while when I get messed up and feel these surges of anger and superiority, I think of a big refrigerator in Rochester, Minnesota, and say: St. Kenmore, or St. Frigidaire, or whatever you were, pray for me ... help me to listen and do what these people are telling me to do. Amen.

Dan M.
Chicago, Illinois

GATEWAY TO SANITY
February 1989

The words of the Second Step struck me with a kind of elemental force— a force I recognized as truth the first time I read them in southern Arizona after my husband had called AA for help. My first reaction was anger toward him for letting "other people," as I put it, share in the secrets of our married life. It was 1966—we knew nothing about AA—and I didn't think it was anyone's business if I drank a little or a lot. And anyway, I had pressure in my marriage and job which made me special, and allowed the letting-off of a little steam each night! My rationalizing, of course, was the mirror image of Step Two: I believed that through the force of my own will and intelligence, I could shape the world into my personal concept of sanity!

But in my heart of hearts, I knew that something was terribly wrong, that my personal life and my marriage were headed for some kind of disaster. My husband's academic career was going nowhere, and our marriage, instead of growing in strength as the years went by, was degenerating into a sodden and nonproductive drinking partnership.

Each morning, we would drag ourselves out of bed, eat something if we could or—if the hangover was too intense—sip beer until it stayed down and the morning "glow" from alcohol temporarily replaced the horror of the early morning shakes. Then we were off to work, trying to nurse ourselves through the day, living first for lunch, always laced with a few drinks, and then for dinner, inevitably preceded by a fifth of Scotch. This was quietly consumed in our little home out on the Arizona desert, blinds and drapes drawn, air conditioner efficiently whirring. Often, even before dinner came around, unconsciousness would overtake us, and we would awaken at dawn, facing the whole dreadful cycle all over again.

But my husband did call AA, and that evening a wonderful man who was to become our lifelong sponsor walked into our lives, smiling outrageously and carrying an armload of AA literature. His obvious delight and happiness with life was at such variance with the absolutely horrendous story he told us of his many years of disastrous drinking that we listened to him in wonder and astonishment. Could this serene man be saying something that had to do with our situation? He left after an hour—we had hidden our drinks in the closet when he came—and we made strong new scotches and sat down to read the literature he had left.

And then it happened—that sense that the Big Book, the "Twelve and Twelve," and the pamphlets had been designed and written with me in mind. We pored over each sentence, as we poured more and more drinks, and we read all the literature that had been left, exclaiming to each other, "Hey, listen to this!" or "My God, doesn't this sound like us!" or "This is exactly the way I feel!" We were utterly charmed, that special AA lightning had struck, and we passed out in the middle of the night, still talking about the magic of the evening—our sponsor-to-be and the literature—not realizing then that we had had, a day at a time, our last drink.

In the morning, we looked at each other in the knowledge that something special and different had entered our lives. Our sponsor was coming in the evening to take us to our first meeting, and we spent most of the day continuing to go over the literature, especially the Steps and Traditions. The First Step immediately made great sense to me because it suggested that I merely admit that I was powerless over alcohol and that my life was unmanageable. But the Second Step posed an urgent problem, I felt, because it suggested I must believe in some strange, far-off power greater than me who could restore my sanity! What is this? Am I insane, as suggested? Why, I had a quite successful career which flowed from my university achievements. I had taken pride in my intellectual attainments, my "superior" brain, the quality of my reasonable and tolerant nature. Now am I to think of myself as insane? And what about this concept of a power greater than me? Formal religion and I had parted company some years before, and I wondered what, if anything, I had to believe if I joined AA.

I went over the first two Steps again. I had certainly come to the realization, subconsciously if not consciously, that I was powerless over alcohol, and when I saw the words in clear black print, I knew that our best attempts to properly manage our lives had come to nothing—that we were in the grip of dark forces over which we seemed to have no control whatsoever. But that Second Step which alluded to the insanity of our present lives and the need of some greater power necessitated for me a leap into what seemed terribly risky darkness.

Yet that early faith in AA was already present. I had the feeling deep down that the program *must* be correct, and that I had little choice but to throw myself without reservation into the full arena of the Steps. I had tried diligently with my intellect to understand myself and my drinking, and to control and properly manage my life. All my efforts had not only failed, but failed abjectly and totally. So I listened to that inner voice saying, "Accept, try, have hope! Just perhaps, something might work here!" And my life of day-to-day sobriety began, a life of satisfaction and joy beyond my wildest, most alcoholic dreams.

When I discovered through reading AA history and listening to old-timers about how the Second Step came to be, tears came to my eyes—and again I had that strange, almost mystical feeling that AA's principles had been hammered out with me in mind! Bill W. tells us that since Ebby's notable visit to him in the fall of 1934, the program was basically word-of-mouth, with most of the basic program ideas coming from the Oxford Group, William James, and Dr. Silkworth. There were six major ideas, ranging from acceptance and powerlessness to the need for a full inventory. The sixth concept seems closest to our present Second Step. It read, as Bill remembers, "We prayed to whatever God we thought there was to practice these precepts." Bill realized, as he put it, that these " ... six chunks of truth should be broken up into smaller pieces." So the first version of the Twelve Steps was written, the number twelve coming up quite accidentally. The revised Second Step read, "Came to believe that God could restore us to sanity," and immediately controversy began. Bill says there were conservative, liberal, and radical viewpoints. Some felt the Christian message should dominate, while others would have nothing to do with doctrinal issues. They emphasized that the Fellowship was spiritual, not religious. Many who read the Steps wanted the word "God" taken entirely out, while others wanted a clear religious statement throughout.

The final version of the Steps reflects the force and value of these heated early discussions, and attempts to strike a balance, making AA open to all, regardless of personal beliefs, or no beliefs at all. And the particular decision regarding the vital Second Step seems particularly providential. Bill doesn't remember who first suggested the actual compromise words, but he says, "In Step Two we decided to describe God as a 'Power greater than ourselves,'" and "we inserted the words 'God *as we understood Him*'" in Step Three and Eleven, deleted the expression "on our knees" from Step Seven, and added, as a lead-in sentence, "Here are the steps we took which are suggested as a program of recovery."

I still feel a bit of a shiver when I read this history, because I wonder if I could have accepted a Step like the Oxford Group sixth concept or the Second Step as it appeared in the first version of the Twelve Steps. No, I doubt it. I needed exactly the freedom and openness and tolerance so beautifully expressed in the Steps as they were finally decided upon. In fact, Bill said—in referring to the heated discussions and final compromise language—that "such were the final concessions of those of little or no faith; this was the great contribution of our atheists and agnostics. They had widened our gateway so that all who suffer might pass through, regardless of their belief or *lack of belief.*"

It is paradoxically the strength of surrender and the acceptance of help from a "Power greater than ourselves" which set me free from those tight bonds of alcoholic thinking and drinking. The Second Step in its careful language, which denies no one, along with the other Steps, similarly structured, provides an infinitely wide acceptance pathway. In reflecting on the final formulation of the Second Step, and the other eleven, Bill says, "God was certainly there in our Steps, but He was now expressed in terms that anybody—anybody at all—could accept and try. Countless AAs have since testified that without this great evidence of liberality they never could have set foot on any path of spiritual progress or even approached us in the first place. It was another one of those providential ten-strikes."

Yes, some time spent reflecting on how the Second Step became so central in our program teaches me again how fortunate I am. We came to believe—perhaps not instantly but in good time—that a power greater than ourselves—however we as free individuals wish to define or perceive this power—could "restore us to sanity." For me, this was the full education of my AA program, the gradual realization of who I was, where I should be headed, and the source of the joy and serenity in my life.

Jan P.
Spokane, Washington

Keeping It Simple   *March 1979*

I am happy to say that after two years of sobriety, I am no longer tortured by the wheels spinning in my brain. One day at a time, AA has relieved me from that terrible bondage of self-analysis. Introspection is no longer an obsession, and God has replaced psychology as my Higher Power. The Twelve Steps have helped me learn how to keep my life, both personal and professional, simple. AA has taught me to "utilize, not analyze," to live life instead of thinking about it and to put faith in my Higher Power, not in my own mind.

AA and my Higher Power have transformed me from a complex person who lived out of her head to a simple person who is trying to live out of her heart. Thanks to this program, I am no longer a prisoner locked within the walls of my mind. Now that I am no longer morbidly preoccupied with self, I can reach out to others and contribute to life. For this miracle, I am humbly grateful.

C.R.
Greenbelt, Maryland

SOBER FOR THIRTY YEARS
May 1968

As noted in my story, "The Vicious Cycle," in the Big Book, I came into the Fellowship in New York in January 1938. At that time AA was just leaving the Oxford Group. There was one closed discussion meeting a week, at Bill's home in Brooklyn—attendance six or eight men, with only three members who had been sober more than one year: Bill, Hank, and Fritz. This is about all that had been accomplished in the four years with the New York Oxford Group.

During those early meetings at Bill's, they were flying blind, with no creed or procedure to guide them, though they did use quite a few of the Oxford sayings and the Oxford Absolutes. Since both Bill and Dr. Bob had had almost-overnight religious experiences, it was taken for granted that all who followed their way would have the same sort of experience. So the early meetings were quite religious, in both New York and Akron. There was always a Bible on hand, and the concept of God was all biblical.

Into this fairly peaceful picture came I, their first self-proclaimed atheist, completely against all religions and conventions. I was the captain of my own ship. (The only trouble was, my ship was completely disabled and rudderless.) So naturally I started fighting nearly all the things Bill and the others stood for, especially religion, the "God bit." But I did want to stay sober, and I did love the understanding Fellowship. So I became quite a problem to that early group, with my constant haranguing against all the spiritual angles.

All of a sudden, the group became really worried. Here I had stayed sober five whole months while fighting everything the others stood for. I was now number four in "seniority." I found out later they had a prayer meeting on "what to do with Jim." The consensus seemed to have been that they hoped I would either leave town or get drunk.

That prayer must have been right on target, for I was suddenly taken drunk on a sales trip. This became the shock and the bottom I needed. At this time I was selling auto polish to jobbers for a company that Bill and Hank were sponsoring, and I was doing pretty well, too. But despite this, I was tired and completely isolated there in Boston. My fellow alcoholics really put the pressure on as I sobered up after four days of no relief, and for the first time I admitted I couldn't stay sober alone. My closed mind opened a bit. Those folks back in New York, the folks who believed, had stayed sober. And I hadn't. Since this episode I don't think I have ever argued with anyone else's beliefs. Who am I to say?

I finally crawled back to New York and was soon back in the fold. About this time, Bill and Hank were just beginning to write the AA Big Book. I do feel sure my experience was not in vain, for "God" was broadened to cover all types and creeds: "God as we understood Him."

I feel my spiritual growth over these past thirty years has been very gradual and steady. I have no desire to "graduate" from AA. I try to keep my memories green by staying active in AA—a couple of meetings weekly.

For the new agnostic or atheist just coming in, I will try to give very briefly my milestones in recovery:

1. The first power I found greater than myself was John Barleycorn.

2. The AA Fellowship became my higher power for the first two years.

3. Gradually, I came to believe that God and Good were synonymous and were to be found in all of us.

4. And I found that by meditating and trying to tune in on my better self for guidance and answers, I became more comfortable and steady.

J.B.
San Diego, California

A God Personal to Me
April 1982

When I came into AA, I had genuinely surrendered. By age twenty-six, my drinking had taken me to the point of a lost career, broken relations with my parents, DTs, and no hope of ever having anything decent and clean in my life. I had no doubt that I was an alcoholic. At my first AA meeting, I found a bunch of people who were not only decent and clean, but sober. They were willing to share their sobriety with me.

Obviously, my drinking had made my life unmanageable. The Fellowship had more power than I had. Its members were staying sober, where I couldn't. They became my higher power. I came to believe that their wisdom could restore me to the sanity of not drinking. I decided to turn my drinking will over to them and let them teach me about not drinking. That was how I took the first three Steps.

At the end of six months, I surveyed the situation. I had been sober longer than I had been at any period in the past ten years! AA was working for me. At nine months, I took an inventory and shared it with a minister. Using a minister was a token gesture to those other people's Higher Power, whom I did not—would not—believe in.

By my first anniversary, I had completed the first nine Steps. With my drinking neatly tucked in the hands of my higher power, which was still the Fellowship and the meetings, I was free. I had started on the quest for all the things my upbringing and my drinking had so unfairly cheated me out of. By my second anniversary, I had a marriage, a stepdaughter, a career in my own company, and cars, and I was in the process of buying a house. I could settle back!

I had fallen into a deadly trap I've seen many fall into since: I had no need for a Higher Power personal to me; the Fellowship was my god and my guide.

Today, I can thank God for the next two hellish years. Without drinking or using drugs, I watched the whole world I had built fall down around me. Divorce, separation from a child I had grown to love, and economic ruin were all made worse by the fact that I was sober and supposedly working the program. On the rare occasions when the shame of failure did not prevent me from sharing, even my AA friends, with all their love, could not keep me from sinking deeper into the pit of despair.

I had cleverly avoided searching for a God personal to me. But as thoughts of suicide crossed my mind, I reconsidered. When my higher power was the Fellowship, I sought through conversation to improve my relationships with these loving people. Our Eleventh Step says "prayer and meditation," not conversation. I tried to improve my "conscious contact," but since I had never had one in the first place, I was led back to Step One.

This time, however, my suicidal depression had gotten me to the point of being as desperate as a man drowning. I became open-minded. As I walked through the Steps with the help of my sponsor, I came to know myself, the futility of life run on my terms, and my need for more than the Fellowship. When I became willing to believe, even as those other people believed, God's power flooded into my life. He became mine.

Today, God is my Higher Power. By His grace, I have not had a drink since December 5, 1971. The "Twelve and Twelve" says, "Nothing short of continuous action upon these [Steps] as a way of life can bring the much-desired result." Now that I trust God, I can continue without fear. My life is worth living. I believe the desired result is "to fit ourselves to be of maximum service to God and the people about us."

When someone asks about problems in sobriety, I say, "Yes, we have them." But in our AA Fellowship, we have a program of living called the Twelve Steps. When we persist in them, we will "presently love God and call Him by name." He will give us the power to get through problems and experience the joy of living a sober life.

M.S.
Baltimore, Maryland

An Agnostic's Spiritual Awakening
October 1990

I was more defiant than ever when I re-entered AA in August 1987, having come in and gone back out twice before. I was convinced that the Twelve Steps—except the first one—weren't for me. I was too intellectual, too steadfast in my agnosticism, for any spiritual experiences. I still equated "spiritual awakening" with "getting religion," and I firmly believed I would prefer dying in the gutter to getting religion.

My two previous encounters with AA—the first in 1976, the second in 1983—had given me about six weeks' exposure to the program. I had heard all you had to say, I thought, about spirituality and the Higher Power. I had read Chapter Four and Appendix II. I was not impressed. Herbert Spencer's observation about contempt prior to investigation was, I agreed, quite correct. But I had investigated. I had even practiced a few different religions at one time or another before deciding that none of it was for me. Still, I maintained an intellectual interest in the subject. I'd become something of an armchair scientist, and humanity's evolution was among my special interests. Obviously, religious beliefs and their development over the ages were a major part of humanity's own story.

Still, like many intellectuals, I felt it was a matter of time before we all outgrew such ideas, if only our high-tech civilization survived. No matter how the theologians dressed it up in modern language, to me religion remained superstition.

What Bill W. had to say in "We Agnostics" was nothing new to me. I had encountered his arguments, and others far more sophisticated, attempting to defend the logic of believing in a Higher Power. I had weighed them all, and found them wanting.

I went back out those first two times because I hadn't hurt badly enough. Still, I was luckier than most. Even my third bottom was a high one. My job was still secure. I had never even been stopped, let alone ticketed, while driving drunk. My physical health was fine. But I was in enough emotional pain to make me desperate, and I had become convinced, finally and totally, that if I kept drinking it would get worse.

Although I was more convinced than ever that I could never take the Second Step, or any beyond it, I came back to the meetings, knowing that if I got nothing else from the Fellowship, you could help me stay away from that first drink. I thought that would be enough, that if I could just stay sober, I could manage my own life.

It took about a month of drying out for me to realize I hadn't finished taking the First Step; to realize that, even if I wasn't drinking, my life still would be unmanageable until I overcame my terminal uniqueness and found a way to make the program work for me. And, at that point, the point at which I began to acquire a little willingness, a way was revealed to me—a way in which I could believe in a power greater than myself without compromising any of the fundamental principles out of which my agnosticism had grown.

Even now, more than two years of happy sobriety later, I cannot begin to explain in a Grapevine-sized article anything about my Higher Power, or how it works in my life. It's not the God of the churches or the theologians. I'm still an agnostic, and there are some parts of Chapter Four I'm reluctant to encourage a newcomer to read. But I have discovered that the program will work for anyone who will let it work. I didn't have to find a way to make it work. It will work perfectly well on its own if I will let it, provided I'm willing to do some work myself.

The first thing I had to do was resign from the debating society. That didn't mean I started agreeing with everything I heard. It means only that I listened without arguing, used what I could use, and filed the rest for future reference.

The second thing I did was to become an active member of my home group, which happened to be my sponsor's home group. (I'd gotten a sponsor immediately. I already knew that was one thing I'd better do right away.) I saw that whatever else spirituality might consist of, it had to include being of maximum service to my fellow alcoholics, whether or not they were still suffering.

Once I did those two things, every question I needed an answer to was answered. Every promise contained in the Big Book has come true in my life, especially the one about being amazed before I was halfway through.

It might be that my Higher Power is the same thing as the rest of you call God. I don't know. That's one reason I still call myself an agnostic. During a discussion, sometimes I'll call it "God" rather than "the Higher Power," just to keep it simple. Whatever it is, whatever you or I call it, it works, just like the Big Book says it will if we're open-minded.

I can see no way I could have had this spiritual awakening if I had not been driven into the arms of this Fellowship by my alcoholism. I know that many non-alcoholics have experienced it, but I don't believe I would have if I had been a normal drinker. So I am grateful today not only for my recovery, but for the disease from which I am recovering. My discovery of a Higher Power that I can use in my life has been worth every bit of the hell I had to go through to get there. (I wish it hadn't been necessary for others to go through this hell along with me, but all I can do now is make amends wherever possible.)

You told me each time I came in that I could experience blessings beyond my wildest dreams. I could only think at the time: These people obviously don't know how I can dream! But, like everything else you told me, it was exactly true. While my material blessings still are less than what I could wish for, my life today is indeed far richer than any I could have dreamed of. And it really did not take much to bring it about. Just a little honesty, so I could finish taking the First Step, then a little open-minded-ness, so I could begin the Second Step, and a little willingness to follow through with the rest of the program.

Doug S.
St. Augustine, Florida

What We Could Never Do

February 2001

> *The central fact of our lives today is the absolute certainty that our Creator has entered into our hearts and lives in a way which is indeed miraculous. He has commenced to accomplish those things for us which we could never do by ourselves.*
>
> — Alcoholics Anonymous

These words from the Big Book are awfully tough for an atheist to swal-low. That so-called "central fact" about a Creator is no part of my life. And anyway, even if there were a Creator, what could he do for me that I cannot do for myself? I'm the one who has to do the Steps and make amends. I'm the one who must go to meetings and do service work. What is it that I cannot do that I need a Creator to do for me?

After some months in AA, I became frustrated when I heard people in meetings talk about God doing for them what they could not do for them-selves. One woman said she is now a good, loving mother for her children. She said there was no way she could have accomplished that herself. She knew because she had tried and failed for years previously. Clearly God was accomplishing for her what she could not do by herself, she concluded.

At first, this caused me to bristle. She was skipping over something important. At some earlier time, she could not take care of her children properly. Now she could. So she concluded that something miraculous had occurred. But in fact, she had learned to take care of her children in the intervening time. She was deluding herself with false modesty, crediting God with what she was doing herself or conversely, crediting herself, by saying that what she was doing couldn't be done except by God.

But she started me thinking. When I thought about myself, I began to see that perhaps there was something to all this. And at last came a breakthrough thought. For me, AA has been like my high school typing class. Before I took the class, I could not type—no way, no how. I could hunt and peck, but I had no inkling of the true technique of typing. In theory, it is possible that I could have taught myself how to type by reading books or watching videotapes. But in fact, I know beyond a shadow of a doubt that I could never have mustered the self-motivation to learn typing on my own.

However, in typing class, there was a teacher who cared about what I was doing. She monitored my progress on a daily basis. And there were other students in the class, so we competed to be the best at typing. We were tested and graded on our work. With all this motivation, I enthusiastically learned how to type over the course of the year. Now I can reel off pages of print effortlessly.

If I compare the time before I took that class to the present, I may be tempted to conclude that a miracle occurred. Since I couldn't do it before and now I can, clearly I am not the one doing the typing. God must be doing it for me, since I can't be doing it myself.

This conclusion is evidently ridiculous. But the example contains a grain of truth. The typing class did not do the work. It did not move my fingers on the keyboard, or put in the hours of practice necessary to learn typing. I did all that myself. Yet I could never have brought myself to do that work without the typing class. The teacher, the tests, the other students, and the report card each played a role in teaching me to type. The class did for me what I could not do for myself: It motivated me to do the work to learn to type.

AA has been a similar experience for me. I have had to do all the work myself. I have had to work the Twelve Steps; I have had to attend meetings; I have had to make coffee, secretary meetings, and serve as GSR for my home group; I have had to call my sponsor every day; and I have had to read AA literature on a daily basis. No one has done that for me. And yet I could never, I would never, have done any of this work without AA to motivate me. There was nothing magic, paranormal, or supernatural about his "miraculous" experience. The other AA members, my sponsor, and

AA as a whole have done for me what I could not do for myself: They have motivated me and given me confidence to do the work necessary to recover from alcoholism.

The central fact of my life today is the absolute certainty that AA has entered into my heart and life in a way which is indeed exceptional. It has commenced to accomplish those things for me which I could never do by myself. AA as a whole is my Higher Power.

Gabriela R.
Seattle, Washington

Three Dimensions of AA   *July 1955*

An AA member once told me that he had been skeptical about the AA spiritual program until he realized that it was the systematic expression of an old Jesuit prayer he had learned as a boy. The prayer was:

"Take, Lord, and receive all my liberty, my memory, my intellect, and all my will—all that I have and possess. Thou gavest it to me: to Thee, Lord, I return it! All is Thine, dispose of it according to all Thy will. Give me Thy love and grace, for this is enough for me."

I told my AA friend that I was afraid of that prayer. I feared that if I made that offering to God at eight o'clock in the morning I would have taken it back by ten o'clock.

"How do you know you'll be alive by ten o'clock?" he said. "How do you know but that God may give you even greater help after making that offering? That's the way that AA has taught me to look at it," he said.

Since then I have not been afraid of that prayer. This AA member had given me an understanding of that old Jesuit prayer, which I had not got in my thirty Jesuit years.

A year later I met this AA friend and told him what our conversation had taught me. "I also learned something that night," he said. "I noticed for the first time that last sentence of the prayer, 'Give me Thy love and Thy grace, for this is enough for me.' That meant that all we were asking from God was nothing, except everything. For with His love and His grace, I do have everything," my AA friend said.

And that is the deepest dimension of AA—God's love and His grace.

Edward Dowling, S.J.

A Not-So-New Newcomer

March 2003

My mom, who died at age ninety, never believing she could have reared an alcoholic daughter, always warned me not to put all my eggs in one basket—which I always did. And therein lies my story.

My husband, also a sober alcoholic, died when I was almost twenty-four years sober. I had followed him into the program of Alcoholics Anonymous nine months after he got sober. As his death from emphysema slowly approached, I was often seized by fear as I lay beside him during the long nights, listening to him struggle for breath. I did not know how I would live without him.

After he died, I found, to my utter dismay, that I could not pray; church meant nothing to me, and what is more, I was unable to concentrate on reading, which had always been a source of great pleasure for me. The only place I felt safe and at peace was at AA meetings. The only books I could read were the Big Book and the "Twelve and Twelve."

I had no family close by, and I had no children. I had no sponsor, as my original sponsor had died years before, and I had no close friends, as my husband and I had isolated ourselves on our farm. We had joked about sponsoring one another, but it was no joking matter now. Life for me after my husband's death was a perfect zero, a big nothing, a terrifying emptiness. At a meeting of my home group after my husband died, when a longtime friend of my husband's commented that I was "a people person and needed to get off that farm," I told him, with scorn, "I am not a people person!" What I meant, but did not understand, was that I did not know how to be around anyone except my husband. All I knew was that I was frightened and I could not share that with anyone, except my dog, Chunky.

Then, about six weeks after my husband's death, the obsession to drink returned, nearly twenty-four years after my last drink. I sat on a hillside on our farm, and I knew I was going to drink. It was the same feeling I had had before I got sober. My dog sat beside me, and I cried into his fur, feeling utterly hopeless and helpless. I thought about how drinking would let my husband and God down. I thought about the first five years of our sobriety in St. Paul, when we had had so many AA friends and so much fun in the program. I thought about my first sponsor, Margaret, who taught me it was possible to watch a husband kill himself, one cigarette at a time, with peace and serenity. I thought about Old Jerry, the Missouri puke, who liked to repeat what his Old Granny had taught him—"What goes around comes around"—and who, after our home burned to the ground, came to my office and without a word, handed me a hundred dollar bill. Most of all, I thought of my husband, who had been two years into relapse, when we picked each other up in a bar. I remembered how we did the Tenth Step after an argument, and how we worked together to mend relationships with his children and our parents, I remembered burying our parents, celebrating weddings and grandchildren, dogs loved and lost, building a new home after the fire, walking through his illness, just the two of us, and then his death, at home.

I knew I couldn't drink, but I did not know how not to drink without him, and I did not know how to make a new life from the total emptiness that was mine. I had put all my eggs in that one basket my mother warned me of.

I don't remember asking God for help, sitting on that lonely hillside on our farm, but suddenly the words "Call Greg" came into my mind. I did not argue; I walked into the house and called Greg, the friend who had made me so angry by telling me I was a people person. I must have had some belief that AA would help, but it was not a conscious belief. I just obeyed the words "Call Greg."

And of course, Greg helped. That moment of obeying the thought to call Greg was the moment of grace for me, when God did for me what I could not do for myself: take the next right action instead of taking a drink. That was the beginning of learning that Alcoholics Anonymous could work for me under any and all circumstances.

As Bill W. wrote in *Twelve Steps and Twelve Traditions*, I actually learned to accept "bereavement with courage and serenity."

I began to understand a problem I had from the very beginning of my life in Alcoholics Anonymous. I believed my life would be manageable if I did not drink—manageable by me, that is. I never gave God a chance to show me what my life could be with God as the manager. So when I found myself without a life to manage after my husband's death, I was totally bankrupt. After twenty-four years of sobriety I had reached the state of "pitiful and incomprehensible demoralization" that finally led me to admit to another human being that I did not know how not to drink and that I did not know how to go on living a life that was totally empty.

Greg and others got me going on ninety meetings in ninety days. I turned to the Big Book for help. I read about "the hunch or the occasional inspiration" and thought "What I need is to be told what to do next!"

At that time, I did not realize that I had made my husband's God into my God, that I had taken the easier, softer way and had not done the work of finding the God of my understanding. So, with almost twenty-four years of sobriety, I became a beginner: I got a sponsor and started to listen to what my sponsor said and what I heard in meetings. I knew I would die if I did not learn how to stay sober through the program of Alcoholics Anonymous. And little by little, I came to believe that it could work for me.

One of the first things I was taught was to pray each morning before I got out of bed, asking God what his will was for me that day, and asking him for the power to carry that out. As in Step Eleven, right? Well, as I said, I was starting over!

After a week or so of praying this way, I got an inspiration. It was to write a history of Alcoholics Anonymous in the county my husband and I had lived in for the past eighteen years. And I did. I interviewed about twenty old-timers, including the man, now fifty-two years sober, who had first carried the message of Alcoholics Anonymous into our county.

Alcoholism Is a Lonely Business *May 1970*

I know without any doubt that somewhere I am written into the book of life. The incredible loneliness I once felt was not of the flesh at all; it was the loneliness of the soul cut off from God. Eternal life isn't some dim, distant concept, but a very real thing. For me, it began the day I walked into that AA meeting. Whether you are in a crowded city or on the windswept deck of a ship, you are never alone from the moment you come into AA.

Anonymous
Tolovana Park, Oregon

Another man had heard Bill W. speak in 1970, not long before he died. This man told me that Bill made him believe that he could get sober. And listening to him, I felt as if Bill W. were speaking to me.

As this project got more involved, I was drawn into service. I became a GSR and began to realize that this project was restoring me to sanity. I began to look forward to getting up in the morning to find out what God had for me to do! I had never thought like that in my life.

And the most amazing things began to happen—chance meetings, "coincidences" (which I learned to call God-incidences) that lead to more involvement in AA, to more opportunities for service, and the gift of sponsoring others.

It is now a year and two-thirds since my husband's death. I have traveled 15,000 miles—7,500 on my own. I have fallen in and out of love. I have sold the farm and bought a mobile home. I have moved 2,000 miles to live near the Pacific Ocean, and by an Alano Club. I found a good home for my dog Chunky, who could not live in a mobile home, and got a cat named Bill and two birds named Hetty and Ebby. I took my twenty-five-year token July 5, 2001, at that Alano Club.

I know now that the idea for this history could not have come from my mind. It was God's idea of how I should spend the first few months after my husband's death. I began to realize I had not given him a chance in the first twenty-four years of sobriety. But my God is a God who does not push or punish me. He waits until I am ready. Then his plan is there for me to carry out, one day at a time.

Dinah N.
Oceanside, California

MAKING AMENDS

March 1975

In the program of Alcoholics Anonymous, Steps Eight and Nine suggest that, to attain peace, I must make a list of persons I have harmed and make amends to them. For some time, I neatly sidestepped the tough amends, saying, "The Step says, 'except when to do so would injure them or others.' Well, I'm others, aren't I? And some of the amends would clearly hurt me, right?"

That is precisely the kind of thinking that prevented me from giving myself completely to this simple program. Angle-shooting and "cool" thinking kept me drunk for six years and, worse yet, let peace of mind elude me for over five sober years. Self-righteousness was blocking me from God's light.

After tenaciously holding on to my self-will until it about drove me insane, I faced the tough amends one by one. I owned up to stealing money via a padded expense account; I admitted character assassination that bordered on libel; I faced the Internal Revenue Service and other creditors. The most difficult part was doing all these things while sober.

Today, I'm learning the freedom that comes with facing my problems fearlessly and without resistance. They are not all resolved, but I've done my part. God will take it from here.

There was one more act of amends—the hardest of all. After a few attempts at sitting down with my father, I was convinced I'd never be able to honestly complete this one. Each time I'd about get to the point of admitting I'd stolen from him, slandered him, hated him, and venomously resented him, my insides would go into knots, and unbelievable hostility would well up. My mind would flash to the years I spent fearing him, the bad things I thought he'd done to me, the ways he'd let me down as a father, and the unforgivable things he'd done to my mother while he was drunk. I simply was still hating him and didn't know how to deal with it.

A few months before my seventh AA birthday, I was alone, praying. Somehow, the words "Our Father" clicked in my head. I'd been saying that prayer since I was five years old, without hearing it. "Our Father" means God to me, not my natal father. If God is our Father, he is then my father's Father, too, and we therefore are brothers. All of a sudden, I saw my worldly father as my spiritual brother, doing the best job he can with what he's got. It has been as hard for him as it has been for me. He's attempting to find happiness, just as I am.

I am very grateful I have found the program of Alcoholics Anonymous as a guideline to living. It has allowed me to learn that God, my spiritual Father, is guiding me through today. With each living experience, I find that happiness and security come as a result of working this simple program.

The next time my dad and I were together, all the hatred and fear were removed. I reached out to him with love—without strings or reservations. It was like an inside shower. Today, we're very good friends. We don't need to either approve or disapprove of each other. Why do we have to put our parents in some unfailing, Godlike role? I'm so glad I've finally seen that we are both God's kids, doing our best each day.

Tom A.
Laguna Beach, California

The Perfect Parent

April 2003

When I first came into the AA program, I believed in a vengeful, punishing, all-powerful God. I knew he could help me, but I was certain that he would not because I was such a horrible person. So, of course, I had turned my back on him long ago.

Around here we open and close our meetings with prayer, and I thought, "God—not him again!" My consequences required that I go to AA meetings or go to jail, so I kept coming back in spite of this reliance on God. After several months, I finally heard the first two words of the prayer we close with: "Our Father." I began to think about understanding a Higher Power as a parent.

My kids had done some pretty hurtful things while they were growing up, but I still love them. They had screamed (on more than one occasion) that they hated me. I still love them. If, as an imperfect parent, I could love and forgive my kids for those ugly scenes, was it possible that God could love and forgive me? After all, he was a perfect parent. Hmmm ....

This was the beginning of my relationship with my Higher Power, whom I call the old HP. I began to see things a little differently. When they were babies, I taught my kids how to walk. I knew that they were going to fall and bump their heads, but I taught them anyway. Why? Because they would have a richer life by knowing how to walk. When they got older, I taught them how to ride bikes. I knew that they were going to fall and scrape their knees, but I taught them anyway. Why? Because I knew they would have a more independent life if they knew how to ride a bike. When time came for school, they were afraid and wanted to stay home the way they always had, but I made them go anyway. Why? Because I knew that education was necessary for fulfillment.

It occurred to me that my job as a parent wasn't to prevent difficulties, but to be there to comfort my children when the inevitable happened. The lessons I taught them were all necessary and yes, sometimes painful. Often, my kids thought I was being mean instead of encouraging their growth. They would go to their room and slam the door in my face. I knew this was all a part of growing up, painful as it was.

I've come to understand that the old HP is the same way. His job is not to prevent my growth or to keep me from learning the lessons in life. His job is to comfort me when the inevitable happens. I still get mad and even slam the door in his face. But eventually I open the door and make up. Life goes on, both of us facing the world together. I do the footwork by staying sober and trying to do the next right thing and then leave the outcome to him.

Cal C.
Fort Wayne, Indiana

Connecting with Miracles   March 1982

Genuine faith in a real Power greater than myself—other than AA—came ever so slowly, through what I can see today as gentle, almost imperceptible spiritual experiences on several new roads. The great gratitude I've always felt made it possible to connect the miracles I saw in my life and so many others' with surrender to the Steps and the practice of their principles. One day, I simply heard myself talking about Step Three to a new "baby," and I knew I believed what I was saying. My new belief made it possible for the Higher Power to further change me. And with more time, as I lived the Steps with greater care and insight, my "whole attitude and outlook upon life" was changed.

P.M.
Sumner, Washington

LET GO AND LET GOD
April 1979

Except for a few doubts that were resolved when I was about ten years old, my belief in God was always part of my makeup. Years of training in the seminary, culminating in ordination to the priesthood, made me feel that I knew a great deal about God and how to relate to him. But it was not until my attendance at an AA meeting that I began to learn how incorrectly I had been handling the relationship.

I was in an alcoholism treatment center for priests. After three days, I went to a meeting in town, and a man used a saying that I heard for the first time: "Let go and let God." I was still in such an alcoholic fog and depression, I couldn't understand him. I thought he was saying, "Let go and let gone," a sort of variation on "Let bygones be bygones." But I listened closely at other meetings and finally heard what he was saying: "Get out of the driver's seat. Let go and let God."

At fifteen, I had gone to an open meeting of AA and realized that my drinking was alcoholic. I always drank to ease the pressures I felt. It took almost thirty years to get me to another meeting. As the disease of alcoholism became progressively worse for me, I turned everywhere except AA for help. I sought the help of psychiatrists and religious directors. And I prayed and prayed and prayed: "God, help me with my drinking problem."

In my arrogance, that was all I was asking help for, help in learning to drink like a normal person. I more or less told God I could take care of everything else. I could handle my personal crisis in the priesthood. I could handle all the financial problems of a huge inner-city parish. I could make people love one another and could break down racial hatred and injustice. I could handle the troubles of the Vietnam war, unemployment, bad housing, everything. All I wanted God to do was handle that one little area: my drinking.

Well, that kind of prayer and relationship to God brought me to the brink of death and insanity.

Now, thanks be to God, I can say each day, "Lord, I am letting it all go, and I am letting you, God, help me to flow along. Let me be a channel, flowing the way you want my life to flow this day." I used to think I was some kind of fountain or reservoir. All I was spouting forth was my own ego and selfishness.

Life is a joy now. It's a joy being a priest. It's a joy being sober. It's a joy knowing that all the good things God has given me through psychiatry and religion and science can make my life happy and productive if I let God be in the driver's seat.

I did not acquire the Third Step of AA in the seminary. Not until John Barleycorn had me flat on my back and the hand of AA reached out to me was I able to see that the only way I can live is by letting God—letting him channel my total life. While that life has troubles still, there is nothing I cannot handle with his help. Each day, it gets better. Hearing him speak at meetings through members of this wonderful Fellowship and turning to him frequently every day have made life worth living, one day at a time.

D.M.
Northbrook, Illinois

A Door Opens   February 2002

In August 2001, AA's Class A Trustee Dr. George Vaillant and two members of the General Service Office were invited to the People's Republic of China to talk about alcoholism and AA. Greg M. is the general manager of GSO.

Grapevine: In your travel report, you describe your trip to China as "a mountaintop experience." What did you mean by that?

Greg M.: It's the experience of sitting across from a man who has been locked up in a psychiatric ward for quite a while—a man with a scar from ear to ear that he got trying to slit his own throat because he could not stop drinking. It is looking him in the eyes and sharing as one alcoholic with another and seeing that glimmer of hope, that little flicker of light go on, and knowing that I, we, and AA here in the United States, had some little part in changing this man. It is believing a seed has been planted in him and that it will grow and grow.

THE BIGGEST WORD IN THE ENGLISH LANGUAGE

January 2000

When I came to Alcoholics Anonymous in 1988, it was at the end of a thirty-year drinking career. Over those thirty years I'd thrown away innumerable God-given opportunities, destroyed two marriages, and generally made a shipwreck of what could and should have been the best years of my life. So it was that when I walked into that men's meeting long ago, I was desperate. It was either go to AA or eat my revolver, and I wasn't ready for the latter. Yet.

Like all newcomers to the Fellowship, I brought an astounding amount of baggage to my recovery. My body may have been headed for retirement, but my emotional maturity was headed for high school. With two postgraduate degrees (both acquired while drinking), membership in a high IQ society and assorted professional credentials, I believed I could think my way through anything. The only thing larger than my arrogance was my self-centeredness. Had I been tested, I would have been found certifiably insane.

None of this mattered in the least to those men at my first meeting. They welcomed me, gave me a half-cup of coffee (I couldn't keep more in the cup), and handed me a copy of "How It Works" to read, which forced me to say out loud those words I'd been saying to myself for many years: "My name is Al, and I am an alcoholic." It was then and there that the miracle of my recovery began.

I quickly ran into a roadblock, however: God. Largest of the wrecks of my past was a seminary education and brief career as an alcoholic minister in a large Protestant denomination. This experience, I believed, qualified me as an utter expert on the subject of God. Given any theological problem, I could readily quote chapter and verse in reply, buffering my response with citations from noted scholars.

Since I knew all about God, Steps Two and Three were No Problem Whatever. Of course I believed that God was the answer to my problems (Step Two), and of course I'd committed myself to God when I entered the ministry (Step Three). No difficulty there. And then I tripped over Step

Four. I didn't have a lot of inner honesty then, but I was forced to admit that deep down I really didn't believe in God. I just had a batch of information. That being so, I hadn't actually completed Steps Two and Three at all.

If I had to be perfectly honest (and I did), I had to admit that the only truth—Truth—I had was that Something had not only removed that uncontrollable, unmanageable urge to drink that had dogged every hour of my adult life, but that Something had somehow brought me to physical sobriety without going through DTs or convulsions. I could not have done that myself; it was an outside job, beyond my understanding. To this day, that's the bedrock of my spiritual experience.

This experience, however, didn't mesh with the classic Western-Christian definition of God I then carried. What to do? My sponsor suggested that I might do what Ebby first suggested to Bill W.: find a God of my own understanding. But how to do this? The key to that came from members in my home group, who said that there was a difference between spirituality and religion. All my life I'd been looking for God in organized religion: perhaps, they said, I might look elsewhere.

To make a long search short, I eventually found my way to Zen Buddhism, a spiritual practice whose core activity is zazen, seated meditation. Zazen, I learned, is nothing more (ha!) than sitting quietly. The difficulty, of course, is what's called "monkey mind," an appropriate phrase if ever there was one. It's taken me years to learn to more or less quiet my monkey mind and keep it calm in the here-and-now—which, of course, is exactly what the program of Alcoholics Anonymous suggests as well.

One evening, the Abbot of the Zen Center I attended gave a talk. In it, he asked what the biggest word in the English language was. A number of words were proposed. Someone suggested "antidisestablishmentarianism." He said, "No, the biggest word in the English language is 'Oh.' We struggle and we think and we scheme and we do everything in our reach to solve some problem, and it's only when we let go that that 'Oh' happens and we find the answer." Moreover, he added, the longest journeys of our lives are invariably those taken to get to "Oh." If there is any benefit to Zen practice, he concluded, it may be that our journeys to "Oh" may become a bit shorter. They usually do, he noted, when we quiet the mind and let What Is settle out.

And that's AA in a nutshell. I struggled with my drinking and thought about doing something about it for years, until one day I finally said "Oh. I'm an alcoholic. I need to go to AA." And the miracle began.

I tried and tried to make my life go my way, and it never did, and one day I said "Oh. I don't need to be in charge. I can just let things happen however they're supposed to happen." And in doing that, I found peace.

I studied and memorized all there was to know about God, and never knew God at all, and one day I said "Oh. God's been there all along." And now I have a Friend who cares for me.

I still practice Zen. The God of Christianity eludes me. The Lord's Prayer makes no sense to me: I haven't recited it in years. But I have found a Higher Power (to use AA's terminology), and through that Higher Power and the Fellowship of Alcoholics Anonymous, I have found a new life. I still struggle with many of the same problems I struggled with when I came into AA, and, without exception, I find that the answers to those problems always begin with the biggest word in the English language: *Oh.*

Al L.
Angels Camp, California

BUILDING AN ARCH

May 1989

I first heard about Step Five from my sponsor. He had recently taken his. It didn't sound like fun. Not being one to suffer alone, my sponsor's immediate reaction to his own "spiritual house cleaning" was to launch me upon a Fourth Step. He wanted to give away what he'd received. I thought, What happened to "this is a selfish program"?

Step Four took a very long time. At all of it I balked. I thought I could find an easier, softer way, but I could not. With all the earnestness at his command, my sponsor became cunning, baffling, and powerful, constantly reminding me that half measures availed me nothing. I hated him.

The day finally came when even I had to admit that I'd completed Step Four to the best of my ability. That's what had me so upset. The best of my ability didn't look so hot in those days. I called my sponsor to tell him I'd finished, expecting to take a six-month to one-year sabbatical from the Steps after this arduous trek into my life. That's when he lowered the boom. "Great," he said. "The best time to take the Fifth Step is right after you finish the Fourth. Meet me at my home tomorrow at six."

Son of a gun! Who do you think you are? I thought, but aloud, I said, "Oh—kay, I'll be there."

I hung up the phone and said to myself, I bet Bill W. didn't have to go through this! I used to think the Big Book referred to Step Five when it said, "What an order! I can't go through with it." I thought, How can talking about all this junk that I never wanted to write down in the first place make any difference?

By the time I finished Step Five, I knew that I was well on my way toward "building an arch" through which I would "walk a free man." What happened? Did God convert me into a religious AA dervish? Was I brainwashed by some mystical technique into an AA true believer? Did I go into permanent shock? None of these things happened. The truth is much simpler. Step Five simply accomplished exactly what I was promised, based on the tried and tested experience of Alcoholics Anonymous.

This is what happened. For starters, I had prepared for Step Five by making a beginning on the previous Steps. I had my Fourth Step inventory which had given me a new awareness, albeit a not completely objective one. Nevertheless, I had it. Though the temptation to avoid sharing with "another human being" was nearly overwhelming, my fear of not following my sponsor's instructions to the letter was even greater.

I arrived at my sponsor's home promptly at six. I didn't want to be late for my "funeral." He ushered me into the living room, and I sat in what was obviously the condemned man's chair. Given to redundancies in times of hysteria, I commented on the weather at least twice, and God only knows how many times I mentioned the state of local AA affairs. Then my sponsor said those terrible words: "Why don't you get out your Fourth Step so we can get started."

I feared that doors automatically sealed themselves during Fifth Steps. But I prayed to God and "asked His protection and care with complete abandon." "Okay, where do you want to begin?" I asked, hoping for mercy. "Why don't we begin with your grudge list," my sponsor said. "But before we begin," he added, "why don't we pray and ask our Higher Power for guidance. After all, this is a three-way deal. God is very much a part of this. It's his grace that brought you here."

Sometimes sponsors can really surprise you. This was one of those rare times. We prayed, then he became his old self again, indicating that it was time I began. We went over my grudge list, item by item. I discovered that he liked "item by item." I read and explained. He listened and commented.

Before we were halfway through the list, I began to realize that the advice, counseling, and experience he shared was not only his, but that of others as well. It was the experience of one drunk talking to another, but it was more than that. It was the resonating voices of countless men and women in AA who had shared their experience, strength, and hope with each other. Was this God-consciousness? I wondered, as I continued my disclosures.

Finishing the grudge list, we assailed my list of fears. To my surprise, I discovered my sponsor and I shared some of the same ones. By this time, occasional laughter interspersed the more serious portions of the unfolding panorama of my life. I was beginning to feel a sense of relief. It continued to grow even as we discussed pertinent aspects of my "list of major human failings—the Seven Deadly Sins."

It was incredible! As years of humiliation, pride, and fear fell away into harmless debris, my sense of isolation actually began to dissipate. I no longer felt like a freak, a pathetic caricature of humanity, incapable of integrating myself into the world about me. The existence of God's presence was no theory; it was fact. God was with us and my cup did indeed run over. It overflowed with his love as it was translated into the experience, strength, and hope of two twentieth-century alcoholics joined in the miracle of a spiritual awakening known as recovery.

Those secrets that I'd sworn to take to my grave were now dead and buried under the fertile soil of a new freedom nurtured by truth and sharing and laughter, moistened by tears of relief and joy, and warmed by the sunlight of the spirit. "Step Five works! It really does," I marveled. I knew now that the man who was leaving was not the same man who had fearfully entered this Fifth-Step sanctuary just a few hours previously.

Today, after many revisits to Step Five, I know that my initial experience was no fluke, that "God does move in a mysterious way His wonders to perform," and that Step Five is one of those.

I have also been privileged to share in the Fifth Step experiences of others. Since there is nothing like personal experience to qualify one for this extremely personal spiritual awakening, I would suggest having done a Fifth Step as a prerequisite for hearing someone else's. We must be prepared to share our own Fifth Step disclosures, laughter, and tears that the experience of others might be as profound as our own. Being able to keep confidential the disclosures of others is also essential. This experience is only between God and ourselves.

Franklin D. Roosevelt said, in his first inaugural address, "The only thing we have to fear is fear itself." If we're willing to expose the pages of our lives to the love and understanding of our Higher Power and a fellow alcoholic, we'll surely know a new freedom and a new happiness. We'll discover that love is never having to feel alone again; that God's presence in our lives has become profound; and that the unity of the Fellowship of the spirit can be ours so long as we are willing to "pass it on."

Chico C.
West Palm Beach, Florida

SUNLIGHT AND AIR

May 1999

I came to Alcoholics Anonymous young in years but sick of soul and full of secrets. Now, in my middle age, I no longer harbor secrets, and my soul is in better health than ever. It's freer, more generous, and able as it never was in my drinking days to receive love and joy and wonder as well as the darker emotions. While all of AA's twelve suggested Steps are crucial to my ongoing recovery, the Fifth Step more than any other has helped me get free of those soul-crippling secrets.

I attended my first meetings with my then-partner. She was older than I, and her alcoholism was more visible. When our physician prescribed AA for her, I went along because except for our jobs and her occasional disappearing acts during binges, we did everything as a unit. I realize now that I didn't trust her to go on her own. I didn't trust AA, either, and knew next to nothing about it. How could those people understand her the way I did?

The first meeting we stumbled (!) into was open to all. I hastened to explain to the group members who greeted us that my partner was the one with the problem; I was just there for moral support. They told me about Al-Anon but said I was welcome at open AA meetings, too. Much as I did need Al-Anon, it was open AA meetings that saved my life.

My partner and I went together to several open meetings a week. We still drank, though, and I still flew into rages and battered her insensible during our drunken arguments, sometimes so badly that we ended the night in a hospital emergency room. These outbursts, I told myself, were caused by her drunkenness. Who wouldn't lose patience with such obnoxious behavior?

At AA meetings, I listened only for what might get my partner sober. But after hearing scores of alcoholics tell their stories, I couldn't help but look at my own drinking. I didn't consider myself an alcoholic—after all, I wasn't as bad off as she—but it did come through to me that normal social drinking did not result in blackouts or fits of violence or the need to drive with one eye closed to keep from seeing two sets of lines in the middle of the road.

At that time, I was a newspaper reporter. My beat was a rural county that voted with paper ballots, and on election nights all the reporters who covered the county brought food and soft drinks to the county clerk's office to share while we waited out the vote tally and then wrote our stories. I had my last drink on an election night when I had decided that my contribution would be a case of beer. No one else ever brought alcohol, nor had anyone suggested that I bring it. Every time I helped myself to one of the beers, I urged others to join me, but they all declined, saying they needed their wits about them while there was work to be done. I defiantly drank several more beers, somehow wrote my stories, and drove myself home without incident—hardly high drama compared to the drunken domestic battles. The next day nevertheless found me face-to-face with the realization that while my colleagues had focused on their work, I had been obsessed with the beer. AA had ruined my drinking! I still couldn't admit that I was an alcoholic, but I doubt now that I could have stopped drinking or stayed stopped without the support I got secretly from attending AA meetings as a spectator.

My partner and I eventually separated, and I no longer had a reason to attend AA meetings—or so I thought. I moved to the city, where I was heartsick and achingly lonely—although I kept that a secret even from myself—but also painfully self-conscious and fearful of meeting people. A few drinks would make all this easier, I thought, and maybe I could drink moderately now that I knew the danger signs. Fortunately, my closest friend was a sober alcoholic I had met at one of those open meetings. Before I resumed drinking, she gently guided me back to AA, suggesting that if I listened for myself this time I just might discover that I belonged here. She told me that the only requirement for membership was a desire to stop drinking, and that I was entitled to the help that AA provides for living without alcohol.

Almost immediately, I accepted the First Step and declared myself an alcoholic, which brought a great sense of relief. I set about working the rest of the Steps, too, but I secretly edited them because I didn't believe in God. People who did, I thought, were just too weak-minded to face hard reality. I would use AA to restore myself to sanity. I would turn my life over to the care of ... well, AA would do as a higher power. My first attempt at a Fourth Step produced a list of my drunken misdeeds, and for my Fifth Step, I recited this list to the sponsor I rarely saw or called, tossing in an amusing detail added here and there to keep her attention. And so on. I went to lots of meetings, but I barely skimmed the surface of the Steps, and above all I avoided close examination of my own soul and any mention of God. My secrets stayed secret, and I stayed sick.

Eventually, meetings began to irritate me. I looked around the rooms and focused on the few sober alcoholics whose lives seemed marginal to me and decided it was crazy to depend on them for guidance. Besides, I had a new partner, who was not an alcoholic, and my life was manageable now. Maybe it was a mistake, I thought, to define myself in terms of a disease. Coping without alcohol no longer seemed difficult. I concluded that I could stop attending meetings and stay sober with the other tools AA had given me.

In truth, I had little real practice with most of those other tools. My moral inventory had been neither fearless nor searching. I had never admitted my most serious shortcomings to myself, let alone to another person or to the God I didn't believe in. The self-centered fears and resentments I had carried through my drinking and into sobriety were still with me, because I could not remove them myself and was far from ready for God to remove them. Now, without meetings and fellowship with other recovering alcoholics to subdue them, my character defects took on new strength.

Any veneer of emotional sobriety I might have developed quickly wore away once I stopped going to meetings. I didn't beat my new partner—at least I hadn't hit anyone since I'd stopped drinking—but I did try to control her every breath and showed no respect for her feelings. My frequent outbursts of obsessive jealousy left me humiliated and ashamed, and so did the romantic obsession I developed with another woman that led me to betray my partner. When my escalating emotional turmoil kept me from concentrating on my work, I made serious mistakes that cost me a job and increased my sense of shame. I had not picked up a drink yet, but emotionally I was worse off than ever. Finally, when I hit what I now know was a spiritual bottom, I went back to the one place that I knew would still welcome me—AA meetings.

This time I was ready to open my mind and my heart to the program in its entirety, to seek serenity and emotional sobriety and not just the quick fix. Now when I looked around the rooms, I focused on people who had what I wanted. I saw that they were the ones who worked at improving their conscious contact with God as they understood Him—or Her, or It. I still couldn't claim even the slightest knowledge of God, but it was clear to me at last that I needed to depend on something much bigger than me. Even AA couldn't fill that bill, because it was made up of people like me. My understanding of a Higher Power is still subject to shifts. Sometimes, I think of it as The Unknowable, or as The Great What Is. Often, I envision it as an indifferent force, something like an electrical current, that is available to all living things and from which human beings can derive strength and generosity and acceptance. The one thing I feel sure of is that it's more powerful than my will or any mere human or collection of humans, even AA as a whole; that's what makes it higher.

Having acknowledged a Higher Power, regardless of how little I understood of its nature, I was ready at last to take the Steps of AA as they are and not as I wished them to be. For starters, I saw that I had not restored myself to sanity, and that I never could. All the Steps seemed different now, including those that don't specifically mention a Higher Power.

The Fourth Step, to me, is like a tour of a haunted house. My first time around, when I heard the scuttling in the walls, I raced alone through the hallways and out the back door. This time, the acceptance of a Higher Power gave me the courage to open the closet doors and even venture into the cellar. I found long-hidden stores of fear and resentment. I found a few hidden treasures, too.

Having uncovered my character defects, I could admit the exact nature of my wrongs, not just their most obvious manifestations. The hardest part of the Fifth Step was admitting the truth to myself. I had to look at the fears and insecurities that led me to hurt that former partner in many ways, not just physically, to harass and betray my current partner, and to hurt others I loved as well. I preferred to see myself as an unfailingly generous friend who had pulled myself up by my bootstraps, required little from others, and never gave in to self-pity. Instead, I had to admit that my need for the love and approval of others felt bottomless, that I deeply envied my friends' achievements, and that I blamed the deprivations of my childhood for my own failure to rise above the level of mediocrity. Admitting these character defects to my Higher Power was easier than admitting them to myself, because my understanding of God has nothing to do with judgment and everything to do with the acceptance of what is. Once I felt secure in the acceptance of a Higher Power, admitting the truth about myself to another human being seemed much less risky.

If the Fourth Step is the exploration of an abandoned house, I have come to think of the Fifth Step as raising the blinds and throwing open the windows. The house has air and sunlight now, and it's no longer haunted. When people come to the door, I can welcome them without shame, and I can even invite them in. Some rooms are private of course, but none are secret, and I live in all of them.

Cheryl M.
New York, New York

MOMENT OF SILENCE

August 2001

The Hocking Hills region of southeastern Ohio has long been a source of emotional grounding for me, a place of introspection and wonder, discovery and rediscovery. While scrambling along its ancient ridge tops and exploring its rocky hollows, I have known moments of such complete joy that I've been left breathless and dazed.

It was there that I chose to take my Sixth and Seventh Steps. Reflecting on the gravity of the occasion, my sponsor recommended that I find a place that would offer few distractions. I decided I would camp overnight and find a secluded hollow within the Hocking Hills State Park. (I should mention that my wife, Annette, has always supported everything AA-related.) After a three-hour drive to the area, I found a campsite, and that evening I prepared for the next day by reading the Big Book and reviewing my moral inventory.

The next morning I loaded my pack with a couple of water bottles, my Big Book, and a topographic map of the area. When I started walking, I had a good idea where I was going. There was a certain remote valley containing a series of hollows that I'd been aching to explore. I've always enjoyed finding and exploring places well off the beaten path.

I hiked to the stream that carved the valley and followed it until I came to a smaller stream draining into it. That stream led into a cool hollow that ended at the base of a high-walled cliff. A narrow falls leapt from the lip of a recessed cave in the cliff wall. The most striking feature of this place was the sand that had piled up in the mouth of the cave behind the waterfall. My map didn't list a name for this place, so I dubbed it Sand Castle Hollow.

After climbing high up to the cave and going in, I knelt in the sand, looking through the falls out into the hollow, and I prayed. I hadn't prayed in a very long time, and never like this. I have no idea how long I was up there. I was in God's presence and I exposed to him my heart and soul. I talked, confessed, laughed, cried, and sang to my God. I gave thanks for my sobriety, my family, and all of my blessings, and then I asked that my character defects be removed. Through all of this, the hollow was filled with the sun's warmth and light, a gentle breeze came through the trees, and the water fell freely through the sunlight to splash on the rocks at the fall's base. And then, quite suddenly, the falls stopped. Everything went quiet. The falls had gone dry.

I was afraid to move or to breathe. After a very long pause, just as suddenly as they had stopped, the falls began to flow again.

I don't know how long the falls paused that morning, but it had a profound effect on me. I reasoned that the water above the falls was temporarily dammed by autumn leaves. That wasn't a miracle. The miracle was that I was there to experience it. I had been quiet and absorbed in my world long enough to actually notice, with all of my senses, something as simple and sublime as the effects of a leaf jam on a little stream. God knew I was there, and he told me so.

I return to this place at least once a year. I don't expect the water to stop falling again, but I like to go back to Sand Castle Hollow and reflect on how my life has changed. And I thank God.

Dennis G.
Toledo, Ohio

A Sense of Wonder   *June 1968*

I am here, today. Nothing can ever change that. I belong here. I'm not a very big part of the universe, but a part, nonetheless, and God wants me here as such. I have a part to play; but it is simply too big for me to discover on my own. So I humbly ask God what his will is for me, today.

That is what AA has taught me—to relate myself to the universe—to God as I understand him. In so doing, I can get things in their proper perspective, and find "the peace that passeth all understanding." The things that used to keep me awake nights now no longer bother me, because I can put them against the backdrop of eternity. The long, lonely winter that was alcoholism has turned into spring—the rebirth, the renewal of my life. It is God's promise. He was there all the time. It just took AA to show me the way.

B.L.
Seattle, Washington

The Circle of Peace
July 1992

For the past year and a half, my spouse and I have been chairing AA meetings at one of the correctional facilities in our city. Recently the inmates have begun taking a more active part in their meetings, such as sharing, reading from the Big Book, and so forth. We have typed "How It Works" from Chapter Five of the Big Book and after the Serenity Prayer and the Preamble the inmates read this aloud.

Last week, at our regular Wednesday meeting, the inmate chairperson declared the meeting an open discussion meeting and said there would be no set topic. Each person would speak out on what was in his heart and then that person would tag someone else. If the person tagged did not care to share that would be okay but he must tag another person.

The chairperson spoke first and his topic was gratitude. He tagged another inmate and for the next half hour several inmates shared. No one changed the topic, so it stayed a gratitude meeting. There were a number of Native Americans attending the meeting, and finally one inmate tagged an elderly Native American. At first the old man sat silent, then he looked up, waved his hand, and said, "I speak no English."

Almost everyone laughed except one young Native American. He got up from his chair, walked over to the old man, and spoke for a moment in another tongue. He turned to the rest of us and said, "The old one will speak and I will interpret his words." The old man began speaking, and the younger man would stop him every few moments and relay the words to us. "I have been here a long time and all because I committed a terrible crime against a brother of mine," the old man said. "I was drunk at the time, but that is not an excuse for what I did because I was drunk a great deal of the time. After I came here [to prison] I started to search for something to relieve the pain I felt for what I had done.

"First I tried the various religions offered here. Then I tried solitary meditations. At no time could I find peace. One evening I heard one of my brethren speak of a meeting that was starting on Wednesday nights. It was a meeting about drinking problems. I came to this meeting. I have been coming back each Wednesday night for over a year. You may ask why I attend a meeting when I could not understand the words that were being spoken. I will tell you.

"From the very first time I stepped into this room and joined this circle of chairs, I felt a powerful spirit. Each time I return here I feel this spirit and the beginning of a wonderful feeling of peace. I need not know the words, although some of them are becoming known to me. All I need to know is that for the hour that I spend here with you people, I am at peace with myself. I feel close to the Great Spirit of my fathers. Words are not necessary. The Great Spirit speaks in all languages. That is all I have to say."

We closed the meeting shortly afterward with the Lord's Prayer and all of us felt a special nearness to our own Higher Power and a true feeling of what spirituality is all about.

J.F.M.
Tucson, Arizona

A Powerful Reason for Faith
May 1982

I am an alcoholic, and I am now a blind alcoholic. With my first drink, a physical compulsion was set up in me. I thought I had good reasons to justify my drinking, but I always felt guilty about it, and it finally reduced me to a nothing.

I came to AA when my husband of sixteen years left me because of my drinking. I thought it was a terrible thing to have to go to AA, but I wanted to show my husband that I was serious about not drinking. I did well in AA, got active in the program, and stayed sober for four years, always with the goal of getting my husband back. When my husband remarried and I realized he was not coming back, I slipped. After eight or nine years of drinking and pills, I became so sick that I begged God to get me to AA again.

In the old days in AA, they used to say that when anything is bothering you, you should get the Big Book and let it fall open to any page. I got the Big Book, and on the page it fell open to were these lines: "When many hundreds of people are able to say that the consciousness of the

Presence of God is today the most important fact of their lives, they present powerful reason why one should have faith."

I was so sick, I wanted God in my life with my whole heart and soul. I forced myself to go to a meeting three days after I said that prayer. At this meeting was a member of the group that I had first belonged to. I talked to him and was able to be honest and tell him where I was at. I became involved in AA work, joined the group, and took on commitments.

After several years of sobriety, I had a part-time job as a teacher's aide, working with alcoholics. I was a busy, happy, seventy-two-year-old woman when blindness struck me—a devastating, traumatic, completely frightening experience. There were days and months when I asked moment by moment for help in trying to cope with the blindness. I was obsessed with wanting to see and could think of nothing else. Although I prayed for acceptance of my blindness, I could not accept it.

After a number of operations, I realized I could not be helped. Despite

Love   *March 1980*

Freely acknowledged mutual dependence—caring and sharing—was the soil in which my seed of love could grow. Through the Twelve Steps, I was shown how to sweep aside the primacy of concern with self, to discard the selfishness and arrogance that stood in the way. All these were obstacles to love, and as I began to learn to turn my life and will over to God as I understood him, the first faint glimmerings of humility began to appear.

And with this came, finally, the spiritual awakening, for the first time in my life, of that unique experience we inadequately call love. It was not the "I want everyone to love me and I'll do anything to get it" love. It was simply "I love you"—without reservation, qualification, or expectation. Love can be offered with a smile.

I don't stand around on street corners just loving everybody today. But in an AA meeting or any AA gathering, I know I am in the kind of community of love that every therapy, religion, and philosophy desperately seeks. Love is our glue.

C.H.

Fairfield, Connecticut

many kind and generous friends and many, many prayers, I despaired.

One day in the hospital, I wrote a small poem for my roommate, in response to her many kindnesses. Other poems followed. It was as though God had said to me, "It would have been worse if you had lost your mind instead of your eyesight. You have a good, creative mind—use it!"

I was no longer obsessed by wanting to see. My prayers had been answered in a miraculous way. I could accept my blindness.

When I got home, I wrote a poem for the hospital, where the personnel had been so good to me. The poem is now hanging in a prominent place in the lobby of that hospital.

I practice the Twelve Steps of AA every day to the best of my ability. As long as I do that, I will not need to drink, no matter what situation I am faced with. I have just had my tenth anniversary in AA, and I would not exchange these ten years for any other period in my life.

Since my return from the hospital, I have taken a course in creative writing, and my instructor tells me three manuscripts I have written are worthy of consideration for publication. I have learned Braille and am now reading stories in Braille. With the help of a cane, I have extensive mobility. I am working with several young people in AA. This is a great joy to me, and I am very grateful. None of this could have been accomplished without AA. In my AA sobriety, I have found God in a very special way.

G.E.
Franklin, Massachusetts

PRACTICAL ENLIGHTENMENT
August 1995

I seem to notice more Grapevine articles on the tensions between AA and its religious traces recently. I read that old-timers threaten newcomers with relapse if they don't conform to the old-timer's idea of a miracle-working God. I read that newcomers are willing to try anything but prayer and meditation, which they insist is pernicious Christian residue they can do without.

Neither one of those positions is the program that got me sober. At the beginning of the Big Book, I see that Ebby didn't preach, but told Bill to choose his own conception of God. At the end of the Big Book, I read a warning about "contempt prior to investigation." On the same page I find that an alcoholic "can only be defeated by an attitude of intolerance or belligerent denial," and I believe that's true at any point in recovery.

Where I learned AA, sharing about religion was frowned on—I think as a way to avoid controversy. But recalling and sharing my own experience helps me, and I know from my life in recovery that my doing so may help others. Not only atheists resist AA.

My parents are Baptist missionaries. The first thing I discovered in alcohol once I started drinking in college, was freedom from the anxious, suspicious, alienated life I'd learned in church. Drunk, I was one of the guys, and life was fun. I became a "Whiskeypalian," so I could drink with the best. I could drink folks under the table, and one day I woke up there myself.

I bottomed out in seminary, oddly enough. When I drank, I knew all I wanted to know about God and was at the top of my class in theology. The faculty didn't know I was a drunk; they just thought I was obnoxiously arrogant. The God I believed in was the "ground of being," the energy of the cosmos, supreme and ungraspable. I believed God was professionally interested in my species, but was as indifferent toward me personally as I was toward bugs—or, to tell the truth, as I was toward myself.

I came to AA because I couldn't stop getting drunk. I hated the oppressive cheerfulness and loud laughter, but I didn't know where else to go. I dismissed what I heard as uneducated nonsense. What kept me coming back was that I was sure I wouldn't drink while I was seated in an AA meeting, not because I believed what anybody was saying, but because I knew no alcohol was available there. At the end of my first week, I realized I had gone seven days without a drink; I hadn't done that for years. As my head cleared during those first months, I realized that "something" worked in those rooms, because more often than not I arrived frantic and left calmer. It dawned on me that what I felt at those meetings kept me sober between them as well, and I realized with surprise that a healing and sustaining power was involved with me directly.

My first crisis in AA came at the Third Step. I knew, having gone through many religious revivals growing up, that turning one's will and life over didn't work. Backsliding was inevitable. I would break every promise made to reform, just as all the people around me (and you, too) would break every promise they made to support me. To me, the Third Step was the same as "conversion," and I wanted nothing more to do with lying offers of salvation that only ended up increasing my shame and despair.

On the other hand, I'd been carried by the program for several months and had come to trust it. I'd taken the first two Steps, and this was the one facing me now. So I said to myself that I would turn my life and will over only to whatever worked in those rooms. I'd trust AA, but I wanted God to stay out of it. I didn't want a decision with cosmic and eternal implications; I wanted only what had worked so far to keep me sober one day at a time. And after several years of recovery, that still satisfies me.

I'm sure God would rather have me sober than not, but I also know that when I hobnob with God as my Higher Power, my notions of recovery tend to inflate dangerously: I begin to think that everyone ought to be in recovery, and that I know they ought to be in recovery, since God, who is my Higher Power, is in charge of it all. So, instead of that heady brew, I reign myself in to "utilize, not analyze." If I wonder about the Higher Power that guides my recovery at all, I imagine it is something like a guardian angel—assigned to me while I'm around, willing and able to help, but "self-supporting" and with "no opinion on outside issues."

Two more comments. I'm glad I have one foot in religion. It gave me a way to understand what I was doing in Alcoholic Anonymous. All religions have spiritual disciplines that orient the practitioner toward enlightenment or union or release. AA offers the possibility of "a spiritual awakening as the result of these Steps." And working the Steps opened my eyes to the human struggles of the writers of the Bible; I found myself identifying with them. They weren't taking divine dictation about transcendent truths and assigned morality, but writing about their own movement from "pitiful and incomprehensible demoralization" to a life "happy, joyous, and free." I came to see them not as grumpy tyrants but as fellow travelers.

Second, open-mindedness seems to me a core spiritual principle of the program. It is the heart of Step Two. Without it I cannot change. The program is pragmatic and experiential: I listen to others share their experience, then "act as if" and "keep what works." But to be open, I must believe there is something to be open to; that's what I mean by spirituality. At the very least, I need openness to my own future. In other words, I believe recovery depends on a sense that a perspective other than my own exists, either "Good Orderly Direction," or the combined wisdom of those in the Fellowship, or the accumulated experience of the program. I needed that the day I walked into my first meeting; I still need it now. I don't expect to outgrow it.

If I am to recover, I must be honest about what works for me, open to other things working, and willing to give those things a try—or at least to let them be. I cannot continue to grow in recovery when theory replaces experience, stubbornness replaces strength, and control replaces hope.

W.

San Francisco, California

Something Extra   *April 1983*

My Fifth Step varied from year to year in format, content, and hearer, depending on what I saw to be my principal character defects at the time. In my fifth year, the leading contender was my lack of connection to a Higher Power—a shortcoming that was making it impossible for me to relate to the spiritual part of the program. "You can't make an omelet without cracking the eggs" was the way I put it to myself.

So I chose for my hearer a clergyman in the program, because clergymen know all about such things. "I have no connection with a Higher Power; I don't really believe in a personal God." That was my opening gambit, and I expected a fifteen-minute lecture on the ontological and cosmological proofs of God's existence. But that's not what I got.

"Don't worry about it," he said. "You have more of a connection than you think. He's walking along the fence beside you. You don't have to believe in God," he continued. "Believe in whatever got you sober and has kept you sober."

We talked about this for a while, and he said a few other things. But I was no longer listening. I was off into my own space. The image "X +" flashed into my mind. This was my Higher Power—X because it meant an unknown quantity, and + (plus) because it was something extra!

S.L.

Manhattan, New York

PART THREE

Practicing

∽⁊

THE SPIRIT IN ACTION

Neglecting our spiritual condition can leave us in a kind of "spiritual kindergarten," Bill W. warns. Here, then, are a group of AAs who share with us how they've grown through the practice of the spiritual principles they have come to embrace.

Practice takes discipline, one writer says, and often "we alcoholics are undisciplined" when it comes to a spiritual practice. One AA describes attendance at religious services as "disciplined devotion to my Higher Power." Another AA, contemplating a poem by Emily Dickinson, observes, "Now, I heard that letting go meant acquiring discipline." One writer remarks that facing difficult times often teaches us to turn to a Higher Power "rather than to one more control scheme."

So how do we achieve spiritual discipline? Develop the habit of prayer, says one AA, for "a prayerful person is like a compass needle, which tends to spring back to true north (the Higher Power)." There's meditation, that "wordless silence" through which another AA achieves "inner resonance and harmony." One writer claims that a spiritual connection is maintained by participating in the lives of others, while other AAs comment that simply feeling gratitude is a form of spiritual practice or that "awareness of the ever-moving and ever-changing now is the spiritual experience."

These are just some of the many ways AAs have brought a Higher Power into their lives. As one agnostic writes, "This 'something' resides within me," and the spiritual habits that we build around this "something," wherever it may reside, work in a very practical way. For as one writer declares, "*everything* both good and bad can happen to us," but, "steady practice makes it possible for us to cope with *whatever* comes."

TAKE STEP ELEVEN

June 1958

When it comes to the practice of AA's Step Eleven—*Sought through prayer and meditation to improve our conscious contact with God as we understood Him, praying only for knowledge of His will for us and the power to carry that out*—I'm sure I am still very much in the beginner's class; I'm almost a case of arrested development.

Around me, I see many people who make a far better job of relating themselves to God than I do. Certainly, it must not be said I haven't made any progress at all over the years; I simply confess that I haven't made the progress that I might have made, my opportunities being what they have been, and still are.

My twenty-fourth anniversary is just ahead; I haven't had a drink in all this time. [Bill died January 24, 1971, early in the thirty-seventh year of his sobriety.] In fact, I've scarcely been tempted at all. This is some evidence that I must have taken and ever since maintained Step One: *We admitted we were powerless over alcohol—that our lives had become unmanageable.* Step One was easy for me.

Then, at the very beginning, I was fortunate enough to receive a tremendous spiritual awakening and was instantly made conscious of the presence of God and restored to sanity—at least so far as alcohol is concerned. Therefore, I've had no difficulty with AA's Step Two, because, in my case, its content was an outright gift. Step Four and Step Five, dealing with self-survey and confession of one's defects, have not been overly difficult, either.

Of course, my self-analysis has frequently been faulty. Sometimes I've failed to share my defects with the right people; at other times, I've confessed *their* defects, rather than my own; and at still other times, my confession of defects has been more in the nature of loud complaints about my circumstances and my problems.

Nevertheless, I think I've usually been able to make a fairly thorough and searching job of finding and admitting my personal defects. So far as I know there isn't at this moment a single defect or current problem of mine which hasn't been discussed with my close advisers. Yet this pretty ventilated condition is nothing for self-congratulation. Long ago, I was lucky enough to see that I'd have to keep up my self-analysis or else blow my top completely. Though driven by stark necessity, this continuous self-revelation—to myself and to others—was rough medicine to take. But years of repetition have made this job far easier. Step Nine, making restitution for harms done, has fallen into much the same bracket.

In Step Twelve—carrying the AA message to others—I've found little else than great joy. We alkies are folks of action, and I'm no exception. When action pays off as it does in AA, it's small wonder that Step Twelve is the most popular and, for most of us, the easiest one of all.

This little sketch of my own "pilgrim's progress" is offered to illustrate where I, and maybe lots of other AAs, have still been missing something of top importance. Through lack of disciplined attention and sometimes through lack of the right kind of faith, many of us keep ourselves year after year in the rather easy spiritual kindergarten I've just described. But almost inevitably, we become dissatisfied; we have to admit we have hit an uncomfortable and maybe a very painful sticking point.

Twelfth-stepping, talking at meetings, recitals of drinking histories, confession of our defects and what progress we have made with them no longer provide us with the released and the abundant life. Our lack of growth is often revealed by an unexpected calamity, or a big emotional up-set. Perhaps we hit the financial jackpot and are surprised that this solves almost nothing, that we are still bored and miserable notwithstanding.

As we usually don't get drunk on these occasions, our bright-eyed friends tell us how well we are doing.

But inside, we know better. We know we aren't doing well enough. We still can't handle life, as life is. There must be a serious flaw somewhere in our spiritual practice and development.

What, then, is it?

The chances are better than even that we shall locate our trouble in our misunderstanding or neglect of AA's Step Eleven—prayer, meditation, and the guidance of God. The other Steps can keep most of us sober and somehow functioning. But Step Eleven can keep us growing if we try hard and work at it continually. If we expend even five percent of the time on Step Eleven that we habitually (and rightly) lavish on Step Twelve, the results can be wonderfully far-reaching. That is an almost uniform experience of those who constantly practice Step Eleven.

In this article, I'd like to develop Step Eleven further—for the benefit of the complete doubter, the unlucky one who can't believe it has any real merit at all.

In lots of instances, I think that people find their first great obstacle in the phrase "God as we understand Him." The doubter is apt to say: "On the face of it, nobody can understand God. I half believe that there is a First Cause, a Something, and maybe a Somebody. But I can't get any further than this. I think people are kidding themselves when they say they can. Even if there were a Somebody, why should he bother with little me, when, in making the cosmos run, he already has plenty to do? As for those folks who claim that God tells them where to drill for oil, or when to brush their teeth—well, they just make me tired."

Our friend is clearly one who believes in some kind of God—God as he understands Him. But he doesn't believe any bigger concept or better feeling about God to be possible. So he looks upon meditation, prayer, and guidance as the means of self-delusion. Now, what can our hard-pressed friend do about this?

Well, he can strenuously try meditation, prayer, and guidance, just as an experiment. He can address himself to whatever God he thinks there is. Or if he thinks there is none, he can admit—just for experimental purposes—that he might be wrong. This is all-important. As soon as he is able to take this attitude, it means that he has stopped playing God himself; his mind has opened. Like any good scientist in his laboratory, our friend can assume a theory and can make an experiment. He can pray to a Higher Power that *may* exist and *may* be willing to help and guide him. He keeps on experimenting—in this case, praying—for a long time. Again, he tries to behave like the scientist, an experimenter who is never supposed to give up so long as there is a vestige of any chance of success.

As he goes along with his process of prayer, he begins to add up the results. If he persists, he will almost surely find more serenity, more tolerance, less fear, and less anger. He will acquire a quiet courage, the kind that doesn't strain him. He can look at so-called failure and success for what they really are. Problems and calamity will begin to mean instruction, instead of destruction. He will feel freer and saner. The idea that he may have been hypnotizing himself by autosuggestion will become laughable. His sense of purpose and of direction will increase. His tensions and anxieties will commence to fade. His physical health is likely to improve. Wonderful and unaccountable things will start to happen. Twisted relations in his family and on the outside will unaccountably improve.

Even if few of these things happen, he will still find himself in possession of great gifts. When he has to deal with hard circumstances, he can face them and accept them. He can now accept himself and the world around him. He can do this because he now accepts a God who is all—and who loves all. When he now says, "Our Father who art in heaven, hallowed be Thy name," our friend deeply and humbly means it. When in good meditation and thus freed from the clamors of the world, he knows that he is in God's hands, that his own destiny is really secure, here and thereafter.

A great theologian once declared, "The chief critics of prayer are those who have never really tried it enough." That's good advice—good advice I'm trying to take ever more seriously for myself. Many AAs have long been striving for a better conscious contact with God, and I trust that many more of us will presently join with that wise company.

I've just finished rereading the chapter on Step Eleven in our book *Twelve Steps and Twelve Traditions.* This was written almost five years ago. I was astonished when I realized how little I had actually been giving to my own elementary advice on meditation, prayer, and guidance—practices that I had so earnestly recommended to everybody else!

In this lack of attention, I probably have plenty of company. But I do know that this is a neglect that can cause us to miss the finest experiences of life, a neglect that can seriously slacken the growth that God hopes we may achieve right here on earth, here in this great day at school, this very first of our Father's many mansions.

Bill W.

DIVINE HOT LINE

December 1977

From time to time, at closed AA meetings, when someone shared his closeness and contact with the God of his understanding, a person sitting next to me has whispered, "He sounds as if he has a hot line to God!" This remark is usually tinged with sarcasm and disbelief.

Recently, when someone said this to me, I kept thinking about it as I drove home and found myself saying, "I do indeed, I have a hot line to my God, and I would not survive without it."

I came to AA bringing, in my sick mind, a mixture of philosophy, psychology, logic, science, and theology so confusing as to put me into the category of an agnostic with mental and spiritual indigestion. Certainly, I had not conceded that there was anything greater than I, at least on the conscious level. The God that I understood then was a frightening entity, separate and apart from me. I had no regular communication with that entity, nor did I give it much thought or feel any need to make its acquaintance. I was "doing my own thing" long before it became popular to say or do so, and this willfullness was leading me into all kinds of trouble and into alcoholism, with its ultimate consequences of destruction—death or insanity.

In my family, there were a number of ministers, of two denominations, but I had failed dogma, orthodoxy and creed. Religions had not failed me. It was I who could not conform to them. Yet all along I had been studying, reading, and talking with others, searching for the meaning of life. The eternal mysteries of birth, life, and death persistently plagued me when I was faced with problems. I longed for answers and some meaning to my life.

Not until my disease of alcoholism was full-blown and the crash landing came did I realize for the first time that I was powerless and that those who loved me were powerless to help me. Admitting and accepting this fact, I turned myself over to AA and soon was praying lamely, "Whatever God is helping these people, please help me." With this simple prayer, uttered time and again, and an almost monotonous repetition of the Serenity Prayer, there entered into my life a presence that had not been there before. This presence came during one of my quiet times, which I disciplined myself to have early each morning before dressing for work. Something loving, gentle, tender, and beautiful came to abide with me. I felt this powerful presence to be God.

I had brought a lot of troubles to AA with me—broken relationships, a lost business, financial problems, a job that was in danger of being lost, no close friends, and no family nearby. Alone for the first time, in an efficiency apartment, I found myself talking to this God in the same language I am using now. At first, it seemed a little crazy to be talking out loud to this unseen friend. But, since I lived alone, there was no one to question my sanity. I poured out my feelings, my fears, my despair, my disappointment in myself and others. This was an ordinary conversation, not conventional prayer. I was talking to a loving, caring, all-powerful friend, and I was reassured and comforted.

For almost five years, I prayed for specifics. All of these prayers were answered in the right way—yes, no, maybe, wait—but I could not see the rightness of some answers, especially the "no" answers, until I looked at them in retrospect. In time, I understood that if I turned my will and my life over to the God I was making my companion, some of my answers would have to be "no" for my highest good, and for the highest good of others.

Turning from formal prayer, the "thee and thou" traditional way of praying in my childhood, to the conversational prayer was a great freedom for me. I could talk to God in simple, direct, and truthful terms, in everyday language, and the more I practiced this, the more I began to understand the admonition to "practice the presence of God." The thank-yous were audibly or silently expressed many times a day, in gratitude for the unexpected answers, the blessings, and, yes, even the trials allowed for my growth. There were small prayers for others I might see as I walked or drove along—for people who seemed troubled or ill or handicapped or just plainly joyful.

I stopped giving a list to God when I fully understood Step Eleven's *praying only for knowledge of His will for us and the power to carry that out.* I could still give thanks for God's love, and pray for sobriety, guidance, protection, healing, and enlightenment; but no longer did I draw a description of what I thought I wanted. My faith in my Higher Power grew so that I trusted God to manage my affairs and became willing to accept his will for me.

As time went on, I felt the need for more. Meditation replaced contemplation in the quiet times I set aside each day. Friends more advanced in this practice taught me how to enter into this, one of man's oldest methods of worship, for a time of quieting the body and the mind and putting myself in a mood receptive to inspiration, and a time, at the end of the meditation periods, for offering up prayers for others who were sick or suffering or having trouble getting sober. I prayed for their highest good, not asking for specific results. And I always remembered Bill W.'s suggestion that when guidance seemed to be strong, we check it out with another trusted AA friend. This safeguard is a necessary one to prevent my ego from stepping in and rationalizing something I might want.

A hot line, as I understand it, is an immediate connection for communication. I can use mine anywhere, any time. I do not hear a thunderous voice in response, but if I wait and listen and observe, replies will come, often in many unexpected and surprising ways. Inspiration or answers may come through the words of a friend or a stranger; a sudden insight may come without effort on my part, may appear in something I am reading, in something someone says at a meeting, or in my dream sleep.

In my hot line conversation, one-sided as it seems, I present my problems or concerns, cite my options as I can see them, and then turn them over to God. When I have done this, I try to let the problems go mentally.

There are times when I find conditions and situations so disturbing that I cannot pray about them. All I can say on my hot line is "God help me," but this is a powerful prayer. That prayer and the prayers of others have brought me through the pain of death of loved ones, the trauma of early retirement on disability, operations, illness in the deep of night when all the world seems to be asleep and far away. But the hot line is always open, always there. It is the greatest source of comfort and security I have—the feeling that my loving Higher Power is always there, ready to comfort, to show the way, to love me without demand.

E.P.
Alexandria, Virginia

LETTING THE SPIRIT JOIN IN
November 1995

Practicing our Eleventh Step develops my ability to do one thing at a time. At meetings, people are sometimes amused when I say that. One man told me, "That's ridiculous, everyone knows how to do one thing at a time." Later on, when I asked him how he meditated, he said, "I can't stop my mind from racing long enough to do that." That remark demonstrates the purpose of the practice.

I wasn't born with the quiet mind needed to meditate. I work hard to develop it. The problem with me is that I'm alcoholic and as *Alcoholics Anonymous* says, "we alcoholics are undisciplined." So the real problem is lack of discipline.

My first sponsor showed me that I couldn't wait until I felt better to work the Steps. He said, "You must work the Steps in order to feel better." And so my work, my new purpose in life, was cut out.

When I decide to sit still, for twenty minutes, it is the alcoholic mind that has the ability to distract me. Distraction usually comes to me in the form of a thought or a subtle sensation, a twitch, or an urge telling me to stop meditating and to do something else. Quieting this alcoholic mind is why I meditate. Following through on a decision to sit still for twenty minutes—no matter what happens—is spiritual practice.

With the purpose of discipline in mind, and without regard to the results, I have a simple method that I use for meditation. Allow me to pass it on.

Before assuming the posture to meditate, I set a timer for twenty-one minutes (twenty-one is a spiritual number). Next, I say a prayer and ask God, as I understand God, for clear contact. Then for twenty minutes twice a day, morning and evening, I sit with my back straight, in my quiet spot, with reverence for the practice. With my chin held level, and my eyes closed, I focus on my breathing.

The only thing that exists now is the breath. When thoughts enter my mind I simply label them as "thinking." I don't chase after them. On the out breath I say, "be done."

This is my formal practice of our Eleventh Step. However, I'm an alcoholic, and when something is good, I want more; so I've learned how to meditate even when I'm not sitting in my formal practice.

For example, I keep rhythm with my footsteps when I'm walking. Doing one thing—walking—with my body, and paying attention to it with my mind, gives my spirit a chance to join in. When I pay full attention to what I'm doing, I'm meditating. I'm united—body, mind, and spirit—with a singleness of purpose. This helps quiet my alcoholic mind.

Another example is when I do the dishes. I no longer view the dishes as an unpleasant task. I see them as an opportunity to meditate. In fact, I stretch the job out. I touch the warmth of the water. I listen to its rich flow. While watching the formation of bubbles, I feel a loving God. I concentrate on washing the dishes and not on what I'm going to do next. The most important thing is what's in front of me—now.

One AA member who frequents my home group describes mindfulness this way: "Wherever you are—be there." Likewise: "When I walk, I walk; when I do dishes, I do dishes." You'd be amazed at the opportunities that are given for meditation during a twenty-four-hour period. Being united in body, mind, and spirit is spiritual; it keeps me sober.

Tom W.
Buffalo, New York

False Courage   *February 1977*

The false courage resulting from too many trips of the glass to the lips seems to be universal. It was true even in the case of a monk who lived in a monastery that made and marketed a well-known type of brandy.

The friar in question had the job of tasting the finished product to make sure it was up to quality. One day, he became over-enthusiastic about his task and began to gulp instead of sip. After a few hours of this, he suddenly slammed his fist on the table and shouted, "I can out-meditate any man in the house!"

Phil H.
Michigan

PRAYER

April 1974

For over five years, the Eleventh Step has intrigued me. Maybe this is the effect of early seminary training and making annual retreats. But the truth is that my own prayer did not become real "contact with God" until I'd begun working with the spiritual plan of AA.

Many years ago, I asked a college student whether he still prayed. Because I knew his heavy schedule of study, debating, and sports, his answer didn't really startle me. Joe replied, "Yeah, father. When I collapse in the sack at night, I always look up and say to God, 'Keep in touch, Man!'"

This probably beat my own prayer record in my drinking days. Vague religious longings did strike the windows of my walled-in soul occasionally, but my desired closeness to God was about nil. After my final hospitalization for drinking, a wise priest talked me into trying the program of AA, which became a spiritual life jacket. After only the first meeting, I tentatively tried praying again—and I liked it! Since that miracle night, I have honestly tried to understand and effectively practice this spiritual language of prayer. It has simply endless expressions.

It's always puzzled me that instant embarrassment is the rule when a member says anything about his or her prayer life. Perhaps it is considered too intimate a matter, or there is fear that it might turn off some new member. Yet, when I twice dared to chair an Eleventh Step discussion, each time it turned into a lively meeting with many helpful, previously buried ideas surfacing. Our members do enjoy praying, and this spiritual activity is of great interest to most of us. If prayer isn't basically fascinating, how does one explain the growing interest in transcendental meditation and other Eastern prayer forms?

Perhaps the rather cold seminary definition discouraged me early: Prayer is any act that raises the soul to God, to glorify him and perfect us. To me, this sounded as inspiring as the definition of a hexagon. Another definition would have me "reflect on the things of God and apply them to myself." Also rather chilly. After I joined AA, I began to like the legendary Irishman's description better: "Just lookin' at God and sayin' a word to

Him." Recently, an old image struck me more forcefully: A prayerful person is like a compass needle, which tends to spring back to true north (the Higher Power) when it is released.

Although theologians would divide prayer into acts of petition, adoration, asking forgiveness, and gratitude, the practical fact is that most of my pre-AA prayers were entirely beggar routines—"Gimme, gimme, God!" Not that God didn't want me to ask favors—quite the contrary. But I discovered that he desired much more than this. One day, I read in the Letter of James, "If any of you lacks wisdom, let him ask God ... and it will be given him." This line persuaded me to ask him for a growing wisdom in practicing prayer according to his good pleasure. The result was that a whole new spiritual horizon crystallized in my mind! How right Bill W. was when he wrote (in *Twelve Steps and Twelve Traditions*, page 104) that meditation "has no boundaries" and that "it is essentially an individual adventure."

An adventure! Hence, I began diversifying my daily prayer. Today, the variety of potential subjects for spiritual meditation truly astounds me. It is comparable to a prayer elevator, in which one can ride from the basement of God's high-rise to the penthouse, free to get off at any meditation floor. Usually, I choose a subject first. If it proves tedious, I try to pray over my most appealing spiritual idea. Or I will switch to what I term "prayerful problem-solving." If I'm bothered by a new resentment or a perplexing decision, I call my Higher Power into consultation. He always comes up with a fresh viewpoint, plus the inner strength for a wise choice.

Occasionally, my God will grant me a vivid light, or an inner feeling of sweetness and consolation. But this is a rare occurrence for most of us, not being saints. Perhaps, in my case, it is rare because God wants me him-centered in prayer, rather than increasingly self-centered. When I get weary of rather dry prayer, I have to ask myself, "Are you sincerely seeking the God of consolations, or just the consolations of God?"

The emotional balance that once eluded me is returning with prayer. Bill W. observed (in the June 1958 Grapevine) that the persistent prayer-maker will "find more serenity, more tolerance, less fear, and less anger." Although some make a daily resolution in meditation, I have not found this always necessary. But what has helped me is to choose a short prayer befitting my meditation, like "O Father, I trust in You." These "one-liners" tend to keep me on the spiritual beam during a busy day.

It is said that, as one grows more experienced in prayer, it takes a simpler form. I failed to really make "conscious contact" in my early attempts at prayer because they were too much like just studying about the attributes of God in the seminary. The heart of prayer is not reflection, but it took me many years to discover this. Today, I realize that the essence of my prayer must consist of spontaneous acts of affection, gratitude, and the like toward God. This is real spiritual contact with him.

These days, I also do a lot more listening—quietly waiting for his unmistakable voice within me. Prayer, as I try to grow, must become a two-way street, without incessant talk on my part. "Be still and know that I am God." Thus, my favorite kind of prayer has become "relaxing in God." Sitting quietly, alone or in a prayer group, I remind myself that I'm immersed in the ocean of God, like a diver miles beneath the surface. Then I simply pay a loving attention to this Higher Power, or offer the activities of my day to him, confident of an enlightened knowledge of his will for me.

It took me a long time to make an enjoyable game out of my prayer, a real adventure in spiritual experimenting and gambling, but it is bringing me happiness now. Certainly, I could never work the Third, Fourth, and Tenth Steps properly if I had not learned to become more God-dependent through prayer. All I have to do now is to persevere in this rich experience—which is also tedious work at times—and I believe that the rewards will be even greater.

Father Bill P.
Seattle, Washington

The Old Fear Had To Go *April 1968*

In AA's Eleventh Step I find that I build today the road I travel tomorrow.

M.M.P.
Binghamton, New York

STEPPING INTO THE SUNLIGHT

November 1989

If someone were to insist on my singling out which is the most important of the Twelve Steps, I'd have to cite the Eleventh. Early in my AA journey I wouldn't have regarded it with such reverence. In fact I scarcely noted it and would never have predicted that it would assume importance in my life because it smacked of religion, mysticism, trances, mantras, and all manner of squirmy things people who can't manage their own lives do. But with time it slowly assumed a status as the first among equals and now plays a pivotal role in what I perceive to be my slow but continuing progress toward some semblance of sanity.

I found that practicing the Eleventh Step functioned for me at two levels. (I prefer to think in terms of *living* the program and *practicing* the Steps, thus avoiding the harsh sharp-edged verbs *work* and *take*, which have onerous connotations to a lazy critter like me.) First, as a daily ritual it works wonders in establishing a tone of serenity for the day ahead and helps me avoid my lifelong tendency to jump on my horse and dash off in all directions at the same time. Whereas I used to function at two speeds— fast and stopped—a daily fix of meditation averages those two extremes out to a more gentle and efficient cruise rate.

At a second and more profound level, daily prayer and meditation offer significant guidance and support. Now this Eleventh Step is not a dramatic one and it can be easily lost among the others.

Like Steps Ten and Twelve it is an essential maintenance Step for me. But even more, I eventually discovered it to be the key to my becoming "weller than well," and to making the journey of Alcoholics Anonymous ever more fascinating and healing. Practice of this Step didn't come to me easily or quickly. The very idea of an invisible means of support seemed okay for you, but somehow I didn't quite need it like you obviously did. Where I was blessed from the start, I later realized, was that I wasn't militant about the idea of not believing in a power greater than myself. And in the first few months of going to meetings (and still taking an occasional drink resulting in an occasional drunk) I wasn't fighting the idea. This unconscious, unperceived willingness was the first of many strange forces for good that started working in my life.

As a formal practice, prayer and meditation had humble beginnings when a member of a stag group I attended gave me his copy of the Hazelden book, *Twenty-Four Hours a Day,* a volume I hadn't then heard of. I took it with me on an extended trip and started reading it daily. And, by George, I found I liked it. I felt better most days just for reading it. And for a man who had never prayed since he crawled out of his World War II foxholes, this was a revelation. I hadn't trudged through much of my adult life disparaging prayer, you understand, just ignoring it.

And what was I praying for? I'm not at all sure. I do know it was not to a God such as memories of my Methodist Sunday school evoked, an all-powerful, white-bearded presence sitting on an imposing white marble throne monitoring and keeping precise score on all five billion souls on this mortal coil. But there were these new forces at work in my life and somehow I began to think of God as a force for good, a creative intelligence, a spirit of the universe and, of course, as a power greater than myself. I had quietly been accepting the proposition that deep down in every man, woman, and child is the fundamental idea of God. Sound familiar? Those are all words, phrases and concepts found in the Big Book's Chapter Four, "We Agnostics."

So I found there was a "target" toward which to direct prayers that made me feel comfortable and refreshed. These daily interludes became a regular part of each day and started contributing to my emotional and spiritual recovery, which in turn also quickly translated into the removal of any hankering or craving for alcohol.

The practice of reading, praying and meditating to improve my conscious contact with my higher power evolved with the months. Among the first realizations was the difference between prayer and meditation made by a speaker that praying was talking to God, meditating was listening to him. And it's really the things I "hear" in meditation that have done the most to adjust my heading in life and elevate my spirits.

But it wasn't until I persevered day by day and practiced and refined the process that I truly began to find ever more peace and serenity in the form of a more centered, purposeful life, at least in the sense that my body, mind, emotions, and soul were all more or less heading in the same direction. I was riding one horse instead of four.

Often I found remarkable results when I utilized meditation for a purpose, usually one of seeking direction. By that I don't mean whether to buy a grey suit or a blue one, but for guidance in some life-quandary or as a compass to lead me out of a quagmire of indecision. I became convinced early in this new and awkward experience that real meditation was a first cousin to self-hypnosis. I often formulated some positive suggestions to implant in my barren psyche and I tried to open up and listen to my innermost self as opposed to my intellect or to logic or to my emotions or to the world-at-large. And I thus achieved an inner resonance and harmony from which often gurgled to the surface a gentle inner leading pressure quietly nudging me in some specific direction or murmuring softly, "Stay the course." Once when I was deeply disturbed over the lack of financial stability in my life, I experienced an unmistakable communication: "It's going to be okay." With that there came a great sense of confidence, followed within a few weeks by a steady improvement in the very conditions over which I had been fretting. There are many possible explanations for these and other "spiritual" realizations, as I choose to call them. They range from divine guidance, to the emergence of a psychic message from one's deep and scarred unconscious mind, to the surfacing of strong intuitive hunches based on common sense. Maybe the meditative process helped remove some psychological debris and created a moment of clarity that had been clouded by self-will and rampant grandiosity.

So beyond any philosophical, metaphysical, mystical, psychic, psychological, or spiritual explanations, this simple time-honored practice has

A Blanket of Forgiveness   October 1992

By what measure I judge others, I judge myself. By what measure I forgive others, I forgive myself.

Rick B.
Minneapolis, Minnesota

proved eminently practical. It can help me put the day in focus. It can evoke calm, confidence and certainty that I can handle the day with composure and equilibrium. It enables me to set out on a broad course of action for the day and then set myself on cruise control, avoiding the stops, starts, sputterings, false starts, screeching halts, and the fussing, fretting, and fuming that once so punctuated my days.

Such a practice of the Eleventh Step can set us on a long-range course in life that is smoother and healthier and more enriching than most of us ever expected possible. As written in the "Twelve and Twelve," "Meditation is our step out into the sun."

E.K.
La Canada, California

MYSTERIOUS ALCHEMY
December 1990

"Frankly, Bill, I don't understand alcoholism. Go to AA."

Those were the words of my exasperated psychotherapist, whom I had been seeing for several years in a futile attempt to stop drinking. So miserable was I that it was a struggle just to get to his office for my weekly appointments. The only thing I knew about AA was that there was a lot of talk about God. Whatever God I had once believed in became a casualty of my scientific training. I no longer believed in a personal God. Yet what did I have to lose? I was desperate.

Leaving nothing to chance, my therapist arranged for an AA member to take me to my first meeting. As I walked into the meeting room my companion explained that AA is a spiritual, not religious program. Yet, staring at me from the wall was a poster containing the Twelve Steps, and I noted that half of them contained certain ominous, capitalized words. When the meeting ended with the Lord's Prayer, surely a religious exercise, I thought, my anxiety turned to despair. Sensing this, my companion told me that I could substitute the group for my Higher Power. Those words gave me hope that there was a way out of my misery.

So I went to meetings, listened to people, and read all the literature. But I found in the "Twelve and Twelve" the strong implication that the group-as-Higher-Power is only a temporary expedient, that in time the newcomer must embrace something above and beyond the group. I was convinced this was crossing the line into religion.

Today, after ten years in AA, I am still of that opinion, and I still do not believe in a personal God. When meetings close with the Lord's Prayer, I stand silent. I wince when I hear the words "... that probably no human power could have relieved our alcoholism ..." For me today, it is precisely a human power that keeps me sober. That power comes in part from all my wonderful AA friends—certainly a power greater than myself. I sometimes say at meetings, "I don't drink because you people don't want me to."

Is the group my only Higher Power? No, there is more, for I have found something "above and beyond." Far from a vaporous deity, this "something" resides within me. It is a power to which I can "turn it over." It gives a nonbeliever like myself a meaning to prayer and meditation. Oddly, I have known this thing within me long before I came to AA. It comes from many years in my profession as a mathematician.

Whenever I am unable to solve a mathematical problem I have found that if I set it aside until another day, the answer will often come. And it comes seemingly out of nowhere, even when I am not thinking about the problem. Insights come while I'm jogging, standing in the shower, or even enduring a long-winded monologue at an AA meeting! Of course, you don't have to be a scientist to know what I am talking about; we all have sudden bolts out of the blue. After coming into AA I discovered that I could "turn over" such things as resentments, self-pity, and personal decisions, to this mysterious alchemy. I now practice a daily meditation, a time of quiet when I try to turn off all verbal chatter. At such times, answers to my problems often appear. Is this what my AA friends would call God's will for me? Or am I missing something? I've thought a lot about these questions.

Sir Thomas Brown wrote, in 1635: "We carry within us the wonders we seek without us." I believe there is in each of us a creative power, a force for good, an innate genius that is unique to the human species. People like

St. Francis, Mozart, and Einstein are extreme examples of that creative force. As a practicing alcoholic I was too engulfed in my own ego to be aware of such a power. I now know it is there if I am willing to listen. This power lies deep in the human mind, and my belief in it is an act of faith, just as my AA friends have a more conventional faith.

I have described my own version of spirituality. I don't argue with those who believe in God. I don't proselytize. Some may think my beliefs incomplete, only half the equation. Others may say that what I have found is no different from a belief in a God, that only my language is different. I really don't care. I am comfortable with it, it works for me, and has given me an inner peace that I would never have believed possible. I am grateful to AA for forcing me to find the spiritual meaning of the Steps. The essential ingredient for my wonderful discovery is quiet—a wordless silence. It may be that I have only rediscovered what the Psalmist knew when he wrote: "Be still and know that I am God."

Bill M.
Creston, California

THE POWER OF GOOD

April 1978

I should like to write a few words of encouragement to you who are unbelievers, as I am. By unbeliever, I mean you who do not take for granted that there is a transcendent God or an ultimate purpose in human existence. You need not alter your convictions or take it lying down when other members of our Fellowship say these are "old ideas," which must be got rid of. I can assure you from my own experience that you can take all the Steps without frustration or hindrance while still maintaining these views.

Let me entreat you, however, not to use this as an excuse to belittle another member's faith. We are not in the business of proving others wrong, or for that matter proving ourselves right. We must at all times keep in mind the maxim "Live and Let Live," and maintain a charitable, unselfish attitude toward all people in and out of the program. Without such an attitude, we are surely courting disaster.

The genius of the Big Book is that it is not dogmatic. Its contents can be tailored to fit just about anyone who keeps an open mind. The chapter "We Agnostics" helps us past our first milestone—the need to form a fundamental idea of a power greater than ourselves. This Power need not be anthropomorphic or substantial. It can remain conceptual only. Its necessary ingredient is that it precipitate a spiritual experience, since the purpose of the program is "to enable you to find a Power greater than yourself which will solve your problem."

This chapter leaves us with several very comforting assurances: that our own conception of God is sufficient; that the realm of the spirit is not exclusive; that we need not accept on faith concepts that are difficult to believe; that we need not be antagonized by others' beliefs. But just what can we use as a Power greater than ourselves?

For myself, I found the answer to this dilemma in *Alcoholics Anonymous Comes of Age*. The Twelve Steps were shown to a Buddhist priest in Thailand. After he read them, he said, "Why, these are fine! Since we as Buddhists don't understand God just as you do, it might be slightly more acceptable if you inserted the word 'good' in your Steps instead of 'God.' Nevertheless, you say in these Steps that it is God as you understand Him. That clears up the point for us. Yes, AAs Twelve Steps will certainly be accepted by the Buddhists around here." It goes on to say, "Alcoholics may be led to believe in God, but none can be forced." If anyone tries to intimidate you by saying you will fail if you don't believe as others do, you might lovingly remind him of this.

So my concept of a higher power is the power of good. The power of good has restored me to sanity; its absence nearly killed me. That part of the Big Book dealing with Step Three emphasizes that I am not to set myself up as a god, deciding what is right and wrong for others. I am to root out selfishness, self-centeredness, and pride. On this basis, I have been able to take a satisfactory inventory and make a verbal admission of my wrongs.

The key words in Step Six are "entirely ready," implying that under no circumstances do we want to hold on to our defects any longer. We want the power of good to push them out and replace them. We no longer put our defects into practice. The firm assurance that good can overcome evil is abundantly clear. That one catches more flies with honey than with vinegar is self-evident. The power of good will drive out our shortcomings if it is sought. Step Seven has now been satisfied. Resentment, pride, selfishness, dishonesty, all summed up in the word "fear," have been rooted up and are being disposed of. The power of good is beginning to take over. We become drawn to make our amends joyfully.

I must now repeat this cycle of Steps as summarized in Step Ten each time I falter. They always work if I take them without balking. Consequently, the power of good can remain with me.

Step Eleven might frustrate you, since it mentions prayer. It need not. Notice that the phrase *as we understood Him* has been reinserted into the Steps at this point, as if to reemphasize the great latitude allowed us regarding our concept of a power greater than ourselves. I have found that reflection on the power of good and how I might use it in my life is a very satisfactory approach to taking this Step. There can be no end to the possibilities of serving my fellows. They are limitless.

By this time, a true spiritual awakening has already manifested itself. In the words of the Big Book, we have undergone a "personality change sufficient to bring about recovery from alcoholism," a "profound alteration" in our reactions to life, and have "tapped an unsuspected inner resource" identified with our own idea of a power greater than ourselves.

Finally, we have a message to carry to others who have suffered as we have, and we hope to be able to transmit it lovingly to our fellows at every opportunity.

A while ago, someone asked me a question, brilliant in its simplicity yet profound in its philosophy. He asked, "Do you think anybody owes you anything?" I hope that my answer will always be, "Definitely not." I expect no rewards, now or ever. I am trying to do what I can to love, today. Can anything else be more important?

Anonymous
Pasadena, California

THROUGH ANOTHER ALCOHOLIC
April 1983

After fifteen and a half years of continuous sobriety, I was in an almost fatal accident and suffered burns over forty-seven percent of my body. Only quick action by two of my three teenage sons, both Boy Scouts with first-aid training, saved my life, by smothering the flames. I must add my sons have all been born and raised during my sobriety.

In the hospital on the night I was burned, my wife was told that there was only about one chance in ten I would survive. That bad news was withheld from me. I was aware, however, of pain of an intensity I did not know could exist. It was with me with every breath I took. I feared for my sanity. Only the pain and nothing else existed. I could not bear to listen to a radio or read a newspaper, since these simple acts could not get through the pain.

Until this event, I had been one of the "resident agnostics" of my San Francisco AA groups. When newcomers entered meetings I attended and expressed concern over whether they could get the program and not believe in God, they were often referred to me on the spot.

Slowly, there in the hospital bed, desperately trying to keep my sanity, I discovered the only relief I could get was the same relief I had when I entered AA. My poor brain could only repeat the clichés I had read or heard (or both) for many years: "Thy will be done;" "This, too, shall pass;" "Not my will, but Thy will." Several times, my conscious brain seemed to want to cut off and end it all, and there would come a blank moment, followed by a chorus from some far-off eternity, getting louder and louder as it came toward me, repeating, "This, too, shall pass."

On the fourth or fifth day, a burn-unit nurse who knew I was in the program came to my door bringing a young man with a badly burned arm. I could under no circumstances concentrate on his features or hear his name. She left us, and the young man began his story, telling me he had a serious drinking problem, had tried AA, and had found that it would not work for him. On the previous night, he had gone to a meeting, left in the middle of it angry, gone to a bar, gotten drunk, become involved in a motorcycle accident, and been badly burned.

My thoughts when the nurse introduced Pat (that was his name) had been the usual—"Poor little burned me. Why can't they leave me alone?"—until Pat started to tell me about his problem. He said he could already admit he was an alcoholic, so we talked about surrender. We had a lively discussion on the absolute necessity of a higher power to help us one moment at a time.

I have no idea how long we talked, but sometime during the conversation, I became aware that the pain was gone! It stopped entirely until Pat left my bedside, when it resumed in all its intensity. Immediately, I started to use my newly discovered escape. It was clear that what I had to do to stop hurting was to participate in the lives of others. My beautiful wife, who had been at my bedside from the first, was next. I started talking to her, sharing everything I knew to share. The nurses set up mini-meetings for me from then on, with hospital personnel who were in the program. I learned that all my regular groups, plus others all over the Bay Area, had been praying for me.

The skeptics will say that after all those years of hearing discussions about God, I was ripe to be convinced by any good old-fashioned trauma. It may be that there was fertile ground at last, but I cannot really get too interested in explanations. The spiritual experiences shared with me by other members of AA over the years have always appeared to me to be extremely personal. This experience was most certainly a spiritual one for me and was also extremely personal. I could not miss the message even if I had wanted to do so. There had been a God in my life all along, patiently waiting to show me again and again his grace, his mercy, his beauty. It was as if he had told me, "Now you see who has been running your life since you came to the Fellowship." Through Pat, he had said, "I will give you your life and your sanity through another alcoholic."

If I needed additional proof, it came about a year after the accident, at an AA meeting. A bright young man said, "Do you remember me?" I told him that I honestly could not remember him but his face was vaguely familiar. He said his name was Pat and he was celebrating a year of sobriety. A year before, he said, he had been in a motorcycle accident and had confessed to the nurse as she bandaged him that he had a drinking problem. She told him she wanted him to talk to me. As she led him to my room, he said, she told him, "Don't stay too long. He is dying of his burns."

Pat said he asked himself why in the world a dying man would want to talk to him about his alcoholism. He told me he asked himself that question several times in the next few days.

I have seen and talked to Pat since our second meeting, and I do not think he would buy for one minute my conviction that he was the instrument by which God went about saving my life. Pat still maintains it was I who twelfth-stepped him!

S.R.
San Francisco, California

OUR SPIRITUAL GIFT

July 1982

Along with the joy of participating in the God-given program of AA, there is often, for me, a deep sense of sadness. This sadness is attributable to my observation that many members struggle and have great difficulty in finding the spiritual part of the program. I think it is a fair statement that those who do experience a spiritual awakening attain a type of sobriety guaranteed by the program. Additionally, it also appears quite clear that the deeper the spiritual experience, the greater the strength of the person's sobriety.

Conversely, what also becomes clear, after many twenty-four hours in AA, is that those who slip or are dangerously close to doing so invariably appear to have forgotten that our disease is threefold; consciously or subconsciously, they have avoided or ignored the spiritual part of our illness.

AA, in its great wisdom, has opted to deal gently with this problem. But we members should not overlook the fact that serious damage can sometimes be done by outspoken, strong-willed members who see and present the illness as solely physical and/or mental. While it is indeed both, we had best never forget the very critical spiritual aspects of our disease.

In my opinion, this program is uniquely successful above any other because it allows each member the beautiful freedom to return to—or meet for the first time—the God of his or her understanding. It is my belief also that without God's great work in the rooms of AA, our Fellowship would have been just another "social rehabilitation" program and would have long since gone by the board.

Part of the problem, of course, is a natural reluctance to speak out in group meetings about one's spiritual AA experiences. Frequently, this void allows the adherents to the "two part" approach to dominate a meeting's thought flow. Very often, there results a decidedly negative mood or at least a lack of uplift for the listeners.

But how many times we observe that when a member unashamedly describes the work of God in his or her life since coming to AA, the ice seems to break quickly; similar, uplifting sharing quickly follows, sometimes dramatically changing the character and mood of the entire meeting. Frankly, it is this AA's opinion that we need more of this type of sharing, much more. The knowledge that God has worked through AA should not be hidden, minimized, or allowed to surface only occasionally.

Some might argue that this position is too strong or that its premise takes AA close to a religious posture. God forbid! Could anything more disastrous happen to AA than its members beginning to proclaim one particular sect or faith superior to all others? We assuredly must leave the work that God has begun in the rooms of AA to his divine plan, trusting only in the believers knowledge that once help is asked, it will be unequivocally given.

Let us who believe in God therefore boldly and often step forward and share with our suffering fellow members the majestic spiritual work started in our lives through the marvelous AA program. To do less is to minimize the gift we have been given and perhaps to deprive spiritually searching sufferers of the opportunity to come to the God of their understanding and enjoy the fruits of long-term serenity.

Anonymous
Suffern, New York

PRACTICE BUT DON'T PREACH
April 1994

Bill W. warned of the spiritual pride that would delude us into thinking we had a direct pipeline with our Higher Power: "In AA's first years, I all but ruined the whole undertaking with this sort of unconscious arrogance. God as I understood him had to be for everybody. Sometimes my aggression was subtle and sometimes it was crude. But either way it was damaging—perhaps fatally so—to numbers of nonbelievers." Bill reminded us (and me too) that "we ourselves need to practice what we preach—and forget the 'preaching,' too."

I need to be reminded constantly that I don't have all the answers just because I consider myself spiritually fit, and that the greatest example of false pride and self-righteousness is to claim, I have the answers! That is what divides us from the cults and religions: No one person speaks for the Fellowship; each member can have a power greater than themselves or not; and the only requirement for membership is a desire to stop drinking. There is no requirement for anyone to believe as I do. We are each allowed to accept or reject what we wish—and that is the great power and beauty and attraction of this program.

In a 1940 letter, Bill W. stated that "we make no religious requirement of anyone.... In such an atmosphere the orthodox, the unorthodox, and the unbeliever mix happily and usefully together. An opportunity for spiritual growth is open to all." Everyone contributes in this unique and special Fellowship. We are guided by principles greater than each person which protect the sanctity of each of us and allow us to come together to do what we could not do alone. We understand, as Bill W. eventually did, that each person's theology has to be his own quest.

Today I've learned tolerance and understanding of those who have an orthodox belief in the cosmos; some need a more structured belief system than others. I've learned to forgive those who turn meetings into testimonials and remind me of my old church days. I try to not judge those who judge me for not having a Higher Power called God, or because I don't pray the Lord's Prayer at the end of a meeting. I think it's in conflict with the Sixth Tradition of our Fellowship. The Lord's Prayer comes from the Bible, and if that ain't endorsing Christianity, I don't know what is. I'm just grateful I don't retaliate and end a group with a Buddhist chant.

This is a spiritual, not a religious program. Let's keep it that way. I won't force my beliefs on you if you don't force yours on me. Say what you want, and so will I with the help of my Higher Power whom I choose not to call God, and together we'll stay sober one day at a time.

Eddie B.
Ahwahnee, California

THE KINGDOM WITHIN
May 1989

By the grace of God, I haven't found it necessary to take that first drink since Christmas morning 1983. For this I owe the program and the Fellowship of Alcoholics Anonymous. I belong to the world's best home group; sponsor people and am sponsored; have been active in general service as a GSR (general service representative) and DCM (district committee member); and attend five or six meetings a week. These meetings, like the ones in other states I've lived in, have opened my eyes spiritually and deepened my trust in God as I understand him. The only problem, for what is apparently a sizable majority of AA members I know, is that God as I understand him is a loving Christian God—and that seems to make many of my AA friends uneasy!

Before you get the wrong idea, I do not use the meetings I attend or my sponsorship opportunities as occasions for "Bible thumping." When I share, I try to convey my experience, strength, and hope in a way that will be of the most benefit to the most people—including the atheist or agnostic newcomer whose teeth are still chattering. I believe our Third Tradition means what it says: "The only requirement for membership is a desire to stop drinking." My own sponsor, a Christian, was an agnostic his first three years in AA—and he's been sober sixteen years now. I respect the right of other AAs to believe in the Higher Power of their own choice, even if that's only the group. As our co-founder says in *As Bill Sees It*, "Honesty with ourselves and others gets us sober, but it is tolerance that keeps us that way."

My question, however, is simple. Are we getting a narrow, distorted idea of tolerance? When the newcomer says he or she has just made a coffee table a higher power, we nod our heads approvingly and murmur that it's perfectly fine with us. Or we'll hear people say they have no idea who or what God is and then say they're comfortable with that. Again we say that's perfectly fine with us. But let someone dare mention Jesus Christ at an AA meeting, and see how fast some chairpersons intervene. Or wait for the awkward silence, followed by nervous putdown of churches. This has happened more than once at meetings I've attended in several states. Is this uneasiness really in the spirit of Step Eleven, where it's suggested that we try to improve our conscious contact with God as we understand him? Are vague notions of God somehow considered superior to specific beliefs? What about "contempt prior to investigation"?

Page 28 of the Big Book, our basic AA textbook, has this to say on the subject: "We think it no concern of ours what religious bodies our members identify themselves with as individuals. This should be an entirely personal affair which each one decides for himself in the light of past associations, or his present choice. Not all of us join religious bodies, but most of

On Religion and Spirituality   *May 1985*

Early in my sobriety, I used to confuse my own Christian religion with the spirituality of Alcoholics Anonymous. From time to time, I still experience some trouble distinguishing the two of 'em.

But I've studied the Steps and Traditions pretty well since I came into AA in a crummy boardinghouse a few twenty-four hours ago. It's a rare AA meeting where I will openly discuss the Christian heritage or the Psalms I now hold privately so dear to me. I don't think that my own religion is any other alcoholic's concern but mine and my AA sponsor's. I once told a person who spoke a bit too openly of her religion at a meeting that "AA isn't Christianity!" After a while she, too, started to mellow out.

M.T.

Cotati, California

us favor such memberships." *Most* of us favor such memberships! Could that statement, true for the first 100 or so members involved in writing the Big Book, be made today? Do we walk that walk, or even talk it? Does the change have anything to do with why AA, in the opinion of long-timers I've talked with, is more of a revolving door than it used to be?

Underscoring their point, the Big Book's authors give this Eleventh Step guidance on page 87: "There are many helpful books also. Suggestions about these may be obtained from one's priest, minister, or rabbi. Be quick to see where religious people are right. Make use of what they offer." Other AA literature—including the "Twelve and Twelve," *AA Comes of Age*, and the pamphlet for clergy members—also praises organized religion. What happened to "being friendly with our friends"—ministers like Sam Shoemaker and Ed Dowling, who were among Bill W.'s spiritual advisers?

By this time, you're probably thinking to yourself that I'm some sort of "Mr. Church." Actually, I devote considerably more time to my AA life than to my formal church life. This, I believe, falls into the category of "First Things First." Although I follow the "Twelve and Twelve's" advice and have brought "new purpose and devotion to the religion of our [my] choice," I clearly remember that two, pre-AA dry years in a church did not, ultimately, keep me sober—and that on Christmas Eve five years ago, I was too drunk to find my way inside the church where I had driven to worship. The next day I hit bottom on a hospital bed.

AA has been my God's chosen instrument in helping me, one slow but increasingly joyful day at a time, to find my way inside—not only inside the church of my choice, with a newfound "faith that works," but more importantly, inside myself. There, as the Big Book notes on page 55, is where "we found the Great Reality deep down within us. In the last analysis it is only there that he may be found." Christ—one-third of my Higher Power, along with the Father and Spirit, all mentioned in the Big Book—said it even more simply: "The kingdom of God is within you" (Luke 17:21).

Having said that, I do not feel the need to apologize—ever—for the God of my understanding. I happen to believe that the God of my understanding is God. Nor do I feel a need to arbitrarily impose that God on you. The last time I checked, though, AA was a place where we share. I don't feel threatened when fellow AAs share that for whatever reasons, they prefer not to give thanks to the God of their understanding, if they have one, in a formal setting. I hope no one else feels threatened when I share with you that following Christ, both in and out of a house of worship, has deepened the quality of my sobriety and that a church is a good place to give thanks for the most priceless gift of my life on earth—the sobriety that God has given me through Alcoholics Anonymous.

John M.
Lexington, Kentucky

The Person I Am

December 1991

I was raised in an orthodox Jewish family with strong religious traditions, but I relinquished my faith about the time that I relinquished everything else as my disease progressed. I remember including my religion as one of the resentments on my first Fourth Step list.

I made a brief attempt at practicing my religion in early sobriety but primarily explored other spiritual paths for a few years. I practiced Christianity for a few years until I had what I consider another spiritual experience. I believe my Higher Power answered the Seventh Step in regard to my longstanding resentment of Judaism. One day, I suddenly understood that I resented certain individuals associated with my religion, not the religion itself. More importantly, I also realized that I had been feeling the shame of being "different" and "inferior" because of my religious affiliation. I think I had been turning this "shame" into "blame." With this clarity, I was relieved of my resentment and shame. I began practicing Judaism with enjoyment and a greater appreciation, thanks to AA principles. What I have experienced is joy in being the person I am, instead of trying to run away from myself. This is growth for me.

Although the Lord's Prayer, shared at most meetings in my area, is derived from Christianity, I have not taken offense at it. It helped save my life when I was willing to grasp anything to maintain sobriety. I incorporated it early in my program as an evening prayer and still use it on a daily basis. I do not think it conflicts with my religious beliefs which rest on the concept of a single deity. I frequently hear at meetings about people praying on their knees. This appears to be stressed for humility purposes. As a child, I was taught that this practice conflicts with traditional Judaic beliefs and customs. I always felt uncomfortable doing it and currently do not pray on my knees. However, there are Jewish customs of prayer available to me which symbolize the same thing: humility before my Higher Power. These rituals had no personal meaning to me before I learned what humility was in AA. I also have realized that my arrogance has prevented me from accepting and utilizing various religious "tools" and beliefs.

I have experienced a unique acceptance by other recovering alcoholics that I have not experienced anywhere else. Religious differences have not interfered with the hand of AA being there for me during my six-and-a-half years in the program. Likewise, I have found an unusual amount of religious tolerance in AA, though it is rarely discussed. The bond of recovery from alcoholism appears to overshadow other differences. For me, religion is no exception.

Although I am not devout in the practice of Judaism, I try to attend synagogue weekly, utilizing the time as disciplined devotion to my Higher Power. This has been beneficial to my Eleventh Step practice. I also learned more about spiritual principles and developed a greater sense of fellowship. It feels satisfying to be a part of the Jewish community and culture once again, just as it feels good to be a part of the general community as a contributing member of society. What a turnaround! I may have a different religion than most AAs and most Americans, but I belong as I realize we are all different and unique. As my sponsor would say: "Isn't that wonderful?"

Richard H.
Tucson, Arizona

LISTENING FOR THE REALITY

April 1991

When the twelfth-stepper who took me to my first meeting arrived, I told her of my atheism and of my fear that maybe AA wasn't the answer for me. She said that AA's teachings are suggested, and the only requirement was a desire to stop drinking. She told me I could believe or disbelieve; I could accept or reject; I could find my own philosophy and make my own decisions. But above all, I could stay sober if I didn't drink and worked toward changing my behavior and the attitudes that kept me a drunk.

I did not drink again, I have gradually changed, and the reward has been almost nineteen years of sobriety in AA. I am still an atheist. Except for some condescension ("What a shame you don't believe") or some assurances that I would one day find God, my atheism has been met with tolerance.

Non-believing members from other places tell me a far different story. They describe being told that they must learn to believe in God or they cannot get sober. They tell about sponsors who quote the Big Book, saying that the way to work AA is prescribed and includes God. They are told to get with the program as written or they are doomed to drink again. Their sponsors say, "Pray and act as if you believe." These non-believers say that those experiences have placed a wall between them and AA and they don't know what to do about it.

I don't have the great conflict with philosophy that these people describe to me. The reception I got was the key, perhaps. I was welcomed by someone who told me that AA could work for me. I heard no prediction that I would fail unless I found God. The past few years I have gotten some further understanding of how and why AA has worked for me despite my atheism.

I learned to see my lack of belief in God as an advantage rather than a hindrance to recovery and to working AA's program. The first advantage I saw was in rephrasing some aspects of the program. I looked for the principle of each Step, reworded it in non-religious terms if necessary and used that as a guide for living. Other non-religious members describe similar solutions. What an advantage over taking the words literally! Each translated meaning ends up ideally suited to my individual needs. In fact, those atheists I know with long-term sobriety often have less conflict with accepting life's circumstances than many who are devout believers.

Another advantage is that I have a greater feeling of participation in my life than I would if I believed an outside entity was running it. Part of the reason I came to AA in the first place was because I had felt so out of control and so much a victim of outside influences from which there was no escape. These feelings had left me suicidal. In my interpretation of AA principles, I play a responsible role in my own destiny, not just a bit part.

Often, believers imply that if I don't rely on a Higher Power, then I must automatically assume self-omnipotence. On the contrary, I don't think that I am controlling outside circumstances. I recognize the uncertainty of the future and of others' behavior and I admit my inability to predict or determine all outcomes. I do think, however, that I have some ability to affect outcomes of anything in which I directly participate. I sometimes err in deciding what I can affect and what action is appropriate, but with experience and advice I learn.

Many people who believe, wonder what atheists do when tough times befall us. To whom do we turn if not to God? I turn to friends and reason and experiences of the past. I now think, based on previous events, that the odds are I will get through whatever comes in my life until it ends. Some people say in meetings that "I trust God not to give me more than I can handle." I do not assign all life events to the work of an unseen something or someone who distributes situations (as tests, perhaps) to struggling humans. I accept that some adversities simply occur in normal living and I try to make the best of them. My view of those events which benefit our lives (often called miracles in AA) is similar to my attitude on misfortunes. I think that not all events can be explained with respect to a reason or purpose. They are simply random phenomena—the luck of the draw.

A large percentage of occurrences, however, are the result of cause and effect, and the causes that effect sobriety seem obvious. When I stopped using alcohol, which distorts thoughts and emotions, a healing process began. When I went to meetings, associated with sober, sane people, and incorporated their way of living into my own actions, the logical result was an improved life through sobriety. Recovery is inevitable, not miraculous, under such a course. It would have been a miracle if the chaos of alcoholism had not abated and my life had not improved.

In retrospect, I see there are at least five points that have enabled me to stay in AA as an atheist. 1) I don't defend or explain the reasons for my atheism. I just state what I do to stay sober. 2) I don't attack the beliefs of those who are comfortable with the idea of God. 3) I haven't abandoned AA because of the jargon that muddles the ideas with terms that offend me. 4) I work out translations of ideas so that they are compatible to my thinking. 5) I try to work within AA to show by example that sobriety and atheism are not mutually exclusive. I have a personal commitment to that and I think it helped me not to drink early on and it helps me still.

Especially I try not to trouble myself with the language of the program. Sometimes I am uneasy when people talk about God's will or when they suggest I pray, but I try to tune that part out. Instead I listen for the reality of what they are describing. I keep working on doing what makes sense. After all, sobriety is the real goal of AA principles and Steps, and it is gained by acting as rationally as possible in all situations, whether or not God is in the picture.

June L.
El Granada, California

Under New Management   *June 1982*

Manageable means capable of being handled or controlled. I realize now that most of the problems in my life were a direct result of my attempts to handle my own life, to be in control of my own destiny. I am grateful that today, sober, I can still say my life has "become unmanageable." The Third Step of the AA program tells me that I no longer have to try to manage my own life; I can turn that job over to my Higher Power. Today, I am able to leave the managing to a proven Manager. As long as I remember that my life is unmanageable—not capable of being managed by me—I know that I will remain on solid AA ground.

L.R.
College Park, Maryland

FAITH IS ACTION

May 1977

Recently, I read a newspaper article in which the writer stated that he could not, of course, will himself to believe. For most of my life, I tried to find the "truth" and the "meaning of life." I went from one religion to another. Initially, I would experience the joy of discovery, but ultimately there always came the despair of disenchantment. My soul sickness grew worse, and so did my drinking.

Finally, two and a half years ago, I came to AA, not to find faith but to learn how to live without alcohol. At first, the group was my higher power. Then, slowly, a deeper faith began to develop within me. Today, I have a faith that I never thought possible. But it came about only after I stopped asking so many questions and started taking actions to change my self-centered attitudes.

Today, my faith amounts to faith *that* rather than faith *in*: faith that if I can continue to live according to certain principles, I can lead the best life possible for me. My faith *in* had always been a kinky bag of intellectual non sequiturs, which is just a fancy way of saying it didn't amount to beans.

Today, I believe that faith is as faith does—it's that simple. The basic simplicity of it all still astonishes me. The final justification for my faith lies in the quality of life it produces. Whether I conceive of God as a set of immutable cosmic laws or as an old man with a white robe and matching beard is totally and gloriously irrelevant. All that matters are my values and attitudes and how I act upon them. That I try to do God's will as I understand it is for me the ultimate meaning of life.

I cannot find words adequate to express my gratitude to God and to Alcoholics Anonymous.

H.I.
Culver City, California

The Power To Carry That Out

September 1990

We were together on a retreat—an opportunity to do an annual self-review, part of my working the Tenth Step—when I said to my sponsor: "I am in the worst spiritual state I can remember being in for a long time. All the joy I had in sobriety seems gone. I'm alcohol-free, but so what? I am starting to wonder if all this effort is worth it. This spiritual bottom is even worse than the bottom that brought me to recovery."

We talked for a long while, he questioning and I answering as best I could. Yes, I was going to meetings regularly. Yes, I continued to pray. "But what use is it?" I wailed. "I do not feel as if I'm in touch with God!" Yes, I talked at meetings when called upon, and sometimes volunteered to speak. I called the people in my support network, and continued to help the people I was sponsoring. I still functioned as secretary of one meeting and was even in the process of starting a new meeting. And yes, I stayed in touch with my sponsor. He knew that I did, since he responded to my daily phone calls, sometimes doing no more than listening as I tried to express painful feelings which I often didn't understand and sometimes couldn't even name or describe.

"You are in a lot of pain, and need to do something about it," he said when I was finished. "But it's emotional pain. Your spiritual life is in good shape—in fact, in great shape!" He saw my bewilderment. "You've confused your feelings with your spiritual state," he continued. "When you feel good, you think that all is well spiritually with you, and when you feel bad you think you're spiritually low. Many people in the program seem to think so, too. But if that's right, then you would have been in spiritually great shape when you were loaded and partying and having what you felt was a wonderful time for yourself. But no matter how wonderful you felt at that time, you were in fact in bad spiritual shape. *That* was your spiritual bottom." We talked at length about what he said, and he urged me to work on coming to a deeper awareness of what constitutes spiritual growth and a healthy spiritual state. "Begin with the Big Book," he suggested, and I was not far into it before I began to get an idea of what spiritual growth might mean.

The first sign of "spiritual growth" was accepting things which seemed entirely out of reach. Some pages later, in the discussion of the Tenth Step, mention is made of a new way to deal with selfishness, dishonesty, resentment, and fear: We ask God to remove them, discuss them with someone, and then make immediate amends to those we have harmed. A very simple formula for spiritual maintenance is given: that we "carry the vision of God's will into all of our activities."

Finally, in the discussion of spiritual awakening in the "Twelve and Twelve" Bill W. wrote: "When a man or woman has a spiritual awakening, the most important meaning of it is that he has now become able to do, feel, and believe that which he could not do before on his unaided strength and resources alone. ... In a very real sense he has been transformed, because he has laid hold of a source of strength which, in one way or another, he had hitherto denied himself. He finds himself in possession of a degree of honesty, tolerance, unselfishness, peace of mind, and love of which he had thought himself quite incapable."

I wondered if there was a single word that could put all of this together, that could describe spirituality, a simple description for spiritual growth. As I reflected on all I had read and heard, and on my experience both before and after I started my recovery, it seemed to me that it could all be expressed in the simple idea of "empowerment."

To be spiritual is for me to be empowered. To be empowered means to find the power to do what I could not do before; it also means that I can do in a healthy and healing manner what I might have done before in ways that were unhealthy or which brought suffering to myself or others. This is why the Eleventh Step, more than any other, opens us to God's power and makes it possible for us to do what we could not do before. It is the Step that leads to "sure power and safe guidance from God."

Spirituality for me is not therefore a question of feeling good (though feeling good is a feeling I like a whole lot). Instead, it is a matter of finding from prayer and meditation, from other people, from meetings—in short, from all the "tools of recovery"—the power to do what is good, what is healthy, what brings joy and healing to myself and others. Spirituality is the power to do these things even though I may be in emotional distress; and one way I have of gauging my spiritual strength is seeing how empowered I am to do God's will for me. Spiritual growth means to increase such empowerment;

and I lose spiritual ground when I lose the empowerment I once had.

As my sponsor reminded me, I sometimes felt wonderful when I drank. But despite this feeling, my spiritual state was then at its lowest, since I did not have the power to stop drinking, or the power to see or stop the harm I was doing to myself and to others. Whatever "power" alcohol gave me, it was not the power I now have in recovery, the power to know God's will and to carry it out.

Even when I am feeling at my lowest, the empowerment that is the meaning of spirituality makes it possible for me to work for others and to try and help them. It can give me the courage to take good care of myself—to go to meetings even when I don't think I need a meeting, to speak up when my alcoholism wants to keep my pain to myself, to talk at a gut-honest level to my sponsor and to the people in my group about painful matters I would rather keep hidden. Empowerment makes it possible for me to pray and meditate even when I don't want to do so, even when I don't "feel" connected to my Higher Power, even when I don't feel that any good is coming from these practices.

My spirituality is in good shape when I can do what is healthy and healing. Spirituality is not a state of feelings. It is a state of being, of empowered being.

James C.
West Henrietta, New York

Balancing Act *March 2002*

Emotional balance is very much like balancing on a bicycle—it is more a matter of what I don't do than what I do do. It involves letting go, getting out of my own way, allowing it to happen without trying to make it happen or even knowing how or why it does happen. Watch someone balance on a bike. It looks as if it would be difficult but, in fact, it is a mindless and effortless achievement. Happiness, joy, and freedom are the same, aren't they?

Russ H.
Walnut Creek, California

PARADOX OF POWER

April 1982

For several years before I began my new life in AA, I taught American literature in a university. One of the writers whose work I enjoyed reading and discussing with students was Emily Dickinson. She captured in a few words the peculiar definitions of experience that I had felt but could not articulate.

One of her poems had a special appeal that brought me back to it over and over. It begins: "I can wade Grief/ Whole Pools of it/ I'm used to that/ But the least push of Joy/ Breaks up my feet/ And I tip—drunken."

Those brief lines describe clearly what kept my drinking habits active. I could wade whole pools of grief and depression; over the years, I had psychiatrists to help me through them. I was used to that. But the least push of joy broke up my feet and tipped me, drunken, every time: a vacation, a raise or a promotion, an anniversary, Millard Fillmore's birthday. Those were occasions to drink. Soon, I was finding a reason to turn every day of the year into a festival. When that happens, none of them is special or very festive.

After being around AA for a while, I went back to the poem one day and found an entirely new way of reading it. I had never realized that all my drinking had begun with the carefree moments of celebration and joy, only to end in those desperate years when I had tried to keep up the pleasure and the fun. The program was giving me an understanding of my dependence upon alcohol, and as a fringe benefit, a new reading of a favorite poem.

But that wasn't all. Several lines further on, Dickinson comments that we must guard against those unprotected times of cheer when we are open to hurt and anguish. I then began to grasp the full meaning of two crucial lines: "Power is only Pain—/ Stranded, through Discipline ..."

I had often used that definition of power to start classroom discussions of its possible meaning for students. But now I seemed to be reading it for the first time. It expressed what I was beginning to understand about Alcoholics Anonymous.

Power is a key word in this program, and its importance is underlined repeatedly in the Twelve Steps. We admitted in the beginning that *we were* power*less over alcohol—that our lives had become unmanageable.* Then we *came to believe that a* Power *greater than ourselves could restore us to sanity.* And in the Eleventh Step, we pray *for knowledge of His will for us and the* power *to carry that out.*

I began to see the emphasis this program places upon force and drive. I realized that anyone who regards AA as only the passive giving up of alcohol has not carefully read the Steps. Our continual dependence upon a Higher Power demonstrates further the importance we place upon action and accomplishment.

The source of power, Dickinson adds, is pain. In my AA experience, I have never met a member who has not experienced some degree of pain. I have never met anyone who decided to come into the program on a beautiful morning in spring when everything was going well. Most of us entered on our knees, and the sharing of this mutual pain is a large part of what brings us back to meetings.

"Strand" means to form by twisting together, as in the strands of a rope. So it is implied that the achievement of power comes by way of mixing pain with discipline. And discipline, the word that all of us dread from our years in school, was the part of AA that frightened me most.

In those early days, I hoped that with harsh discipline and self-will, I might be able to stop drinking. I was prepared to sit through meetings holding on to my chair with the grim determination to see this thing through, no matter what. As a child, I had been taught that if I worked hard enough and disciplined myself, I could accomplish whatever goal I set. Maybe that principle would hold true for my desire to stop drinking.

But the members of AA surprised me with a new definition of the term. Instead of holding on, I was told to let go. Instead of using self-control, I was encouraged to turn my will and my life over to God. And at the end of Chapter Six in the Big Book, I read that "we alcoholics are undisciplined. So we let God discipline us in the simple way we have just outlined."

That was a definition I had never heard before. "Letting go" had always meant self-indulgence: polishing off the rest of the bottle, eating the whole cake, sleeping until noon. Now, I heard that letting go meant acquiring discipline. I had to redefine the term in light of what AA members were telling me.

"Power is only Pain—/Stranded, through Discipline ..."

I have been around the program for a few twenty-four hours now, and I'm beginning to understand the meaning of those lines. The renewal of discipline is a process that I must set in motion every day. But I'm learning to wade each pool of grief, to take each painless step of joy, with the power given me through the discipline of Alcoholics Anonymous.

D.H.
Delmar, New York

AWARENESS

September 1974

In his article "The Act of Surrender," Dr. Harry Tiebout was correct, as usual. Surrender and free will are mutually exclusive. There is no way to surrender deliberately. Surrender—admitting, "I'm a drunk"—happens spontaneously. If we try to bring it about, it won't happen.

Awareness usually dawns through a clear recognition of the futility of constantly being painfully jostled about in the world of opposites: drunk-sober, pain-pleasure, success-failure. Futility clamps its icy fingers around our throats until, in total despair, we spontaneously stop fighting. We hit bottom. Surrender into sobriety follows.

Dismissing the past (dead) and the future (nonexistent) and having nothing else, we begin to live now (all that there is). The 24-hour program of AA unfolds, and living now (eternity) brings with it the pure joy of sobriety. Surrender now *is*. We have turned our will and our lives over ...

Awareness of the ever-moving and ever-changing now is the spiritual experience. Our clear, total, uncritical awareness that we are drunks and our spontaneous surrender (which blossoms from intense pain) are the spiritual experience. Each of us understands that experience in his own unique way—God as we understand him.

If we dwell on the past or the future, we put ourselves back into the torture chamber. We stop changing. Boredom, pain, and futility take over again. We have been ... We will be ... We no longer are. The 24-hour program disappears. Anxiety, anger, and a desire for revenge replace the spiritual experience. Awareness and surrender cease. We are on a dry drunk.

Is it the world's fault? Each one of us is his own world. Who else could be? No one. There is nothing bad about who we are. There is nothing good about who we are. "Good" and "bad" are man-made concepts. We simply are who we are. No more, no less. Being aware of the ever-changing truth of what and who we are ("Continued to take personal inventory") and doing so without criticism or commendation is the essence of living in surrender.

All turmoil comes from the deep, nagging feeling that we should be different from what we are. Our minds chatter so noisily! If we could totally accept who and what we are (changing each instant), we would find ourselves moving in the silent immenseness of now.

Look clearly at what you are now. Accept it totally. Neither criticize nor condone what you see. Just look at it and let it alone. From that looking, from that watching, from seeking "through prayer and meditation," grow a spiritual freshness, a spiritual newness, and a spiritual innocence beyond the terror of the world of opposites. Opposites now meet and fuse. Self-absorption is replaced by total, glorious awareness of the ever-moving now, by a constantly renewed spiritual experience.

Demands, hopes, yearnings, and desires tie us to the static horror and the utter futility of the forever departed past and the never-arriving future. To want nothing—to know that we cannot *make* anything happen—brings inner and outer joy, total fulfillment. The earth and the heavens and ourselves become one, and in this state of spontaneous surrender, we discover the deep, spiritual constancy in everyday living that we were looking for all along.

Dr. Earle M.
Vietnam

GRATITUDE TREE

December 1981

I called my friend one summer night with a big problem. AAs had been telling me, "Unload and share when something bothers you," and I had my person picked for the job. Just listening to this friend's wisdom at the meetings during those early sober weeks had convinced me that he could "fix" anything—he had it all together. But he didn't even let me come to the end of my woes. He interrupted me, saying, "You should see my Christmas tree. It's the most beautiful tree you've ever seen. You should really come over and look at it sometime. I just turned on all the lights."

Was this guy crazy? Maybe he belonged to a special religious group that celebrated Christmas in the summer. Here it was the middle of summer, and he still had his Christmas tree up. And all the while, I'd been thinking he was one of the wellest persons I'd met in the Fellowship.

Pretty frustrating! There I was, all tied up in a knot because I had this problem I'd been told to share with another AA member, and I couldn't wait to unload the garbage. And the person I'd carefully selected for that privilege was babbling on about his beautiful Christmas tree. "Let me tell you about some of the trimmings on it," he said. And he did:

"There's Mary's pretty ribbon from her second-anniversary corsage, and Joe gave me a pretty card for one of my anniversaries, and I put that on a string and hung it on a branch. And a pretty young lady gave me a silk rose, which I stuck in to the center of the tree. On top of the tree is a little angel from a Christmas present I received from Anne. She had a hard time getting the program and had to work through some difficult stuff, but she stuck with it. She's sober today." On and on he went, telling me about his sober friends who had contributed to the trimmings of his beautiful Christmas tree—among them, a little toy I had given him. It was just a small tree on a table in the corner of his room, he said, but by the time he got finished telling me about all the trimmings on his tree, its form in my own mind grew into the most gigantic and, yes, the most beautiful Christmas tree I had ever in all my life seen.

Precious sober years have passed, and I have accumulated my own Christmas tree trimmings, contributed by all the friends I have been privileged to meet on the AA road to happy sobriety. I have my own tree of gratitude and can turn on all its lights anytime, any season, celebrating and sharing the miraculous gift of life, of sobriety, with you.

L.N.
New York, New York

WHY GOD SAYS NO

February 1958

The first real awareness, for most of us, of the tremendous potential continuing assistance from a Higher Power came when we realized that something beyond ourselves was removing the baffling compulsion to drink. As practical results developed, we began to respect the practical side of a spiritual life. Later we learned that God's help is not limited to our drinking problem alone, but extends into all phases of our lives.

And right there a lot of us begin to get into a certain kind of trouble.

Somehow, since we got an immediate answer for our drinking, we conclude that similar answers should come immediately—for anything else that might be disturbing us at the moment. We learn that with God all things are possible, and therefore why should we have to be disappointed at all?

So we offer up prayers for assistance, and our requirements may be as lengthy as a child's list to Santa Claus. But God doesn't meet our demands, so we become a little miffed. And our agitation is likely to increase when we see others getting many of the advantages we'd like to have. Worse yet, we see people who aren't on a "spiritual basis" at all enjoying an outpouring of luck in all directions ... a state of affairs that can lead us into blind alleys of self-pity and envy, feeling that God has cheated us.

After all, we say to ourselves (and to the Higher Power who seems to be denying us), aren't we trying to lead good lives? We're doing our best to be moral, kind, courteous, helpful, and honest. Shouldn't good things come our way, even material things? (We conveniently avoid the admission that we are trying to lead good lives only because alcohol had us trapped, backed into a corner, with no alternative except to reach out desperately for AA.) We may also have been misled by some of the current books on positive thinking, many of which contain glowing accounts of how countless perplexing problems were solved simply through spending a few minutes each day in prayer and meditation.

But first, shouldn't we consider the real meaning of Steps Three and Eleven in the AA program? In these Steps, we commit ourselves to God's will—whatever it is and regardless of the consequences. Our own plans may seem worthy, and our own immediate desires may be modest, but even these may somehow conflict with the plans God has for us. It may be that in his strategy, the ultimate victory hinges on losing, not winning, some of the battles along the way. Today's disappointment, viewed six months hence, may turn out to be one of the best breaks we ever got. And at the proper time, our own grateful hindsight will let us see the workings of God's unerring foresight.

AA's early history carries some good object lessons revealing how this principle works. At one time Bill W. and several other AA pioneers decided to solicit wealthy people for contributions to the struggling movement. When they weren't able to raise a single dime, they must have wondered if God hadn't forgotten the desperate needs of the embryo society. Yet, as it later turned out, this experience helped teach AA to be self-supporting. It certainly must have been one of his mysterious ways of performing wonders.

Or, take the example of Bill's business reversals in Akron, just before he met Dr. Bob. Why should God let a man sustain a defeat like that, especially a man who had known many successive defeats and was doing his level best to live a new kind of life? No considerate person in his right mind would permit a man to get in a situation like that. But God permitted it, and in groping for a way out of the mess, Bill fell back on his spiritual sources and the soul-restoring technique of helping others. Today we beneficiaries of AA's redemptive power can see that this supposed adversity was really God's heavy hand molding a magnificent movement into being.

But let's suppose, just for illustration, that God did give us immediate answers completely in accordance with our wishes, a blank check to do and have anything we want. How well would any of us come out on a deal like that? Since selfishness is a primary defect of alcoholics, and most of us are experts in using people and circumstances to feather our own nests, wouldn't we do the same thing to him? We would bombard him with unlimited demands, ranging from material gains to dictatorial control over the lives of others.

Since we're an impatient breed, we'd use his help to run everyone else off the road, although we'd smugly rationalize it by saying we were merely receiving what was due us. We would gloat over business successes, romantic conquests, prestige, and other "breaks"—giving little thought to the unpleasant suggestion that our gains might be defeats for somebody else. Yes, we would manipulate God as spoiled children make demands on foolish and indulgent parents.

But God is neither foolish nor indulgent, and has the wisdom to say NO. And his answers are always for our own highest good. None of this is to say that God's answers must always be "no" ... for all of us have known numerous times when the answer was an immediate "yes." But these requests were gratified because they were right, and were undoubtedly made in a spirit of humility and unselfishness.

Some AAs seem to achieve beautiful harmony almost immediately when they expose themselves to God's will. They develop such profound spiritual insight that they receive answers to almost all their prayers. The rest of us admire their serenity and wisdom, but continue trying to inveigle God into doing things our way. Then we start getting the true realization, perhaps, when we too examine the course of our lives and discover God's unerring wisdom in times past, when he has had to listen and shake his head.

Anonymous
Jackson, Michigan

Patience   *June 1980*

Not until I became aware that God's delay is not necessarily God's denial of prayer, was I willing to let a Power greater than myself determine how and when I was to receive the things I truly needed, rather than the things for which I howled.

C.C.
North Hollywood, California

MORE THAN I CAN HANDLE

April 2000

"God never gives you more than you can handle" proclaims an AA slogan. For me, that slogan is misleading and is contradicted by my spiritual growth in the program.

God has given me more than I could handle—several times. And I thank God that I couldn't handle those situations, because my inability to do so left me only one refuge, to turn to my Higher Power with the simple plea, "Thy will, not mine, be done."

Being forced to turn to my Higher Power at these desperate times has enabled me to put aside many of my lifelong compulsions to control and manage, allowing me to learn to turn to my Higher Power rather than to one more control scheme.

With four years' sobriety, I couldn't handle a situation in which a severe asthma attack left me unconscious and put me in the hospital in Colorado Springs, Colorado. The last thing I remember before I lost consciousness was saying "Thy will, not mine, be done." The next thing I remember was waking up in a hospital bed in time to see a magnificent sunrise over Colorado's Eastern Plains.

I remember not being able to handle being a hit-and-run pedestrian victim, waking up in restraints in a hospital bed five days after I was run down on a nighttime walk. I couldn't handle the burst of emotions that the accident had released in me. I was forced to admit my powerlessness and to turn to my Higher Power as I began struggling toward emotional sobriety after over seven years of physical sobriety in Alcoholics Anonymous.

A few years after my accident, I couldn't handle my first marriage ending, at my then-wife's request, and I couldn't handle my son's slide into heroin addiction. My inability to handle these situations led me to participation in Al-Anon and to psychotherapy, two tools necessary for me to fulfill AA's promises and to emerge "happy, joyous and free."

And I have. My second marriage, the happiest event of my life, is two years old, and my wife and I have returned to Santa Barbara, California, our home, after a sojourn in the Midwest that was a powerful learning experience.

That experience taught me once again that when God gives me something I can't handle, I can take the next right step each day, asking God for the courage to change the things I can. And, as always, I must end my Serenity Prayer as it does in the Third Step of the "Twelve and Twelve," with "Thy will, not mine, be done."

John M.
Santa Barbara, California

THESE TWENTY-FIVE WORDS ...
April 1979

The Serenity Prayer has always played an important role in my recovery process, but only lately have I recognized the true value within these twenty-five words. The more I say it, read it, hear it—the more profoundly I feel its effectiveness as it relates to the handling of my one-day-at-a-time living experiences.

If I refuse to accept what I'm powerless to change, I am negating the opportunity that God gives me to do so. He always grants me the serenity that goes hand in hand with the acceptance of that which I am incapable of changing. However, the key question I must ask myself is: "Am I willing to accept this serenity that he so graciously offers me?" I must remind myself of this whenever I think I have accepted something and then discover that my serenity is nil.

If I am sincerely trying to live according to the guidance of our AA principles, I will recognize that I have chosen not to accept the unchangeable, but only to tolerate it. To merely tolerate a situation or a person's shortcomings is to settle for a half measure. And there is the reason for my serenity deficit.

As for the second part of the prayer, "the courage to change" certain circumstances comes from inner strength—my abundant source of supply that my Higher Power constantly nourishes. But I must choose to draw upon his strength. It is always there—I need only be willing to use it.

The third part, "wisdom to know the difference," is the divine key to acceptance and courage. For me, this wisdom is revealed through the practice of our Eleventh Step, *Sought through prayer and meditation to improve our conscious contact with God as we understood Him, praying only for knowledge of His will for us and the power to carry that out.*

Because this is an honest program, I must admit that I fall short many times in applying this interpretation of the Serenity Prayer. I realize I am still growing emotionally and spiritually. After several years of sobriety through the grace of God and AA, I am only beginning to acknowledge the God-power within me.

But by simply expressing my personal concept of this traditional and meaningful prayer, I am enabled to view with more clarity where I am

A Program of Action   *March 1989*

Countless numbers of people have told me they recite the Serenity Prayer as a tool for engendering an attitude of turning it over. I now regard the statements in that prayer, except for the part about asking it to be a grant from God, as a description of a completely sensible way to approach life. Even atheists can learn to recognize the futility of nonacceptance, the value of risking changes, and the way to tell the difference between things we can affect and those we can't. When I begin to worry about things I can do nothing about, I tell myself to "accept what you can't change." Often I have used the ideas in the Serenity Prayer as a trigger for relinquishing my need to control and as a reminder to take action when some discontentment can be remedied.

I find I actually do very little that is different from the actions of those who believe in God. I just think about the actions in a different way. The words of the Serenity Prayer are a concise way to tell myself to do what makes sense because sane and sensible action has a track record of success. When I make a decision to quit trying to control, I do not expect anyone or anything will oversee events and take care of me. I make the decision because it is the reasonable action to take. I get relief from anxieties and fears the same way the believers do—I stop concentrating on what dismays me and direct my attention to activities that are productive.

J.L.

El Granada, California

today and where I was yesterday. Tomorrow is yet to be, but should God grant me another day, then hope, courage, and strength, through the implementation of the Twelve Steps and the Serenity Prayer, will be sufficiently provided to meet my every need. This I believe.

L.T.
St. Petersburg, Florida

BE STILL AND LISTEN

December 1975

Ships are my thing. I've loved them for a lot of years. I've cruised in them while in the throes of alcoholic insanity—and also with the comfort of sobriety, the AA program, and a loving God as I think I understand him.

Recently, I was given a writing assignment that took me around the Pacific on one of my favorite ships. A seven-week cruise! People say this sounds like plush work. It was. But, as for all good things, a degree of responsibility was the price. Prior to sailing, I found myself uptight. I had commitments that seemed beyond me. I allowed myself to feel pressure. By the time we sailed from Los Angeles, I was a nervous wreck. Upon arrival in Honolulu five days later, I was tempted to scuttle the project, jump ship, and fly to the security of my home group.

Instead, I attended a meeting at a club for AAs, located at Aloha Tower, not more than a couple of hundred feet from the bow of my ship. We sailed directly after the meeting. I waved farewell from the ship to the new friends just met at the clubhouse. They had quieted me, helped me bring rusty tools from the AA storehouse. The white liner passed the reef, bound for exotic-sounding places like Tahiti, New Zealand, Australia, Fiji, and Samoa. Instinctively, I knew the program would supply my needs.

Late that evening, I was alone on the upper deck. Under tropical stars, gentle trade winds tickled my senses. I reviewed the meeting, Chapter Five, and the Twelve Steps. And that night I commenced a format that worked fantastically throughout my "Forty-Three Days Before the Mast" efforts.

Here's how it worked. When my evening was done, I discarded my cruise finery, donned comfortable deck clothes, and went topside to practice what was to become a rewarding ritual. The deck was large, usually mine alone at that late hour. I would look at the starlit heavens and ocean surrounding me, and feel awed with the wonder of the universe. It was simple to say the Lord's Prayer into night breezes. As I walked, I spoke aloud the words of the first part of Chapter Five, including the Twelve Steps. Thus, character defects that I could not allow to fester would be revealed, and I was shown a way to handle them.

After an hour of this meditation, I sat quietly on a bench to relax and be still. I called this my listening period. It was here that I received "messages from topside." When whatever fit the occasion came into my mind, I was careful to think over and repeat the words that came through. Then I would go directly to my room to record them. These are the notes I share now.

Lack of confidence made me wonder whether I was capable of achieving that which I had set out to do. The first message received was: "You do your best—I'll do the rest." Nights later, when I was wondering whether I had really done my best, another answer came: "Don't analyze the results of your best—let me be the judge."

Writers are often treated as VIPs aboard ship. This can be devastating to an alcoholic ego. I have to be very alert against ego trips. And a cruise ship on a long voyage can become a tight floating community. Keeping principles before personalities can be difficult. On occasions like these,

Listen for the Still, Small Voice   *January 1978*

It is often hard to find the time to be solitary and listen for the still, small voice that tells you what to do and how to do it. It takes a certain amount of practice to be aware of this prodding, which comes from the Higher Power, and I am still practicing. I know I'll never be perfect at it, but there have been times when I feel I am gaining a deep and permanent relationship with him. I intend to continue to seek solitude at times, but I never want to be lonely. I had enough of that when I was drinking.

F.T.
Missouri

some of the messages fed were: "Look for me in others," "Be quiet, gentle, kind, tolerant—you are not the center of the universe," "Don't take yourself so seriously," and "Keep your heart open for love—do not be afraid."

Self-doubt would creep in from time to time. The answers: "Trust me—I hear you" and "I will give you every assistance you need."

Another evening, I found that because I am, by nature, a long-winded character, I was praying for everyone I could think of—not simple prayers, but prayers complicated with many suggestions for whoever was on my mind. Another answer: "When you put a soul in your heart, you've already prayed for him—and I hear you."

Life on this luxurious ship continued to all the ports, through all the days and nights. The other passengers did their thing: mostly drinking, living it up, and having a ball. I did mine: had fun, worked, and accomplished what I had set out to do.

In the beginning, forty-three days stretched ahead like eternity. Then my messages from topside made them pass quickly and successfully. But the real beginning was twelve years ago, when AAs opened their hearts and shared their tools. And the most exciting thing is: *This* journey isn't over yet.

Henry A.
Lompoc, California

TUNING IN TO THE SPIRIT
June 1986

After putting it off until there was no other viable solution to the problem, I came into AA in April 1980. I know today that each of us recovers differently, and for me a spiritual recovery was apparently the thing to be handled first. I, of course, didn't know that, nor did I engineer it. My Higher Power did.

I found myself instantly attracted to the Third and Eleventh Steps, and began to really think about and attempt to practice the suggestions contained in these Steps. But as I attempted to return to prayer, I found myself feeling awkward, empty, unable even to concentrate on what I was doing;

unable to quiet the noises in my head of a thousand yesterdays and to-morrows; unable to stay in the now even for a few minutes. This realiza-tion led me to explore the possibility of using meditation to "get things quiet up there," and I picked up two paperbacks, which became my guide for the first two years. I began to meditate a lot—whenever I could find a few minutes to sit and the will power to clear my mind of all thoughts—just sitting in the silence and trusting what others through the ages have said: "Clear your mind of your thoughts, and God's thoughts will have room to enter."

Two years later I found myself living in New York, very much im-pressed with the efficiency of meditation as a tool for relieving myself of worry, depression, anxiety and other negative emotions which I had rec-ognized as being a large part of that which I was. I entered a Zen center, studied meditation there, and went on several of their retreats. I gained a better understanding of the dynamics of meditation as a pathway for the entrance of that reality which most people call God. After Zen, I studied Yoga, and commenced to be more aware of the diverse groups of individu-als the world over, all striving for a better communion with a higher source of belief, understanding, love, etc. Meditation had become, for me, the main focus of my life. I felt that AA gave me right thinking, stability, right action; and meditation gave me answers to my soul's questions of peace, love, and charity.

When I shared in AA meetings, I frequently mentioned meditation, and people would come up to me afterward with questions about how they might learn to meditate, or what I might suggest in the way of read-ing material or places to study. Also, when I attended Third and Eleventh Step meetings, I always wondered why the group talked about prayer and meditation rather than actually doing it together and then sharing that experience. All this eventually led me to believe that there were a sufficient number of AA members interested in meditation, but not sure how to pro-ceed with that interest, that an active meditation workshop founded on the Eleventh Step would serve a worthwhile need.

Along with a co-chairperson, I opened the first meeting in November 1984. We began by reading the Preamble, welcoming newcomers, and then reciting the Eleventh Step: *Sought through prayer and meditation to improve our conscious contact with God as we understood Him, praying only for knowledge of His will for us and the power to carry that out.* We then said that we would meditate, each in his own way, for half an hour, and then share round-robin for the following hour. We decided to add a very brief "suggestions for entering meditation" statement for the benefit of those who had never tried getting quiet and sitting in the silence. That statement went something like this: "For those of you who have never tried meditation, we suggest you sit comfortably in your chair; close your eyes and try to release any thoughts which might be running through your mind. Imagine yourself as a television set tuned to a blank channel. This channel is being left blank so that God may tune in to it and contact you through your thought system, your intuition, your feelings, or whatever. If you find it difficult to quiet your thoughts and think of nothing, then we suggest you dwell on your incoming and outflowing breath, just mentally watching it enter and leave your body; and, if it helps, mentally count those inhalations and exhalations up to ten—then backward down to one. Your mind will definitely quiet down after a few minutes."

What Is Meditation? *November 1999*

In my own case, I can remember a time when nothing was happening during my daily meditations. There were no special sights or sounds, no feelings of elation. Nothing is all that happened. During the day, however, a wonderful process was taking place in my mind. As I was busy working or driving the car, repressed memories began to come to the surface. These memories were of times which earlier had caused great guilt and remorse, the sort of thoughts that could—and did—contribute to my having to drink to suppress them. Now, after my meditations, these horrid times of my life came into my consciousness fully healed and forgiven! It was as if I could see all of these events of the past from a totally new perspective, a new point of view which now contained grace and forgiveness. God seemed to be doing for me what I could not do for myself.

Sim G.
Pittsburgh, Pennsylvania

The meetings were a great success from the very first. People were generally amazed that they could actually sit quietly and experience, without any prior practice, a sense of tremendous peace and comfort. Afterward we shared either about our experiences during the meditation or, of course, anything at all pertaining to our AA experience.

The enthusiasm and comments over having one more tool in the program have been considerable. Participants have often said that they are grateful they can now find within the AA context a place to practice their meditation which does not require any type of allegiance to a particular guru or to an unfamiliar theological belief system. This is consistent, of course, with AAs wish and suggestion that every member seek God or a higher power, as they understand it.

Other comments have focused on the good feelings of oneness and safety that arise from doing a new thing together in a group with one's peers. Members who have become regulars to our Thursday night group often say that meditation has become a regular or indispensable part of their daily routine, and that it has brought peace and a new insight to their lives. Others report that they believe they have a form of contact with a Higher Power now that they did not have before.

I am grateful to that Higher Power, which I call God, for leading me to where I am today. In five years' time, the Big Book promises have come true for me and I have tried to dedicate my life, one day at a time, to serving the power that now guides my life and destiny.

J.M.
New York, New York

THE BUTT GUY

May 2003

I had a young sponsor once. He was a real butt kicker. Somehow or other, he got the idea that I was rather "uppity," over-intellectualized, proud, rebellious and, of all things, defiant.

He was deeply involved in area service work and told me all about the great meetings, the lunches, the laughter, and the fellowship. He had some ambitions too. He knew exactly what steps to take to get to be delegate, which sounded real important, like being local emperor for a couple of years. He kept putting out the bait until I asked him when I could go with him. He told me he would let me know when I was ready. Meanwhile, I should just do what I was told.

Finally, after months of my being "good"—that is, willing, humble, and obedient—he pulled me aside and told me that there was a service job opening up that would be just right for me. I was enthralled. I saw pictures of myself running up the ladder of AA success—after him, of course.

It turned out the service job was the butt detail. The bank we met in didn't allow smoking and complained when any cigarette stubs were left on the ground. So the butt guy (it was always a guy) had to put out a few number 10 cans before the meeting and check around during the break and after the meeting to make sure all the stubs were in the cans. Then he would empty the cans, wash them out so they wouldn't stink, and put them away in plastic bags. That was my job.

This was a Sunday Night Young People's meeting, mind you. My sponsor had me meet him there. I must admit, I might have been just a little bit inclined to pontificate once in a while from the vast stored up wisdom of my many years and graduate studies. I didn't take to the job too kindly. I downright resented it. I was filled with defiance inside, but knew that if he saw it, things could and would get worse.

The job was most difficult on rainy nights, when puddles formed in the parking lot. Experience taught me that wet butts in puddles were better retrieved right away. The longer they soaked, the more they disintegrated and the harder they were to pick up. So I tried to be on hand for quick rescue service. But some of the young characters would still flip a butt into a puddle and say: "There's one for Jim." The kids would laugh, and I would burn.

With time, a change took place in me. I stopped pontificating at the meetings. I mean, how can you talk down to a kid whose cigarette butts you pick up any time he decides to toss one? After a while, I saw the humor in it all. Humor is "the coming together of contradictions": me, with my age and degrees; the young "punks," some of them drop-outs, flipping their butts for me to pick up. It took me some time, but I began to laugh. Six months later, my sponsor questioned me about my change of attitude and told me I could come to a lower-rung service meeting with him. And what's more, I could pass the butt job on to someone I sponsored.

I learned from experience that every service in AA is a butt job. Maxine, a wonderful delegate from Orange County, California, put it this way: "Delegate—big deal. Two years of a lot of work and a little glory, then back to cleaning ash trays." I'll always be grateful for that young hotshot sponsor. He taught me that defiance is useless. What is useful is to surrender fast and suffer less. AA is all about picking up butts.

Jim H.
Adelphi, Maryland

SWEATING IT OUT
April 1987

A friend who had just returned from a three-week learning experience around issues of nonviolence on an Indian reservation told me that she had been acutely uncomfortable during the prayer sweat. The ceremony is a ritual physical cleansing which takes place in the sauna-like sweat lodge. Heated stones are placed in the center fireplace of a small round building which seats from four to ten participants. As the waves of heat soar and ebb and new rocks are brought into the lodge from the fire out front, an experienced guide leads the group in the ritual ceremony of four rounds of prayer.

"I couldn't pray out loud," my friend said. "It seemed false." She comes from a Catholic background and I from a Protestant, but as I sat there watching her relive her obvious discomfort at this inability to adapt to the ways of her hosts, I realized suddenly that Janet didn't belong to AA. It's too bad she doesn't belong to AA, I found myself thinking, then she might not have had such a problem.

Several years ago, the first summer I was sober, I had the opportunity to participate in a sweat ceremony led by a friend who is a Choctaw Indian. It was a women's sweat and six of us sat nude and cross-legged on the bare ground inside the lodge as my friend explained the ritual. When it was time to begin the rounds of prayer she told us to think of our prayer as having a conversation with someone—someone present, someone far away, the spirit of someone who had died, an animal friend, a distant ancestor, it didn't matter.

Then she began. She greeted the spirits as grandmother and grandfather. She thanked them for our good health and our presence together and invited them to join us. My friend is also a member of AA and she spoke of our mutual journey toward sobriety. I began to relax. This was feeling almost familiar.

When it was my turn I didn't know what would be "correct" to say, so I thanked my friend for leading the sweat ceremony and talked about my hopes for my own future—that I would be able to resume my career, live in a loving relationship, and grow as a sober adult. I don't remember each of the four rounds, or what the other women "talked" as their turn to pray came around. I do know that by the last round I could say something I'd wanted to for a long time. I told my mother, who had been dead for five years, that I was sober. To say these words out loud in front of others who might "judge" me made my heart race with fear; but I'd known from the beginning of the ceremony that this was the most important conversation I needed to have.

Like my friend Janet, I wasn't used to praying out loud. I never imagined having that intimate conversation with my mother in front of others; and I don't think I could have done it if I had not sat for nearly a year in my women's AA group and listened as each woman responded to the problem or topic of the evening. Some nights the subject seemed profound, some nights trivial, but every night we all listened as each woman spoke from her heart. That speaking, for me, is what prayer is about; for nearly four years now I have practiced speaking honestly what is in my heart and listening when others do the same.

J.M.
Albany, New York

AMENDS IN PARADISE

February 2002

I hit my bottom on the island state of Chuuk in the Federated States of Micronesia. I lived on Moen, the largest island. You can comfortably jog around Moen in two and a half hours.

Chuuk is everything you ever imagined about a tropical paradise—except that it is plagued by alcoholism. And as we all know, alcoholism is a disease that touches many more people than just the alcoholic. The women of the island, despite the fact that they didn't have the vote, had encouraged their husbands, fathers, brothers, and sons to pass a law making Chuuk a dry state. However, as with Prohibition in the United States, this law did not stop the devastating impact that alcohol was having on the population and the culture. Instead, it brought in criminal waves of bootlegging. Every patrol boat had a machine gun mounted on the front of it because bootleggers on boats carrying illicit cargo—151 proof rum—were willing to shoot it out.

It was a common Friday night occurrence for some young men who had gotten hold of these goods to come ranting and raging through the village, throwing rocks at anyone who came in their field of vision. The islanders truly knew that their young men were possessed by spirits. We learned later that the tribal chief of our village, who was in his early seventies, felt so responsible for our safety in the village that he would patrol around our home in the wee hours of the morning. We came to love this man for his tremendous graciousness and generosity toward us.

Unfortunately, I was not even close to recovery when I was his guest on Chuuk. Quite the contrary, I deeply abused his hospitality by indulging in my alcoholic behavior as often as I could get my hands on some of that bootlegged booze.

As a periodic and binge boozer, I would hold out as long as I could, and then I would go on a depraved run looking for as much booze as I could consume in as short a time as possible. My method of operation was to get blind drunk, make an absolute fool of myself (when I thought I was being brilliant and entertaining), and humiliate myself with some form of lewd behavior. On one of these runs, I embarrassed the lieutenant governor and followed up by dropping my pants in front of a senator who was trying to escort me safely home.

I had done worse in my years of alcoholic drinking, but I had never before woken up on a tiny island having to face the music. The next seven years were a dry run before I found AA. I had six beers in seven years and every one of those beers looked like a live cobra about to strike. I did not know why, but I was scared to death of alcohol. I only knew that when I took a drink, I had absolutely no control of my behavior.

Finally, after I left Chuuk, I found AA and began working the Steps. Thinking about my drinking on Chuuk, the question arose: how do I make an amends to a whole state, country, and people? Even with the help of my sponsors, I couldn't work this riddle out for myself. The amends I knew I needed to make lay dormant and unresolved for five years after I came into AA. I'd think up one approach after another but never felt secure about how to do this amends without causing even more injury to myself and others. It was all so foggy, confused, and painful. Then, about two months ago, the Goddess stepped in and just took over the whole project. It was obvious that I wasn't getting the job done despite my willingness.

It all started with a remark by a close colleague that he was going to Chuuk. Going to Chuuk? I rarely met anyone who even knew Chuuk existed! And here was a good friend taking a trip there. I could feel the hand of the Goddess in just this one sign. I leapt at the opportunity his trip offered. With that one piece in place, I called my grand-sponsor and asked for his help putting together a packet of information about Alcoholics Anonymous. He suggested a Big Book and an information packet for starting and conducting a meeting. Great! My sponsor kindly put together enough packets for all five villages on the island.

But there was still one piece I couldn't feel settled on. I didn't like the idea of being another outsider telling an indigenous culture what to do, no matter how well-intentioned. The Chuukese were just discovering their own cultural voice and political autonomy. I wanted to honor that while carrying the message. So here I was, holding up the boat again with my obsessive perfectionism and lack of trust in the Divine.

The weekend before my colleague was flying to Chuuk, some friends invited me to an AA conference in San Francisco. Going into the city is one of my least favorite things to do, but spending time with AA friends and having a day of recovery together was irresistible. So, off we went.

In the second hour of the conference, we were taking the elevator up to an Al-Anon meeting and exchanged a lively and welcoming hello with a woman in the elevator who I could have sworn was Micronesian. I assumed she was an employee of the hotel because she was wearing a white jacket with a Mandarin collar. Then I saw her up at the podium as the keynote speaker for the Al-Anon meeting.

She opened by identifying herself as a double-winner, a member of both AA and Al-Anon, who was an indigenous tribal person from the Philippines. My heart started to pound furiously. I knew instantly that, once again, the Goddess had done for me what I could not do for myself. This woman's story could carry the message in ways I could never dream of.

Her share could have been from any of the island nations along the equator in the South Pacific. Her story was heart-wrenching, terrifying, and magnificently inspirational; her sensitivity, humor, and wisdom touched me at every moment. She had gone from devastating abuse and poverty to the self-actualization of becoming a fine artist.

It was hard to believe that the woman standing before us had survived, much less come to know herself as an artist who had a vision and passion to give to everyone she met. She was absolutely explicit that all of this was due to her recovery in AA and Al-Anon. Afterward, I asked her permission to send her tape with my packet to Chuuk. She was delighted with the request and so, the last piece slipped into place.

My colleague graciously carted over ten pounds of books, leaflets, and tapes on his seventeen-hour-flight. He assured me that it had been a dream of his since being a little boy to be an ambassador to another country some day. He felt that this trip was giving him that opportunity.

Following my map (hand-drawn from memories of fifteen years ago), he located the retired attorney general of Chuuk. This man had held the top legal post for his nation and was one of the people I hoped would welcome the packets and know the best way to distribute them. Within days I received an e-mail from this good man warmly thanking me for the packets and saying that he knew just where to place them.

I still laugh out loud and wonder what the Goddess had up her sleeve on this one. The miracle of recovery and her delightful ways of making sure that the message gets carried are truly beyond my wildest dreams. I am quite certain that the story does not end here.

Shawn B.
Jenner, California

TOWARD REALITY

April 1980

The speaker at my group's closed meeting recounted her sponsor's advice for dealing with her fears: "Don't drink, go to daily meetings, and nothing bad can happen to you." Not long before this meeting, dear AA friends who don't drink and do go to many meetings had experienced probably the worst thing that can happen to anyone—they had lost a beloved child through a tragic accident. Consequently, I was seriously put off by the remark. But it set me thinking nonetheless, and I have continued to ponder it. As I see it, *everything* both good and bad can happen to us no matter how conscientiously we practice the program, but that steady practice makes it possible for us to cope with *whatever* comes.

We are told from the beginning that AA is a simple program for complicated people, but to make the simple simplistic can lead to seemingly unyielding complications down the line. In our zeal to help newcomers cope with fear and anxiety, do we hold out unrealistic expectations and magical answers that bear little relationship to life and the world and people as they really are—a seemingly inseparable mixture of good and bad, true and false, just and unjust, creative and destructive forces?

When I had been sober in AA four months, the secretary of our group was murdered by an insane husband, who immediately killed himself. In a kindly effort to calm and soothe, an older member of the group told me that I should try not to question what happened and should instead accept it as God's will. This was not the answer to me then, and it isn't now. The God of my understanding suffers and grieves with me and is not the cause and source of my pain.

The beginning of maturing for me was becoming willing to try to face the realities of my own life, a day at a time, and letting go of my childhood fantasies of living happily ever after in a perfect world made up of perfect people.

AA's Twelfth Step speaks of having a spiritual awakening as a result of practicing the first eleven Steps. This awakening is experienced in countless different ways by AA members. For me, it was a gradual realization that I was emancipated from the comatose state of my drinking years, so that I could respond to and perceive the world without the anesthetic of alcohol. In a sense, we are more fortunate—better armed, better prepared—than most people are in facing the suffering and problems that no one can escape, because we, in our own deep sickness, have already experienced the darkest kind of trouble and have been led out of it by a Power greater than ourselves and, by way of the Twelve Steps, into the light.

We have a proven way through the AA program to face whatever life sends us, a day at a time, with the hope that the way will be smooth and with the belief that we won't walk the rough spots alone.

C.B.
New York, New York

Progress Not Perfection   *July 2000*

A spiritual relapse involves isolation, judgment, resentment, ridicule, envy, and a desire to get even. It doesn't come all at once. It is as cunning, powerful, and baffling as alcohol. The ego has remarkable powers of recuperation and is bolstered by self-righteous rationalization. Sometimes, I just get stupid, boring, and short with people. On the other hand, three or four times a year I sink into a pit of despair from which I seem incapable of extricating myself. I get depressed and irritable. But I don't do anything about all these things until they start to bother me, as they invariably do. Thanks to my training in AA, I know what to do. Get on the phone. Speak at meetings. Pray. And eventually I am restored to sanity. What is that if not a spiritual experience?

Jim N.
West Springfield, Massachusetts

THE POWER OF THE PROGRAM

July 1978

I had come to the AA program and had found a new way to live. Life was good. I experienced a level of freedom and happiness I had never before known. Then, after almost five years of peaceful, contented sobriety, the honeymoon was over.

In my first year of sobriety, I had worked on the Twelve Steps. Upon the advice of a good sponsor, I had written an inventory. I had discussed my inventory with my sponsor in the Fifth Step. I continued on through the amends Steps. I did about all I could see to do with those Steps at that time.

I was convinced from the beginning that the power of the program works through the Twelve Steps. The compulsion to drink left the day I consciously took the Third Step. My life seemed to become more comfortable as I worked my way through the rest of the twelve. I had what I consider a real spiritual awakening, i.e., a great change in my outlook upon life, people, and God.

It all came to an abrupt end, however, when things started happening in my life that I could not accept. I had enjoyed four years of sanity and sobriety and now fear, frustration, anger, resentment, and depression became the ruling emotions of my life. People who were important to me rejected me. All around me, people were doing things I didn't like or approve of. I reacted with every conceivable negative human feeling. The misery of these emotions was even more intense than it had been during my drinking days, because my senses were not sedated by alcohol or other chemicals.

I started out trying to change the unacceptable circumstances around me by attempting to manipulate people and situations. Nothing worked. I became lost in a maze of confusing emotions. There seemed to be no way out.

I could argue quite convincingly that the problems in my life were being caused by the conduct of others. "If only those people would straighten up," I would tell myself. When I talked of my problems with others, I sometimes received sympathetic agreement. "You are absolutely right," they would say. "You have a right to be upset." That kind of sympathy I didn't need. (I don't want to exercise my right to be upset. What kind of "right" is that?) The effort to justify my resentments did nothing but intensify the problem.

For three or four months, I pursued the frantic search for my lost serenity. Because I had heard and believed the "spiritual axiom," I knew that something was wrong with me. To find out what was wrong and where the answer might lie, I read extensively in psychology, philosophy, and theology. With each new theory or dogma I encountered, I thought, "maybe this is the answer." There are many interesting, plausible, and possibly valid ideas available from many sources. But every time I thought I saw a glimmer of hope in some new system, I fell back into the pit of my black emotions. I considered seeing a psychiatrist. It seemed to me that the battle was no longer worth it. Five years without alcohol, and I was an emotional basket case.

Where had I failed? Had I missed something in the AA program? I continued to go to many meetings. I was doing much Twelfth Step work. I was still seeking through prayer and meditation for guidance in my life. I thought I was working the program.

Then I started to suspect that despite all the outward appearances, I was not really practicing the principles in all my affairs. The Twelve Steps were things I had done, not something I was doing. In the Step study group I attended regularly, I had begun to talk of the Steps in the past tense: "When I took this Step ..."

I had begun to study, analyze, and expound upon the Steps, but I had gradually ceased to make them a part of my life by actually working them and keeping them current each day. Perhaps the answers I had been seeking in more esoteric realms were back where I had left them, in the Twelve Steps. Indeed, they were.

With the renewed commitment, I started again with Step One. By the time I had written a new inventory and taken the Fifth Step, I began to receive convincing demonstrations to the effect of reworking all the Steps. People began to appear in my life who eloquently expressed the continuing need to keep working on all the Steps. They urged me on and told me how to apply the Steps to my life today.

It works. As a result, I have acquired an enthusiastic new faith in the AA program. I have personally experienced what is available at any time, at any stage of sobriety, when we honestly approach the Twelve Steps as the solution to the condition of our lives today.

Now, when a particular Step is discussed at our meeting, I ask myself, "What am I doing about that Step today?" or "What do I need to do about that Step today?"

Perhaps our groups should be Step *application* groups instead of Step *study* groups. I have seen others start to really work on the Steps either with renewed commitment or for the first time. You don't have to ask which members are doing it. You can tell. Lives are noticeably changed, far beyond the removal of alcohol, when we work and rework the Steps. People change.

Now, the important thing for me to remember about the program is that I must continue to work it and live in it and grow in it, or I will slide backward. It is not in the nature of things for me to get my life "fixed" and have it stay "fixed." If I don't keep working on it, it will, sooner or later, fall apart. How do I work on it? With the simple kit of spiritual tools offered to me by the AA people when I first came—the Twelve Steps. I have tried other tools, but they don't work too well for me. Of course, I reserve the right as an individual to practice any form of religion or study any science, pseudo-science, or mental discipline. But I have discovered that knowledge acquired through such study does not really solve anything in my life. Knowledge alone never does.

If I am to have a share of those promises enumerated in the AA book, there is a price I must pay. That price is "destruction of self-centeredness" (Big Book, page 14). The roadway to freedom, sanity, peace of mind, and serenity is not traversed by intellect. AA directs me toward a goal of greater humility and less self-centeredness. It means replacing some of my self-will with God's will for me. Acquisition of more knowledge has very little to do with that goal. My acceptance of a Higher Power came, not from understanding how God works, but from a simple faith based upon the premise that I need not understand as long as I have faith that "the Great Reality" is at work in my life.

Sometimes, I have deluded myself with thoughts of a lofty spiritual realm where I could rise above the problems of ordinary people and attain some exalted state of being. Such thinking, I now believe, contradicts the idea of the AA program—humility. It also seems to abandon the AA method of attaining some degree of that humility. The method, I'm told, is the practice of this simple program.

When I learned about the Twelve Steps, I had the knowledge I needed to keep me sober. That same knowledge will give me maturity, sanity, freedom, serenity, and real happiness—but only if I keep applying that simple set of spiritual principles to my life today.

I will remember, I hope, that life is not always 100 percent built to my specifications. God doesn't work well under close supervision. When things do go my way, and when I have the pleasure of realized hopes and dreams, I want to meet those conditions with gratitude born of the realization that the good things are now possible because of God in my life and the AA program and the AA people. But when the disappointments come and the pain starts to reappear, they bring real opportunity for growth. The pain can also be a cause for gratitude. Without it, I probably wouldn't grow much.

I am grateful today that I have been forced by the circumstances of my life to find a deeper meaning in the AA program.

Bill W., AA's co-founder, once said that we measure our progress in AA by two words, "humility" and "responsibility." May I ever keep my eye on these yardsticks as I continue to seek only knowledge of his will for me. Where I found it before is the most likely place to find it again—in the Twelve Steps.

C. S.
Tulsa, Oklahoma

THE TWELVE STEPS

1. We admitted we were powerless over alcohol—that our lives had become unmanageable.

2. Came to believe that a Power greater than ourselves could restore us to sanity.

3. Made a decision to turn our will and our lives over to the care of God *as we understood Him.*

4. Made a searching and fearless moral inventory of ourselves.

5. Admitted to God, to ourselves, and to another human being the exact nature of our wrongs.

6. Were entirely ready to have God remove all these defects of character.

7. Humbly asked Him to remove our shortcomings.

8. Made a list of all persons we had harmed, and became willing to make amends to them all.

9. Made direct amends to such people wherever possible, except when to do so would injure them or others.

10. Continued to take personal inventory and when we were wrong promptly admitted it.

11. Sought through prayer and meditation to improve our conscious contact with God *as we understood Him,* praying only for knowledge of His will for us and the power to carry that out.

12. Having had a spiritual awakening as the result of these steps, we tried to carry this message to alcoholics, and to practice these principles in all our affairs.

THE TWELVE TRADITIONS

1. Our common welfare should come first; personal recovery depends upon A.A. unity.

2. For our group purpose there is but one ultimate authority—a loving God as He may express Himself in our group conscience. Our leaders are but trusted servants; they do not govern.

3. The only requirement for A.A. membership is a desire to stop drinking.

4. Each group should be autonomous except in matters affecting other groups or A.A. as a whole.

5. Each group has but one primary purpose—to carry its message to the alcoholic who still suffers.

6. An A.A. group ought never endorse, finance or lend the A.A. name to any related facility or outside enterprise, lest problems of money, property and prestige divert us from our primary purpose.

7. Every A.A. group ought to be fully self-supporting, declining outside contributions.

8. Alcoholics Anonymous should remain forever nonprofessional, but our service centers may employ special workers.

9. A.A., as such, ought never be organized; but we may create service boards or committees directly responsible to those they serve.

10. Alcoholics Anonymous has no opinion on outside issues; hence the A.A. name ought never be drawn into public controversy.

11. Our public relations policy is based on attraction rather than promotion; we need always maintain personal anonymity at the level of press, radio and films.

12. Anonymity is the spiritual foundation of all our traditions, ever reminding us to place principles before personalities.

Alcoholics Anonymous

AA's program of recovery is fully set forth in its basic text, *Alcoholics Anonymous* (commonly known as the Big Book), now in its Fourth Edition, as well as *Twelve Steps and Twelve Traditions, Living Sober* and other books. Information on AA can also be found on AA's website at www.aa.org or by writing to: Alcoholics Anonymous, Box 459, Grand Central Station, New York, NY 10163. For local resources, check your local telephone directory under "Alcoholics Anonymous." Four pamphlets, "This is A.A.," "Is A.A. For You?," "44 Questions," and "A Newcomer Asks" are also available from AA.

AA Grapevine

AA Grapevine is AA's international monthly journal, published continuously since its first issue in June 1944. The AA pamphlet on AA Grapevine describes its scope and purpose this way: "As an integral part of Alcoholics Anonymous since 1944, the Grapevine publishes articles that reflect the full diversity of experience and thought found within the A.A. Fellowship, as does La Viña, the bimonthly Spanish-language magazine, first published in 1996. No one viewpoint or philosophy dominates their pages, and in determining content, the editorial staff relies on the principles of the Twelve Traditions."

In addition to magazines, AA Grapevine, Inc. also produces books, eBooks, audiobooks, and other items. It also offers a Grapevine Online subscription, which includes: four new stories weekly, AudioGrapevine (the audio version of the magazine), Grapevine Story Archive (the entire collection of Grapevine articles), and the current issue of Grapevine and La Viña in HTML format. For more information on AA Grapevine, or to subscribe to any of these, please visit the magazine's website at www.aagrapevine.org or write to:

AA Grapevine, Inc.
475 Riverside Drive
New York, NY 10115

Index